Infinite Dendrogram

15. GAME OVER

Sakon Kaidou

Illustrator: Taiki

"Code II: Shelter."

Half a second later, countless beams pierced into her. They carried enough power to turn her into burnt Swiss cheese... yet that didn't happen.

"Don't touch the... *GAME OVER.*"

Character

Ray

Ray Starling / Reiji Mukudori

A young man who began playing Infinite Dendrogram.
He's generally a calm person, but he has a strong
sense of justice that renders him unbreakable when
striving to do what's right.

Nemesis

Nemesis

A girl that manifested as Ray's Embryo. In her base form, she
was capable of transforming into a greatsword, but now she's
capable of becoming a wide variety of weapons. She's a bit of a
glutton.

Elizabeth

Elizabeth S. Altar

Second Princess of the Kingdom of Altar.
A carefree, tomboyish princess. She has a deep love for her
sisters, even if they worry whenever she sneaks out of the castle.
Presently engaged to Canglong, Third Prince of Huang He.

Xunyu

Xunyu

A Superior hailing from the Huang He Empire.
Presently assigned to protect Prince Canglong. Their duelist
ranking is exceptionally high, and they once contributed to the
death of a SUBM.

Zeta

Zeta

A member of Illegal Frontier, a heinous clan of criminals.
She's a Superior, and the King of Thieves.
At the Dryfe Empire's behest, she's presently leading a
group of insurgents to attack Altar's royal capital.
She once held the top duelist ranking position in Dryfe,
and has contributed to the death of a SUBM.

Infinite Dendrogram

15. GAME OVER

Sakon Kaidou
Illustrator: Taiki

Infinite Dendrogram: Volume 15
by Sakon Kaidou

Translated by Andrew Hodgson
Edited by Sarah Tilson
Layout by Cheree Smith
English Cover by Chi Tran

First published in Japan in 2021
Publication rights for this English edition arranged through Hobby Japan, Tokyo.

Find more books like this one at www.j-novel.club!

Managing Director: Samuel Pinansky
Light Novel Line Manager: Chi Tran
Managing Editor: Jan Mitsuko Cash
Managing Translator: Kristi Fernandez
QA Manager: Hannah N. Carter
Marketing Manager: Stephanie Hii
Project Manager: Kristine Johnson

ISBN: 978-1-7183-5514-9
Printed in Korea
First Printing: May 2022
10 9 8 7 6 5 4 3 2 1

Contents

p.09   Conjection: The Game Board They
                       Know as This World

p.13   Chapter Eighteen: Values

p.31   Chapter Nineteen: Hero

p.51   Chapter Twenty: The Fiery Dance of the
                           Jiangshi and the Mummy

p.79   Chapter Twenty-One: The Blades and Shields
                               of Altar

p.108   Chapter from the   Memories of Fire
        Past:

p.124   Chapter Twenty-Two: What Was Sought

p.148   Chapter Twenty-Three: The Humanoid Irregularity

p.165   Chapter Twenty-Four: Don't Touch the
                               GAME OVER

p.174   Chapter from the   What Is Untouchable,
        Past: What Shouldn't Be Touched

p.203   Chapter Twenty-Five: The Incarnation of
                               Maelstroms

p.226   Chapter Twenty-Six: Supernova

Contents

p.248   **Chapter Twenty-Seven:**   **A Life of Fire**

p.265   **Epilogue**

p.287   **The Final Epilogue:**   **Him, Her, and...**

p.294   **Afterword**

The Gaol, Café "Dice"

Two figures were sitting in a café and playing a game of chess.

One was a black-haired man with a smile on his face, while the other was a tired-looking young woman.

"Board games are profoundly simple," said the man, moving his knight to take the lady's bishop. "Wouldn't you agree?"

This man was none other than King of Crime, Sechs Würfel — the proprietor of this establishment and the leader of the Illegal Frontier clan.

"...Not at all," the lady replied. "This is actually pretty hard for me..." She was Gerbera, a member of the aforementioned clan, as well as a freeloader here. As she played, her eyes were glazed over.

This was a slow business day, so the two had decided to pass the time with chess, but Gerbera was less than an amateur at the game. Even with handicaps, she was losing badly.

"Chess is simple," Sechs insisted as he took another one of Gerbera's pieces. "After all, there are only two factions on the board, and only one king for each of them to take. In reality, the number of factions can never be known, and there might be multiple kings that must fall in order to take each faction down. Also, there is a chance that the world itself — the game board, if you will — would bare its fangs, as well. I've seen it happen before."

"The world itself, huh…? You mean natural disasters like earthquakes? Oh, that reminds me — my dad told me about how he barely survived something like that back when he was a kid. Japan gets earthquakes all the time, doesn't it?"

Being half-Japanese and half-British, Gerbera had a certain degree of knowledge about Japan from her father. He always told her that the people there feared a few things: earthquakes, lightning, fire, and their fathers.

Would I also be afraid of my dad if I lived there? she wondered.

"Natural disasters… Well, I suppose you could call them that," said Sechs.

"…The way you're phrasing it is making me curious," Gerbera replied — as though Sechs's description of the world "baring its fangs" wasn't intriguing enough to begin with.

"It *was* certainly a disaster… But at the same time…I think it was the game board's 'king.'"

Sechs's words were truly bizarre — he seemed to be implying that the *world itself* was another player. That would be akin to the very chessboard they were using joining the game and playing against them.

…How would it move its pieces? Gerbera wondered, completely serious.

"Oh, right. I've yet to tell anyone in I.F. about that encounter. I'll have to distribute the information later."

"…Huh? You were talking about *this* world? Not reality…?" Gerbera asked in surprise.

"Yes," Sechs nodded. "Back then, I believe I saw the 'king-piece' of this world… Though, I suppose it's more fitting to call it *the final boss*."

Sechs casually stated something very shocking.

Gerbera's tired eyes and mouth went wide in surprise.

"…Am I reading too much into this, or did you just drop a bombshell on me? This game has a *final boss*? Seriously? Something above raid bosses like the SUBMs…?"

"Yes. The term 'final boss' suits this quite well, actually. Though, according to a friend of mine, it's the final boss of the world this game *used* to be. Observers like the Red King are the final bosses of the game this world is *now*."

Presenting information he'd gained from the most ancient monster of all — The Skydragon King — Sechs took a sip of his coffee.

"...*Dendro* isn't the first game in the series...? And...a 'friend' of yours? I... Are you sure you should be telling me this? I really wouldn't want to get a death penalty or something for knowing too much..."

"There's no need to worry about that. The control AIs would never do anything to affect the Masters irreversibly. Though, I suppose that doesn't apply to psychological damage."

"Hm?"

"I mean, the trauma from things like a tian friend of yours dying a horrible death."

"...Ohh. Well, there are lots of people who can't handle gore... But...where did you encounter this final boss, anyway? Some created dungeon...? Oh! I know! You're from Altar, so it's probably the Tomb Labyrinth, right?"

"I'm sorry, but no. It was in the capital, but not in that dungeon."

"Huh? What do you mean?" Sechs had just implied that the final boss was in the city of Altea itself, and Gerbera couldn't help but wonder how anyone could possibly run into something like that in such a mundane place.

"The final boss I met had a human form and led a human life," Sechs said with a smile on his face.

"...Wh-huuhh?" Her companion's words made Gerbera freeze up.

As he looked at her with amusement, Sechs remembered the latest report.

I believe today is the day Zeta will fulfill Dryfe's request and assault Altea, he thought. Zeta and La Crima — two core members of I.F. — had combined forces to attack the capital of the kingdom.

Dryfe's goal in this was to bring a certain entity out into the open and — if possible — finish it off.

Sechs was fairly certain that this "entity" was none other than the thing he'd seen back then.

I suppose I ended up talking about it because the memory was in the back of my mind... he thought.

Sechs believed that through this event, Dryfe would find out what he knew. That would cause a drastic shift in the world, much like it had during the war in which Sechs challenged Shu to a battle he couldn't refuse.

Does that mean it would also be stirred into motion? I'm far away from it all at the moment, though. It would be quite a bother if everything ended while I'm still stuck here, he thought as he looked outside, at the scenery of the gaol.

A false sky, a false horizon...a false world, built by Red King using walls of spatial fixation.

"I suppose it must be starting right about now," he muttered, looking out at the closed world — though he seemed to truly be seeing something far beyond its walls.

The Royal Capital of Altea, City Quarter

Shortly after the peace talks at the border fell apart, Altea was thrown into a state of chaos when it found itself under attack by grotesque hybrids of bee and human — Apis Ideas.

They killed people using their poisonous, spear-like stingers — and upon death, their victims exploded violently, causing damage to anyone nearby. It would be accurate to call them murderous bioweapons. The guards and Masters inside the city fought back against them while attempting to get the inhabitants to safety, but each and every Apis Idea possessed stats that surpassed even Demi-Dragon-tier creatures. Of the Altarian tians, only the Royal Guard had any chance of fighting them one-on-one, so they were forced to face the monsters in groups.

Even Masters who could take on an Apis Idea each weren't having it easy.

"Riser! They're not just strong — they blow up too! We can't fight 'em close up!" shouted Lang, the hippogriff-mounted Gale Rider and member of the Babylonian Battlegroup.

"Tell the other members to fight with guns, bows, and magic. Anyone without a ranged attack can use the Gems in the clan's storage!"

"Roger that!" Lang was talking to a man riding a motorbike smuggled from Dryfe. Another Gale Rider, this man was Masked Riser, number six in the duel rankings, as well as the acting leader of the Babylonian Battlegroup. While he drove the bike through the streets and shot at the bee-men with a rifle, he used a magical comms device to talk to his clan members.

…Good thing I got Fuso to heal me, Masked Riser thought. Tsukuyo had healed all the wounds he'd sustained in his fight against Chrono Crown. With his Embryo damaged, he wasn't as powerful as he could be, but thanks to her healing abilities, he could at least still fight.

As a temporary replacement for Hermod, Masked Riser was using an MP-powered motorbike that had been leaked from Dryfe.

Things really aren't looking so good right now, though, he thought. At the moment, there were few combat-capable Masters in the capital.

Most of the duel rankers had been assassinated the day before yesterday and their death penalties had yet to expire, while The Lunar Society and Death Period — the first- and second-ranked clans — were at the peace talks. The third, K&R, was missing their two Superior Jobs.

And because The Lunar Society and K&R were both based in Altea, most of the other ranking clans had chosen to set up in other cities. Because of this, the only Masters around who were capable of fighting this wave of enemies were the members of the Babylonian Battlegroup, the rest of K&R besides Kashimiya and Rosa, and a handful of others.

As for the kill rankers… Most of them aren't here, but I guess there aren't many of them who can fight in a city. Like the very top ranker — King of Destruction, Shu Starling — most of the kill rankers possessed immense firepower that was best suited for taking on swarms of monsters. The majority of them would only be of limited use in this situation.

"Damn it! This is too much for us! It's like we're playing chess and our side hasn't got a queen!" Lang said, his thoughts running similar to Riser's.

In response, Riser swallowed his worries and said, "That still leaves the knights, the bishops, the rooks, and the pawns. Let's show them what we're made of."

"…All right!" Lang said, trying to pull himself together.

"I'll go east. You meet up with squad B and head west."

"Roger that!"

After about a minute of driving, Riser arrived at a barricade blocking the road.

Beyond it was one of Altea's several town halls; it seemed like it was being used as a shelter and the barricade was there to protect the people inside.

Near the roadblock stood several people, all of them dressed in the uniform of the city guard.

"You are…Masked Riser!" one of them said as Riser came close. His unique-looking mask and long history as a duel ranker made him well-known among the kingdom's tians.

"How's the situation here?" he asked, dismounting from the bike.

"We repelled the first and second wave, but we've suffered some casualties of our own…and a third wave might be on the way."

"Are you saying that this place is being targeted specifically?"

"Yes. It's not just here, though. They seem to be prioritizing locations where there are a lot of people."

It looked as though the bee-men were attacking at random, but they were actually trying to be as efficient as possible — efficient at killing people, that is.

They had enough sentience to attack where they would do the most harm, and they exploded upon death to do even more damage.

15

"According to guards stationed elsewhere, these bee-men are coming in everywhere, even the rear entrances, and—"

"The bee-men have appeared at the national church's shelter! The explosions are threatening the evacuees!"

"Damn it…!" the guard captain cursed. This wasn't the first time today he'd received news like that.

Among the bee-men, some of them had been bee-men from the very beginning, and others had started out looking human.

The latter often blended in among the evacuating citizens to hide inside shelters before revealing their true forms in a fatal explosion.

Their efficiency at slaughter was as impressive as it was fearsome.

The shelters can't refuse to take in the evacuees, but it's difficult to tell them apart from the disguised bee-men… This is bad, Riser thought.

Not even Reveal could expose them. It only showed their names and a low job level that didn't reflect their true stats, and unlike monsters, their names didn't display above their heads. That latter fact made it extremely difficult to tell them apart from normal humans — and it was also proof that, despite their grotesque appearance, these bee creatures were also human.

"What are they, anyway?! Some Legendarian tribe?!" The guard captain's words left Riser deep in thought.

If they're not monsters, that's the most obvious assumption… but that can't be it. According to a Babylonian Battlegroup member who had a job from the researcher grouping, the post-transformation bee-men had the "insectoid" typing. That just wasn't normal.

No matter how insect-like they looked, a humanoid tribe would always be of the "human" type. There were jobs that changed this, such as Lich, which turned the humanoid that had it into "undead," and Ogre Samurai, which did the same with "Oni." However, according to Reveal, the bee-men had no such jobs.

Even if it was some kind of job, it wouldn't explain the transformation ability or why the stats don't match their levels... Hold on, he thought to himself as he realized there was another possibility — that these might be humans who had been warped by Embryos or UBMs.

It was unlikely, though, that UBMs would commit such a complicated act of terrorism. Riser had been in this world a long time, but even he could only think of one such example — the Exodragon King that had schemed behind the scenes in Gideon.

But that would mean that these bee-men were created by a Master, and...how could anyone like that actually exist...? Riser didn't want to believe that. If that were true, it would mean that there was a Master who turned tians into living weapons. He was a solid worlder and really didn't want to accept that someone so callous really existed in *Dendro.*

"...Whatever the case, I have to stop these attacks on the shelter." Even if the bee-men were transformed tians, he'd already resolved to stop them from harming any more innocent people.

What he needed right now was a means of telling evacuees and the bee-men apart, but his Babylonian Battlegroup didn't have anyone with an Embryo that could help in that regard.

Right as Riser began to fear that the bee-men would retain the element of surprise all the way through...

"U-Um...!"

...a girl called out to him.

"Hm? You're..." She seemed familiar to him.

This girl and Riser both knew Ray and had been in each other's presence several times now.

"I'm Kasumi...from Death Period..." Kasumi was a member of Death Period who had been unable to participate in the peace talks due to real life circumstances. She was accompanied by Io and Fujinon, who also couldn't join Ray for similar reasons.

"Yeah, I remember you. All of you," said Riser. "So you stayed here in Altar, huh?"

"Y-Yes…! Umm… I have something…to say…!"

"You do?"

Kasumi nodded before showing Riser the board in her hands — her Embryo, Taijitu.

"My…my Taijitu can show the locations and levels of nearby Embryos…!" Before, it could only pinpoint the Masters themselves, but its recent ascension to a high-ranking Type Angel-Arms had expanded this ability to their Embryos as well.

Riser instantly understood what she was getting at.

"Those bee-men…" Kasumi said. "They're all marked as 'VII'… Superior Embryos…!" Taijitu was reacting to the fragments of a certain Embryo within the bee-men and displaying their locations.

"Superior… Wait, more importantly, you're saying that you can tell them apart from regular humans even when they're disguised?!"

"Yes…!" That was great news. The greatest threat right now were the bee-men blending in with the evacuees, so dealing with them would greatly reduce the casualties.

"Can you tell us where they are?" Riser asked.

"Yes…! I'll mark them…! So please…inform everyone else!" Kasumi said before looking into her Taijitu and touching its surface.

She traced her finger over the many "VII" signals it was displaying.

"Taijitu…Marking!" The moment she used that skill, their surroundings slightly changed.

A downward-pointing triangle, looking like something straight out of a GPS app, suddenly appeared above one of the evacuees heading to the nearby shelter.

That was it — the mark distinguishing the enemies blending in among the tians.

"…There's one!" Kasumi called.

"Got it!" Io and Fujinon quickly leaped into action. Fujinon — now a high-rank job, Geomancer — used earth magic to bind their target in place.

"BZzzZZzzZz…" The moment he was bound, the man instantly transformed into a grotesque human-bee hybrid.

However, a moment later, he was split in half by a giant axe — none other than Io's Embryo, Five-Ring.

It exploded as it died, but since there was no one nearby, the explosion did no further harm.

In fact, Five-Ring was so large and long that the explosion didn't move it an inch, and Io was so far away that she almost didn't feel the shock wave from the blast.

"A-A mark…? What *was* that…?" This sudden turn of events perplexed the guards, and Riser realized that the situation had now shifted in their favor.

Kasumi's Marking skill didn't contribute to the battle directly, but it allowed them to neutralize the bee-men hiding in shelters before they could do too much damage.

"…Can I assume that all the bee-men in the city are now marked?" Riser asked.

"Y-Yes! Taijitu covers the entire city… But the five 'VII's at the castle were too fast for me to touch…"

"The castle…" The bee-men were powerful, but not absurdly fast.

Does that mean that the "VII"s at the castle aren't just these minion bee-men? Could they be actual Superiors…? No, I can't focus on that right now…! Riser had many questions, but they were less important than the task before him.

19

He grabbed his comms magic device and said, "Attention, all members of the Babylonian Battlegroup: the tians with arrows above them are actually bee-men. Question and bind them just in case, and neutralize them if they expose themselves!"

With that, the members of the Babylonian Battlegroup scattered all over Altea now had the necessary information.

The guards at Riser's side were also busy contacting their fellow guards all over the city.

"Thank you," he said, turning to Kasumi. "You really turned the tide in our favor. Hm…?"

For some reason, the girl wasn't listening to him. She was just staring at her Taijitu with her head tilted to the side.

"…Is something wrong?" Riser asked.

"L-Look…" she said, pointing at a particular location on the map, her finger shaking.

Riser, Io, and Fujinon all came to see what had made her so unsettled.

Kasumi was pointing to the fountain plaza at Altea's southern main street — the place that functioned as the city's save point.

There were a large number of "VII"s clustered all around it. They were overlapping in a way that made them hard to count, but there couldn't be fewer than a hundred, at least. That was no doubt a much higher number of monsters than had been initially released.

"Th-They weren't there before…" Kasumi said.

"Hmm…" If they had been there from the start, Kasumi would've certainly noticed them when she was marking the others. That could only mean that they did indeed just appear suddenly, without warning.

If that save point was the place where the bee-men emerged from hiding…

"…That could very well be the source of the invasion." If they ignored this, the situation could become unsalvageable.

Riser made his decision. Then, he grabbed the comms device connecting him to his clan members.

"Attention, all members of the Babylonian Battlegroup! It's likely that the source of the bee-men is near the fountain in the southern part of Altea. Anyone who can move quickly, go straight there and prepare to fight. I'm heading over too!"

Riser then leaped back onto his motorbike and headed towards the fountain.

Upon seeing his swift departure, Kasumi, Io, and Fujinon looked at each other and nodded before jumping on their own Landwing mounts and spurring them towards the same destination.

A few minutes later, they all arrived at the fountain from the northern side of the main street.

The other Babylonian Battlegroup members were nowhere in sight, but if they were following Riser's instructions properly, they were surely moving to surround the source from every direction.

"What…?" said Riser, struck by the odd sight before him.

Over a hundred bee-men stood in an orderly fashion, like a well-trained army.

"Oh my. Oh me oh my. Oho ho ho ho!" The sound of laughter began to echo from somewhere beyond the line of soldiers. The sound was unpleasant — like a mix between a human voice and the buzzing of an insect. "Congratulations! You are the first humans in the whole city to have the honor of an audience with me. Oh, how splendid. Truly delightful!"

This speech was quite unlike the incoherent buzzing of the bee-men. Garbled though it was, it was still easily recognizable as human speech.

The owner of the voice was sitting elegantly on the edge of the fountain, surrounded by the bee-man army. "Sitting" might not even be the correct word for the figure's pose, as its body was terribly warped.

The speaker appeared to be a mixture of a well-proportioned human woman and *several* bees. The resulting discord in its form made it hard to tell if it was actually "sitting."

It even had a bee-like abdomen — or rather, *several* of them.

Compared to this creature, even the bee-men didn't look grotesque.

"What... Who are you?!" Riser yelled.

"'Who?!' *That* is your first question when faced with such a beautiful being?! Oh my! Such ignorance!" The buzzing, mumbling voice made it difficult to read her emotions, but it was fairly obvious that the question had made the creature upset.

"But I will forgive you," it added. "This is the kingdom of Altar — a place so dreadfully unlike the wondrous fairyland I call home. I cannot fault you for not knowing me. Ignorance is not exactly a sin, after all."

"Fairyland...?" Riser didn't miss that word. There was only one country that it could apply to.

"Indeed. I am Eh Teln Pare! As the holder of the Insect General job, I once served Legendaria's army, but the foolish queen and those who follow her branded me a rebel and chased me out of the country!"

Riser had now obtained the enemy's name and job. However, that information was nothing compared to what it...*she* said next.

"And now, I serve I.F.! Especially La Crima, who recognized my beauty, saw that I was in the right, and granted me these new soldiers!"

"I.F....!" Riser knew of the clan — a group of Superior villains.

That was enough to be certain of who was behind this incident.

"And now…ohh, and now…!" Eh Teln Pare went on as though intoxicated, "I am Regina! Regina Apis Idea! The queen bee! And the true queen of fairyland!"

She proudly revealed the name she had been given as a modified human. "I will use this fight to grow stronger, then free my ancestral home from that misguided queen! I can't allow my beloved Legendaria to continue along its wayward course any longer…!" Eh Teln Pare practically sang out her true desires. "And you will be the first sacrifices towards achieving that end!" Finally, she unleashed her Apis Ideas onto Riser's group.

The ten Apis Ideas in the front of the formation were the first ones to attack. Ten was more than double the size of Riser's group, and the ones that remained were more than enough to protect Pare…or rather, Regina Apis Idea, the queen bee herself.

All of the Apis Ideas were affected by the Insect General job's skills: Insectoid Enhancement and its final skill, Even a Worm Will Burn.

At skill level EX, the former ability merely doubled all of their stats, while the effect of the latter was more complicated.

It was one of the few Superior Job final skills for which someone else, not the user, paid the price.

When an insectoid within the party died, the skill made them explode with a force proportional to their stats. The collective firepower carried by the Apis Ideas, all above Demi-Dragon-tier in stats, was simply immense — as evidenced by the many Masters they had already destroyed.

And now, all of this power was focused on Riser and the three girls.

"Ngh…!" Under normal circumstances, a high-ranking duelist like him might have been able to easily repel these Apis Ideas. However, his Embryo was still damaged, so he lacked the firepower needed to destroy them without a great deal of effort.

"Keep your distance from them! I'll slow them down!" Despite this setback, he still had means of fighting them — one of which was an inventory filled with high-rank offensive ultimate job skill Gems.

He reached into his inventory now and took out a stark white Gem before tossing it towards the ten Apis Ideas as they charged forward.

A moment later, the spherical area surrounding the Gem was flooded with white.

"BzZz... BzZ..." The ten Apis Ideas were instantly covered in frost, which greatly slowed them down.

The spell contained in the Gem was White Field, the ultimate job skill for Cryomancers. Though it was weaker than Crimson Sphere in the same tier, it had the effect of ridding an area of its thermal energy and inflicting the Frozen status.

Though the Apis Ideas had Demi-Dragon-tier stats, they were human-sized and possessed the insectoid weakness to low temperatures.

"Riser! Get down!" Io shouted, putting her Five-Ring under her arm and swinging it horizontally.

The heavy weapon, specialized in offense, easily split and pulverized the Frozen insectoids.

The Apis Ideas scattered and died...

"Huh?"

...but unlike the others, they didn't explode.

Their severed top and bottom halves *were still moving towards them.*

"Get back!" Riser shouted, and the girls immediately created distance between them and the Apis Ideas.

As they fled, Kasumi summoned a Balloon Golem to act as a shield, while Fujinon used her earth magic to create a barricade.

Both of them stopped the Apis Ideas in their tracks, and after ten seconds or so...they all exploded, as per usual.

It was as though *their deaths had been delayed.*

"I know this…!" As an experienced Master, Riser was familiar with one job that made this possible.

"They're Death Soldiers!" The Apis Ideas the queen had at her side — the ones she called the "Queen's Guard" — were different from the other bee-men in two ways.

First, they had their transformation ability removed in exchange for doubling their stats.

And second…all of them were Death Soldiers.

That was the job used by suicide troops in the wars several centuries ago. It was perfect for the purpose because of its Last Command skill, which allowed movement after death.

Having this job would make it impossible for the Apis Ideas to blend in among normal people, for skills like Reveal would instantly expose them. However, the Queen's Guard couldn't transform and thus had no need to blend in, so they lost nothing from becoming Death Soldiers.

This was the greatest advantage Apis Ideas had over ordinary monsters.

Being originally human, they had the ability to acquire jobs. They were still experimental creatures, and Death Soldier was the only job they seemed to utilize so far, but the future held the promise of amazing, fully optimized builds.

Their ability to take Death Soldier was terrifying enough, however. As long as Last Command was active, the Queen's Guard were able to charge at their enemies even if torn to pieces.

Additionally, since Last Command only allowed for the movement of parts still connected to the brain, the Queen's Guard overcame this limitation by having their central nervous system distributed around their body.

Of course, that made human-like thought impossible. Their intellect was arguably even lower than that of actual insects, but that didn't affect their ability to act as the Insect General's pawns. The morality of their creation aside, Apis Ideas were extremely potent soldiers under Regina's command.

"Oh? Ten wasn't enough? You're more skilled than I expected. How commendable," she said, nonchalantly releasing more Apis Ideas from her Jewel.

She seemed to think nothing of the ten former human beings she had just seen die. It was as though they were nothing more than actual insects to her.

"...Fiend!" Riser shouted, unable to restrain himself any longer.

The Apis Ideas were no doubt his enemies, and he was determined to protect Altea from them — but thinking about it from another perspective, they were the nauseating creations of a truly warped mind, and thus victims in their own right.

"Fiend? Certainly not," Regina said, clearly irritated. "Legendaria is the truly fiendish power here. I am fighting to *fix* it, so I cannot be in the wrong."

"What does Legendaria have to do with this?!" Riser raised his voice in anger. Even if she was right about Legendaria, it didn't make her any less of a fiend. There were many conflicts, past and present, where both sides were evil.

"My motherland is overcome by madness! The machinery has come undone, letting foolish ideas spread unchecked!" Regina continued, clearly ignoring what Riser was trying to say. "I had to right this wrong, even if it meant becoming a rebel and initiating a coup d'état! My will to do so has not wavered, even now that I have sworn loyalty to La Crima!"

Riser had heard rumors that there was a secret feud within Legendaria's ruling class, so he could only guess that Regina wanted to set things right.

Still, that was no excuse for her horrific actions.

"Indeed! I *had* to resist! I had no choice! My country has gone mad, and it is traveling down the wrong path!" Regina continued to bare her soul in a buzzing monologue — as if Riser and the others weren't even there.

"Yes! Legendaria is making a grave mistake. After all, they..."

And so...

"They revere Titania instead of me — the beautiful Pare!"

...she revealed her ultimate motivation — one that only she herself could ever see as righteous.

Riser, Kasumi, Io, Fujinon...everyone present could barely comprehend what they'd just heard. They felt as though their ears were failing them.

After all, Regina had just said that she rebelled because people fawned over the queen of fairyland more than her.

To them, as well as to most other people, this motivation and the actions taken on behalf of it were completely incomprehensible.

"It just isn't right, don't you think?! *That* ugly creature — beautiful? Lovable?! Worthy of *idol-like adoration*?! Utter madness! The entire country has lost its mind!"

Riser was still at a loss for words. Images of Titania could be found all over *Infinite Dendrogram*, as well as on the internet in reality. Riser had seen them too, and remembering what she looked like, he thought, *If not finding her ugly is madness, then I guess I also need professional help.* The queen of the fairyland was just *that* beautiful.

It actually felt wrong to compare her to Regina — this monstrosity of warped insect flesh.

"I tried asserting my beauty, but nobody listened! If that isn't madness, I don't know what is!" Regina exclaimed.

"B-But...if your beauty was so important to you...why did you transform into this...?" Kasumi meekly asked.

Like the other Apis Ideas, Regina was marked on the Taijitu as a "VII." It seemed as though she used to be human and had been transformed into what she was now, but...

"What do you mean?" Regina tilted her head in confusion. "My beautiful form wasn't changed one bit."

Her response made them even more perplexed.

"I specifically asked the one who gave me power and this army to let me keep the beautiful form I was born with. I was told that might limit how powerful I could be, but that didn't matter! Nothing in this world is more valuable than my beauty!"

Regina's words were laden with confidence in her righteousness.

Riser just looked at her, saying nothing. Everyone had different values. What was good in one's eyes was bad in another's, so in a way, Regina wasn't *completely* in the wrong.

"Anyone who suggests otherwise is misguided! And I will correct everyone who does!"

However, her greatest error was misjudging the outlook of the vast majority.

"Those who don't accept my beauty are the source of this terrible wrongness, and I will kill them all. I will free Legendaria and the rest of the world from their madness! I am beauty! I am justice!"

She was clearly insane, and yet she believed that everyone *else* was — and she never doubted this for even a second.

Kasumi had Truth Discernment, and the fact that Regina's words didn't trigger it sent a chill down her spine.

Regina truly believed that she was more beautiful than anyone else, and that she should be adored by everyone. If that wasn't how things were, she would rather destroy the world than let it continue in ignorance.

The powers she gained, the Apis Ideas she commanded, her repulsive appearance that she thought was beautiful...many things here could be called "monstrous," but none of them compared to her alien mind.

"...I see," said Riser. He realized that he was facing someone who would mow down everyone in her path for the sake of her own values... and if that wasn't evil, he didn't know what was.

With that in mind...

"Babylonian Battlegroup, attack!"

...he used his comms device to send out an order.

A moment later, the Babylonian Battlegroup members who were surrounding the fountain plaza showed themselves and charged towards Regina. They had assumed their positions and prepared for an ambush while Riser and the three girls distracted the bee queen.

Twelve Masters all attacked Regina from every direction.

No matter how modified, not even a Superior Job could withstand the combined might of that many ultimate high-rank jobs and Embryo skills. And Regina herself had admitted that she wasn't as enhanced as she could be.

She fought back with her squad of Apis Ideas, but Babylonian Battlegroup's Masters, experienced as they were, easily broke through... and aimed their entire assault straight at Regina.

Multiple Masters all played their most powerful cards in their bid to defeat her.

...And a moment later, *explosions resounded from all across the city.*

Some of them were close at hand — a number of the Queen's Guard had blown up, taking several of the attacking Masters with them.

"Oh, what a surprise. There goes a hundred of them," said Regina — who, unlike the Masters, was completely unharmed.

It was as though the damage she should've sustained went somewhere else.

"What? This is…" Riser instantly understood what happened just now, and it was terrifying.

"…Lifelink!"

"Not exactly, but close enough," said Regina.

The skill she was using was called "Colony for One."

It was the Insect General's passive skill, and it made it so that any damage she suffered would instead be transferred to any in-range insectoids under her command. It had a far greater range than Lifelink and wasn't as restrictive about what types of minions it worked on.

As long as there were Apis Ideas within range, Regina wouldn't receive a single point of damage.

And since any damage to her was transmitted straight to her minions spread all over the capital…

"But that…that means that…"

"If we attack her, we'll just cause more explosions in the city?!"

…It meant that any attacks on Regina could result in disaster.

"Oho ho! So, what will you do now? I wouldn't mind if you keep fighting me just as you have been. No one can sully my beauty!" Regina laughed, summoning more Apis Ideas, which instantly readied their poison stingers and aimed them at the Masters.

Regina couldn't be harmed — she held the capital hostage and could increase the size of her army as she wished.

Those facts made Riser realize that, Gloria aside, he was up against his most fearsome foe yet.

September, 2044

On that day, the Babylonian Battlegroup was fighting a UBM on a plateau near the city of Claymill.

The clan was a force to be reckoned with, and many powerful UBMs had already fallen to them. In most cases, the MVP special rewards for those victories went either to Foltesla — their leader and the third in Altar's duel rankings — or Shulka — the clan's sub-leader who formed the backbone of the group.

However, things were different with the UBM they fought this day — Jetdragon, Valcan.

This monster was a landdragon that had mutated and gained the ability to fly at supersonic speeds by releasing the energy within it to propel itself, much like a rocket. Valcan fought primarily by combining the tough body of a landdragon with immense speed, creating fearsome charge attacks.

Since arriving in the area surrounding Claymill, this UBM had caused tremendous damage to the local ecosystem and greatly affected the lives of the citizens. That was why the Babylonian Battlegroup had set out to vanquish it, but that turned out to be easier said than done.

After all, Valcan was a landdragon that could freely fly through the air. Foltesla and Shulka's attacks couldn't reach it, any power-focused skills always missed, and those with skills focused on accuracy couldn't penetrate its hard outer body.

Battles in *Infinite Dendrogram* were always strongly influenced by compatibility, and it seemed that the Babylonian Battlegroup as a whole stood no chance against Valcan...but there was one among them who was capable of battling the creature.

His name was Masked Riser.

His Embryo was still only in its fifth form, but its skills made it possible for Riser to briefly fly at supersonic speeds and deliver powerful attacks.

Because of that, the clan created a strategy centered around him, and the result was a resounding success.

Though the other members of the Babylonian Battlegroup were barely even able to touch the monster, they could still use their abilities to limit Valcan's movement enough for Riser, fully buffed by Shulka, to deliver an attack that brought it down to the ground. This created an opportunity for the rest of them. Shulka used Lahmu to bind Valcan before it could take to the sky again, letting the others lay into it with everything they had.

When it was defeated, Riser was chosen as the MVP.

He himself was perplexed by this, but everyone else — the leaders included — believed that he richly deserved the award, and that was the end of the battle against Valcan.

However, Riser then found himself perplexed by something else entirely.

His MVP special reward — the first he'd ever gotten — wasn't some powerful piece of gear, but a *material.*

"...What am I supposed to do with this?" he said, frowning beneath his mask. He was sitting in the lounge of his clan's headquarters and staring at the object placed on the table — the item called "Compressed Remains of Jetdragon, Valcan."

It was slightly larger than an adult man and looked like a statue of the dragon who had borne the same name.

Despite that, it was no doubt his MVP special reward: an MVP special *material*, to be precise.

The summoner grouping could use items of this kind as catalysts to summon weaker versions of the UBMs. The necromancer grouping could use them as remains to create undead. If any crafting jobs somehow managed to become MVPs, they could use the material in their production efforts.

As a result, this kind of MVP special reward often went to players with these kinds of jobs.

However, Riser was a fully battle-focused Master. Neither his build nor Embryo had any production capabilities, so there was nothing he could do with the Compressed Remains.

This was his first MVP special reward, but it was completely wasted on him.

"What's wrong, Riser?"

"Leader..." Suddenly, he was approached by Foltesla.

"Oh, that's the MVP reward you got yesterday," the clan leader said. "You still haven't asked someone to work on it?"

"Yes, it's the reward... Wait, what do you mean 'ask someone to work on it?'" Riser said, not sure if he actually heard that right.

"Hm? You didn't know?" the leader said. "Other people can work on MVP special materials, but only the MVP who received it can use the final product."

"Is that how it works?"

"Yeah. Totally battle-focused Masters only get material like this when they know someone who can work with it. I once got an MVP reward that could be turned into medicine and had my wife make it for me. I bet you know someone who can do something with this material too."

"I see," Riser said. A particular individual did indeed come to his mind immediately. "I'll go and put in the request right away."

"See you later, then," said Foltesla. "Show me the final result, okay?"

The Fortress City of Claymill had been built several centuries ago as a defensive base. Because of that, it had a strong equipment production sector; supposedly, it had the most tians with crafting jobs of any city in Altar.

Riser brought the Compressed Remains to the workshop of one of the city's most skilled craftsmen. He opened the door, looked at the many people hard at work, and said, "Excuse me, is Mr. Zola here?"

"Oh, well if it ain't Riser! I'm here, laddie. What brings you in today? Your mask seems all right to me."

An aging man polishing what looked like a piece of armor replied to Riser's call. He was the exact person Riser had been looking for — High Armorsmith Zola. The man was the owner of this workshop and spent day after day working alongside his apprentices there to fulfill many equipment requests from Masters and tians alike.

Riser had known Zola since shortly after he arrived at Claymill, which was more than two years ago by that point. The metal mask Riser was wearing right now — based on those worn by heroes from action-heavy tokusatsu shows — had been created by none other than Zola.

In the early days right after *Infinite Dendrogram's* release, most Masters could only craft things based on designs that already existed. In order to create something that had no established recipe, one had to wait until exceptionally skilled craftsmen appeared or until some sort of technological innovation made the process easier.

The same principle applied to customization of existing designs. Even turning a standard full-face helm into a mask without compromising its stats required a skilled hand.

Creating an item that functioned like a metal full-face helm but *looked* like a mask worn by tokusatsu heroes was too challenging for the first wave of Masters, so Riser had no choice but to rely on a tian craftsman.

However, that came with its own problems.

In hindsight, Riser felt that he had been quite unreasonable back then.

I asked him to make me a hero mask when the concept of "tokusatsu" didn't even exist here, he thought. The word "hero" only makes most tians think of "The Hero," which was a Special Superior Job.

Because of that, he and Zola went through many clashes of opinion before they reached a mutual understanding and began making progress. After much experimentation based on Riser's poor drawings, they eventually created the mask Riser wore now.

As Riser leveled up, he also had Zola create improved versions of the same mask design using better materials. They even had a Recipe for it now, making it easy to create replacements in case the mask was destroyed.

Through their many interactions during all this, Riser and Zola had become such good friends that he was even welcome to join the smith's family and apprentices at his dinner table. There was no craftsman Riser trusted more, and he believed Zola was the perfect man for this job.

"I have a request," Riser said, presenting the Compressed Remains and asking Zola to make equipment out of it.

"Hrm..." However, Zola didn't seem too thrilled about it.

It looked like he was conflicted...even *hesitant* to accept this job.

"Lad... Wouldn't it be better to get someone else to do this?" he asked.

"Why?"

"This material's too much for me...simple as that," he said, placing a hand on the headpiece of the remains. "I've heard of UBM special materials before, but it's my first time seeing the real thing. Never worked with stuff this good. I'd be biting off more than I can chew."

"But…"

"And…I ain't a Superior Job," Zola said with a sigh. "I'm just an everyday craftsman who can't even reach max level. This is a one-of-a-kind material. Don't leave it with me. You're better off taking it to a Superior Job or a Master with an Embryo good for smithing."

Unlike Masters, tians had individual differences in talent that could cap their level below 500.

Zola was well aware of the limits of his abilities and tried to refuse Riser's request because he didn't consider himself good enough. An unskilled craftsman would only waste the rare material, after all.

However, looking into Zola's eyes, Riser also saw an artisan's desire to create something truly unique.

Fully understanding the smith's point, Riser…

"That doesn't matter to me. I want you to create it."

…refused to back down.

"I'm telling you — I'm not good enough…"

"Look at this mask," Riser said as he pointed at his face. "*You* made this. On the other side, I got in an accident and had to give up on my dream of being an actor. But thanks to this mask, I can still be a hero in this world."

At first, Riser's reasons for creating the mask were rather negative.

He wanted a reminder of the dream he'd lost and the possibilities that were now out of his reach.

However, that changed when he had finally donned the first mask that Zola had created for him. It had reflected his dream so strongly that he found it dazzling, and as he wore it, he realized that he now had superhuman stats, a trusty Embryo to take into battle…*and the face of a hero.*

Instead of becoming a reminder of what he'd lost, the mask whispered to him that his dream was now within his grasp.

Thus, he resolved to become someone worthy of that mask.

He put it on, requested that Zola create a suit to go with it, and went out to act as a hero.

He protected people by fighting monsters and bandits, even going on regular patrols.

Both Masters and tians alike saw him as a weirdo.

In time, however, he found friends in Bishmal — who liked Riser's style and joined him on his patrols — as well as Foltesla — who heard rumors about him and invited him to his clan.

And as he continued his activities, he eventually began to be called a hero.

Not "*The* Hero," but just a friendly neighborhood hero — a champion of Claymill.

The mask that was supposed to be just a reminder of a dream he'd lost had given birth to a hero known as Masked Riser. And that was why…

"You're the one I want to create the equipment I'll use when I wear this mask…"

"Lad…"

…Riser insisted that Zola accept this task.

Zola hesitated at his earnest request for a second before saying, "I can't say no to that! Just don't complain if it turns out bad!"

The aged smith had accepted.

"All right! We'll have to give it all we got! Lads! We're starting with a sketch! Gather here once you're all done with your tasks!"

"Got it, boss!" the apprentices replied, all with smiles on their faces. They also wanted to work on something made of MVP special material.

"Design comes first. That's what's most important for a hero, ain't it, lad?" Zola asked.

"Oh, feel free to make it in a way that's easier for you…"

"Don't be an idiot! It's gear for you and you alone! It's gotta be all hero-like!" Zola laughed, poking at Riser's chest. "Even though I dunno if we really understand what 'hero-like' means! We'll make a bunch of designs at the workshop, so you come and choose whichever you like, all right, lad?"

"Okay… I'll be looking forward to it!"

"You better!" And so, Zola and his apprentices took to designing the piece of equipment using Valcan's remains.

It was an arduous task that took almost a whole month.

The result was Valcan Air — armor designed to impart the traits of the Jetdragon to its wearer. It was intended to be used alongside Riser's Hermod and, perhaps most importantly, to look like the apparel of a hero.

In many aspects, it was the perfect armor for Riser…if it weren't for a single flaw.

"Sorry…we messed up."

The flaw was so big that Zola and his apprentices were crestfallen over it.

One of the skills the armor had was called "Destruction Resistance."

MVP special rewards were supposed to have an auto-repair function that recreated them for the owner if they were destroyed, but Valcan Air was merely *resistant* to destruction.

That made it quite durable, of course, but it also meant that it couldn't be repaired. It could even potentially be lost forever.

The remaining durability was actually displayed, so its limits were clearly visible. Once the durability was gone, it would break.

Some would say that this flaw alone made it far worse than any other items in its tier.

"I messed up the most important part…" Zola felt awful. If he'd been a better craftsman, he might've left behind a treasure that matched actual MVP special rewards — a power that could never be lost.

Riser's reaction, however, wasn't what Zola expected.

"No. This is perfect."

"What…?"

"There are things that are precious *because* they may break someday." Not everything lasted forever. There were some things that could break or be lost for all time. However, that also made those things all the more irreplaceable.

To Riser, this armor was as dazzling as the dream he'd lost.

"Lad… You like it?" Zola asked.

"I will treasure this armor…this suit of yours," Riser replied without hesitation.

"…Ha ha hah!" After a brief silence, Zola laughed. "I see. Well, I'm glad the client likes it," he said with a relieved expression and gave Riser a light hug. "All right, let's celebrate a job well done with a party! Drinks are on me!"

His words were met with cheers from his apprentices.

"None of you mind if I bring along my wife and kids, right?"

"Of course not!" said Riser. All smiles, they went to call Zola's family and set out into the evening-tinted city of Claymill.

They chatted and celebrated as they walked — the very picture of a simple, peaceful day-to-day life.

But that was then. Now…only one person from this image was still alive.

A month later, Claymill was attacked by the greatest calamity Altar had ever faced — Tri-Zenith Dragon, Gloria.

The people of Claymill, those who had loved Riser and called him a hero, were snuffed out by its devastating light.

He'd lost his dream.

He'd lost people dear to him.

But there was still something he had.

It was…

The Royal Capital of Altea, Fountain Plaza

"Oho ho! Whatever is the matter? Your movements seem worse than before."

The battle against Regina Apis Idea was turning against the defenders.

Regina redirected any damage done to her towards the Apis Ideas spread all over Altea, making them burst in an explosion that could potentially cause a great deal of damage.

The Queen's Guard standing between them and Regina were a serious threat, as well. Having the Death Soldier job allowed them to move even after dying, giving them time to act before they finally exploded.

They used that time to either charge at Riser's group or run towards nearby buildings like suicide bombers.

It was like they were holding the entire capital hostage. The defenders couldn't recklessly attack Regina, so Riser's party had no choice but to stay on the defensive.

As the battle wore on, Riser tried to find a way to win this.

Maybe we should use some kind of debuff? he thought.

They did have the option of using debuffs instead of attacks, like the White Field Gem he'd used against the Queen's Guard.

However, restricting Regina would probably change nothing. Even if she was Frozen or Petrified, the Apis Ideas would still move on their own and explode upon death.

There was even a chance that they would fight even more erratically and aggressively without an active leader, causing even more havoc inside the city. The Apis Ideas could only be stopped if Regina was defeated.

It might be possible to neutralize them with Charm…but not many people have that skill. Riser only knew of two people who used Charm: Catherine Kongou, the second in kill rankings, and Rook from Death Period.

He hadn't seen the former in a while, and Rook was at the peace conference.

Spells like Death Sentence can kill without dealing damage… but putting them into circulation as Gems is against Altarian law, so I doubt that anyone here has those. Their options were limited — and even those limited options weren't available. It seemed like they were completely powerless against this threat.

"R-Riser…" Kasumi whispered to him, Taijitu in hand. It seemed like she didn't want Regina to hear what she was about to say. "I-I noticed something about the explosions."

She pointed at the surface of the Taijitu and drew a circle before continuing.

"All the bee-men that exploded after the attack were within a radius of three kilometels from here…! The ones in the north were almost completely untouched."

"Really…?!" Riser looked at the map and saw that indeed, the distribution of the Apis Ideas was uneven. When he'd looked at it before going to the fountain plaza, they were spread out more or less randomly. Now, there was a donut-shaped area centered around Regina where the Apis Ideas were more sparse.

41

That was clearly because they had exploded due to Colony for One — meaning that this area of about three kilometels was the skill's active range.

It might have a long reach, but it was indeed limited. That knowledge alone was a blessing.

"We should be able to reduce the damage to Altea if we lure her away from here...!" said Kasumi. "But..."

"Thank you."

"...That would be diffi—huh?" Kasumi realized that Riser had cut her off and thanked her before she was even able to finish her sentence.

He knew what she was trying to say.

Kasumi wanted to suggest taking Regina out of Altea while avoiding the Apis Ideas and preventing her from giving the order to destroy the city.

That would be difficult, no doubt — but Riser saw hope in Kasumi's words.

He knew of something that would let him overcome this challenge. He still had an ace up his sleeve that would let him save the city.

All he had to do now...was gather his resolve and use it.

"...Zola," he said as he took out a little cube — an inventory dedicated solely to the most precious objects.

Inside it, there was something irreplaceable. Something he cherished dearly.

It was a memento of people that were gone forever — a piece of equipment that had been through many battles and was currently at its utmost limit.

Even so...

"I'll use this...one last time."

Even so, Riser decided to equip it.

"And this time...I *will* protect everyone."

He grasped the inventory and called its name out loud, even though he didn't have to.

"Instant Wear…Valcan Air."

A moment later, his gear changed.

He was now clad in armor reminiscent of a tokusatsu hero's suit.

The parts that resembled Jetdragon's propulsion truly gave him the appearance of a hero who had just assumed his powered-up form.

However, the suit was the opposite of pristine. Every armor piece was cracked, and several parts were missing, showing clearly just how many battles Valcan Air had survived.

"R-Riser!"

"Riser, you… That's the…!" Lang and the other Babylonian Battlegroup members raised their voices in shock. They all knew just how precious Valcan Air was to him.

However, they didn't stop him. It would surely break the next time it was used, but Riser equipped it regardless. As his long-time comrades, everyone present knew that he was truly resolved to end this.

"What is *that*? Such shabby armor! It isn't beautiful at all," Regina said, ridiculing Riser's crumbling suit. "How *dare* you try to fight me with such an ugly appearance?"

"I am Riser," he said. "Masked…Riser. A man who was called 'a hero' by those dear to him."

Riser told her exactly what he held most dear — the proof of his dream.

"The Hero? Oho ho ho ho! Reveal tells me that you aren't even a Superior Job. You could not be a worse liar if you tried…but even if you weren't, The Hero is a loser!"

He was killed by King of Plagues, after all, and the fact made her burst into laughter.

Riser also felt something upon hearing the word "loser."

He'd fallen against a mighty dragon without being able to protect the people he loved.

He'd run into an impassable wall in the arena rankings and then continually lost at the hands of those who outranked him.

He'd been slain during a battle which would decide the fate of Gideon, leaving more work for those who survived.

And just recently, he was defeated alongside his friend and Embryo before he could even go to the conference that would decide the fate of Altar.

He had many defeats to his name, and he felt powerless because of that.

Despite that, he had never once changed his attitude.

"So you truly believe that you can surpass someone as beautiful as me and an army as powerful as La Crima's?" Regina said, sneering. Riser, however, seemed unfazed.

"It doesn't matter who I am facing…"

He slowly increased the space between his legs.

"It doesn't matter that I am not a Superior Job…"

He lowered his center of mass.

"It doesn't matter how many times I am defeated…"

He moved his hands…

"I will never retreat."

…and assumed a stance.

"Because…I AM *THEIR* HERO!"

In that moment, as he roared out his challenge, he had the aura of a true champion.

He'd lost his dream.

He'd lost people dear to him.

But there was one thing he still had.

It was…*himself, the hero he knew he could be.*

The ally of justice, who was always ready to protect the weak from the ravages of evil, was still here.

"I see that you are nothing but a fool," said Regina. "Get out of my sight, and take your brazen attitude with you!"

She sent the Queen's Guard to surround him.

Riser wasn't able to break out of their assault — and if he tried, he'd likely cause a chain explosion.

This situation meant certain death for Riser...

"BOOST!"

...but he escaped it by *flying away.*

"What?!" Regina exclaimed as she watched Riser with surprise in her eyes.

Multiple parts of Riser's suit were releasing white smoke, propelling him through the air.

"Boost" was the main trait of the Jetdragon, Valcan. Valcan Air, designed to work in tandem with Hermod, had inherited this trait.

Even though it was reaching the limit of its durability, it was still as effective as the craftsmen designed it to be.

"A-Apis Ideas! Stop this man!" said Regina as she went on the defensive, knowing that she was Riser's target.

She couldn't avoid contact with him, but all damage done to her would be transferred to the Apis Ideas.

Even if he tried to take her away from the city, away from her minions, they would stand in his way and stop him.

Regina was surprised that Riser had suddenly taken to the air, but she was still certain that she couldn't be killed here.

However, it didn't take long for that illusion to be shattered.

After all...Riser wasn't planning on taking her *outside* the city.

"OAARGH!"

"Egh! Gh...?!" With a short roar, Riser instantly closed the distance to Regina and sank his right foot into her stomach.

He then kicked off the ground and twisted his body...

"Valcan Air... FULL BOOOOOOOST!"

...and swung that same foot towards the sky.

A moment later, all the propulsion engines on Valcan Air roared to life; Riser was rocketed upwards, taking Regina with him. The gear built by people he cherished freed him from the chains of gravity and rocketed him up to the sky.

"...Ghhh?! Y-You... What are you *doing*?!" They were heading straight up into the sky, almost perpendicular to the ground.

This was the quickest and simplest path outside the range of Colony for One and the range from which Regina could control the Apis Ideas.

Riser intended to defeat Regina high in the sky.

"Y-You... Get your ugly leg off of me...RIGHT NOW!" Regina quickly realized where this was going. Riser was soaring upward at an overwhelming speed — in the first few seconds alone, many Apis Ideas were already outside the range of Colony for One and even the range of her control entirely.

Eventually, she wouldn't be able to redistribute any of the damage done to her and would finally be the one to die.

"I-I'm too beautiful to die like this!" Despite the boot sinking into her stomach and propelling her upwards, Regina was able to take out her weapon — a spear made of Mythical metal, as poisonous as the stingers of the Apis Ideas. She wasted no time in thrusting it at Riser's head.

He had no way of dodging, and the spear struck him straight in the face.

"I did it...!" Regina exclaimed — only to realize that something wasn't right just a moment later. "...Wait, huh?"

The mask made by the craftsmen of Claymill began to crack… but Riser himself was completely unscathed.

The mask was far less tough than the spear, but it somehow protected its wearer.

It was like a miracle the late craftsmen had left behind them.

"OOOOAAARRRRRGGHHH!"

"Gh…?!" With part of his mask shattered, Riser roared once again. Valcan Air accelerated, driving his foot even deeper and taking them both even higher.

Suddenly, Regina felt an intense pain in her stomach, forcing her to drop her spear. The reason why she actually felt pain in that moment was simple — they were now too far away from all her minions to distribute the damage to them.

"N-No! This…! Ghh…!" Spitting blood, Regina truly began to panic.

However, she wasn't the only one.

This isn't enough… We're not high enough! Riser thought.

Valcan Air was crumbling, unable to withstand the power of its own propulsion.

However, Regina was still alive.

Soon they would begin to lose altitude, bringing Regina back to the range of Colony for One.

If that happened, all damage done to her would once again be distributed to the Apis Ideas, and that would be the end of Altea.

He'd already used the ace up his sleeve, so there was nothing that could —

"…Not yet!"

No…there was still one more thing.

"Come…!" It was something that had been with him ever since he'd appeared in this world.

It had been with him through thick and thin.

It was...

"HERMOOOOOOOOD!" Riser called, and his Embryo answered.

Recently destroyed by Chrono Crown, it was awakened once again.

Though inorganic and silent, it heard the call and returned to its Master.

It seemed both miraculous and inevitable at the same time — a true display of everything that an Embryo was.

And so, Riser, his Embryo, and his armor all moved as one and resumed the acceleration.

It was the ultimate flight, sustained by the power of Hermod, the crumbling Valcan Air, and Riser himself.

Their acceleration was so immense it felt like the world was falling away behind them.

"RISEEEEEEEERRR..." The air here was sparse, but since he still had just enough oxygen to speak, Riser used it to roar once more.

"SKYWAAAARRRD..." Delivering his final, strongest attack, he reached higher than ever before.

"KIIIIIIIIIIIIIIIIIIIIICK!" And finally, like the true hero he was, he pierced straight through Regina's body.

The rumbling of Hermod and Valcan Air were suddenly silenced as he left the world and its soundscape behind.

"No... No..."

Regina, however, was still within the realm of sound.

She had been split in two before she could reach that high.

None of her minions were close enough to prevent this fatal blow.

"Th-This is... I-I'm too beautiful to... Not here... Not now..." As her HP dropped to 0, there was a change in her body — it began to release a red light.

"Ahh… No… No…" She knew better than anyone what that meant.

It was the Insect General's final skill, Even a Worm Will Burn.

She herself had been modified into an insectoid, so obviously it would work on her, as well.

"No… NO!" It was as though she was getting her just deserts for treating the once-human Apis Ideas like disposable objects.

"This… THIS CAN'T BE HAPPENING!" With that final scream, Regina Apis Idea detonated high in the Altarian sky.

Riser heard a faint explosion from far below him.

"…This time, I did protect them all," the hero whispered right before his consciousness faded.

His face bore a pure expression of relief.

Chapter Twenty

The Fiery Dance of the Jiangshi and the Mummy

Royal Capital, Altea, Castle

While the city was thrown into chaos by the swarming Apis Ideas, the castle was facing an even greater threat — King of Blaze, Feuer Lazburn, now known as "Ignis Idea." He'd broken into the castle through the main gate and was currently drowning it in flame.

Besides him, there were two other Ideas — one spider-like, the other with the twisted form of a bat— that had broken in along Feuer and afterwards split up to kill the guards within. Tians like the Royal Guard fought back as best they could, but it was clear that they lacked the power to overcome this menace. Even the Masters that had rushed from the city to join the defense effort had been ultimately defeated by the three Ideas.

Things might've been different if Altimia had been there, or if the Celestial Knight or Arch Sage had still been alive — any of them might've been able to repel these attackers.

However, none of them were present, nor was anyone with a comparable level of power. The castle, at the very heart of the kingdom, was in real danger of falling.

Infiltration successful.

Using the chaos as cover, *someone* had infiltrated the castle.

It was none other than King of Thieves, Zeta.

Code III: Mirage is still active, she thought. *The system that would prevent skill activation has either been deactivated…or it was never there to begin with.*

She'd sneaked into the castle using a mix of a job skill that removed her presence and an Embryo skill that made her invisible to all mundane sight.

Normally, she would have triggered the castle's magical defense system, but due to the assault from the three Ideas — most notably, the bat-like Idea's attack on the magic distribution equipment — the system's range was shot. That, combined with *visible* attackers drawing the guards' focus, had allowed her to enter the castle completely unnoticed.

They really are potent, Zeta thought as she considered the Ideas she had let loose and thought back to an event from several months ago — the very moment that La Crima had given her these Ideas.

Soul Trader, La Crima was a well-known name in the business realm of society's underbelly, standing shoulder-to-shoulder with the arms dealer known as The Weapon, Rascal the Bloodonyx.

In truth, La Crima was actually a *pair* of people acting as one.

One of them was a lady in a wheelchair. The most notable thing about her appearance was her *paleness*. She was wearing a white hat with a wide brim, a white dress, and white bandages that covered the upper half of her face — eyes included. The exposed lower half had a shape that many would describe as "beautiful."

The other person was a man pushing the wheelchair. In stark contrast to the lady, he was noticeably *black*. Standing over two metels tall and completely covered in black leather belts, he looked like some kind of mummy.

One was a Master, while the other was most likely an Idea the Master controlled, but it was considered something of a taboo to ask which was which. Everyone who had found out was met with a grim fate.

As the Soul Trader, La Crima dealt in modified slaves.

Their Superior Embryo was "True Form Alteration, Idea." Its type was a mix of Chariot and Guardian called "Advanced Legion," and it was focused on humanoid modification. They modified countless tians and sold them off as high-quality slaves.

A certain clan member had once called them a "merchant of death," to which they responded, "A merchant of death? What a strange title to give me. What I do is uncover people's latent potential and give them a chance to live their lives to the fullest. Would it not be more apt to call me a merchant of *life*? -life?" La Crima talked in unison, with one of them falling slightly behind.

The person they were talking to at the time — Gerbera — would have laughed if it had only been a morbid joke, but the fact that La Crima was completely serious merely left her speechless. That, combined with their warped mindset and strange appearance, made them stand out even among the oddball criminals of Illegal Frontier.

However, few people had ever even laid eyes upon this bizarre duo. La Crima did business using their Idea subordinates as representatives, so not even their business partners knew what they looked like.

Despite being such a mysterious figure, they had been placed on wanted lists and had their supposed hideout in Caldina targeted by King of Termination and King of Revelry — only to somehow make it out alive and cross the strait to Tenchi.

There were only two types of people that knew that La Crima were two people acting as one. The first type was their comrades — the core members of I.F.

The second type was a select few "foundations." Most of La Crima's modifications were done remotely by having someone carry a piece of their Embryo to the target, but they always showed themselves to tians with Superior Jobs, who formed some of the most important "foundations" for their work.

That included four of the Ideas that would be released onto the capital, Regina Apis Idea being one of them.

Zeta, in fact, had met up with La Crima in person to acquire these Ideas.

"Question. I have something to ask you."

They were at a port town in southern Huang He. Zeta was preparing to head west after having stolen a number of the Treasurebeast Orbs left behind by the Draconic Emperor that came before the previous one. La Crima was currently operating in Tenchi, and they had actually come all this way just to meet Zeta and give her the Jewel containing the four Ideas based on Superior Jobs. Included as well was the Jewel holding all the Apis Ideas that would serve Regina.

They also informed her that three other Ideas would meet up with her after finishing their tasks.

Those three Ideas would go on to be defeated by King of Light, F...but that was another story.

"What is it? -it?" One of La Crima's voices again lagged very slightly behind the other.

"Explanation. Tell me the concepts behind the four Superior Job-based Ideas and how to use them."

"That certainly does need explaining. -ning," La Crima said as they both nodded. "Regina was designed to make the best use of her skills as Insect General. However, the majority of the modifications went into the Apis Ideas under her command. Regina herself was mostly untouched. I merely increased her ability to control the Apis Ideas, slightly buffed her stats, and changed her type into insectoid to make her own skills apply to her. -her."

"Question. Why?"

"Because she refused any modifications to her appearance. Idea's modifications work by redesigning the target's physical body.

Whether a slave is optimized for beauty or battle, the more they are modified, the more their appearance changes. If I cannot change the appearance, the modifications I can do are limited. -ted."

"Another question. Why did you not ignore her refusal?"

"Because of a promise. -mise."

"I see…" That answer was enough for Zeta.

She knew that despite having a warped sense of morality that made them unable to recognize true villainy, La Crima always fulfilled their promises. They did tell lies — as evidenced by the mystery of their true identity — but when they gave their word, they kept it.

After remembering something that related to La Crima, Zeta simply said, "Next."

"Very well. -well," said La Crima, seemingly unconcerned by Zeta's brief silence. "Before the modification, Aranea had to use tools to deliver his potent poison and binding abilities. I spliced him with materials from an upper-Pure-Dragon-tier spider, allowing him to use these abilities by default and without limit. The materials needed are automatically created and provided by an inventory implanted into the body. -dy."

And that was the genesis of King of Venom — Aranea Idea.

"Vespertilio had his sensory organs enhanced and was given the ability to avoid being spotted. By creating an unperceivable space, he can force himself to enter a state of invisibility. Like this, he has increased potential for ambushing and ability to continue fighting beyond that. He also has a magic-sensing function that lets him act as a radar for living creatures and magic installations. -tions."

That was the description of King of Raids — Vespertilio Idea.

These Ideas were a few steps more powerful than they had been as tian Superior Jobs. The modifications given to them greatly improved the abilities they possessed.

It was as though these tians were granted Embryos that meshed perfectly with their builds.

Since tian Superior Jobs were often far above Masters in terms of battle technique, these two were truly fearsome foes.

They were below Regina in overall battle potential, but they were no doubt far above her as individual combatants.

However, neither of them were the strongest out of the tians La Crima had just given to Zeta.

"Ignis is actually my most powerful magic-based Idea yet. Out of all the Ideas, he's behind only Ferrum and Cantus. -tus."

That was La Crima's evaluation of Ignis Idea — King of Blaze, Feuer Lazburn.

"He was modified according to his own wishes. He asked for magic power that surpassed that of the Arch Sage. -Sage."

"Confirmation. Was that even possible?"

"The method was quite simple, actually. -lly." La Crima's words seemed absurd on their face. How could surpassing the magic power of Altar's legendary Arch Sage be "simple?" The answer lay in the words that followed.

"I merely used ten of the Sacrifice slaves I cultivated. -ted," they said, as though this was nothing special. "I connected them to his heart and the core of his brain as MP sources. This was no different from implanting monster abilities. Though, I didn't expect all the extra MP to be counted as part of Ignis's own pool and actually *increase* his maximum. I removed the parts of the Sacrifices' brains responsible for thinking, so I believe they might've been recognized not as individual people, but as Ignis's own organs. The fact that this could be the case while they still maintained the Sacrifice job surprised even me. I did some experiments on tians with other jobs, and when I removed their ability to think, they either lost their jobs or simply didn't have their stats merged with the subject who received them as implants.

I believe that Ignis turned out the way he did due to the nature of the Sacrifice job. Also, though I was already using Idea to reduce the risk of transplanted organ rejection, I matched the implants' blood type to Ignis's to reduce the risk even further. Because of this, I'm currently short on Sacrifice slaves with blood type B and...ohh, that information is unnecessary. -ary."

Possibly feeling obligated to do so, La Crima gave Zeta a long-winded explanation. Even contemplating the acts they described would make some people nauseous, but they didn't seem to even think about that.

Though she'd never admit it, even Zeta found this side of La Crima to be truly unnerving.

In fiction, there were mad scientists that mistreated their guinea pigs to satisfy their sadistic tendencies, and Zeta felt that La Crima wouldn't be nearly as disturbing if they were anything like that — she'd merely write them off as "just that kind of person."

Their behavior just wasn't the same as that. If you got past the fact that La Crima were two people acting and speaking as one, you would note how serious and sincere their words were. It was as though they truly thought nothing of what they were saying, no matter how morbid it was.

Their leader — Sechs — was similar in that regard, but...

...*No point in thinking about it too deeply right now,* Zeta thought.

I.F. was a gathering of people like this. Everyone here had come to *Infinite Dendrogram* seeking things they couldn't find in reality. Sechs sought a goal. La Crima sought love. Gerbera would never say it, but she was seeking "a special version of herself."

Zeta was no exception. She was here because she was seeking something within *Infinite Dendrogram* — some would say that her goal was greater than that of the others.

Everyone had such goals, some bigger, some smaller, but the members of I.F. — the wanted Superiors — didn't hesitate to harm others for the sake of what they sought.

That was why they were wanted, and that was why I.F. was the way it was.

As a fellow member of this clan, I really can't say anything about La Crima's sense of morality, Zeta thought.

"Back to the matter of Ignis, the Sacrifice slaves were all modified to have more MP. I also used pre-ancient civilization MP-increasing items that were given to me by Rascal. As a result, Ignis has more MP than even spellcaster Superiors. -ors."

La Crima instantly realized that they had misspoken.

"Oh, that doesn't count The Earth, of course. -course."

"Exception. You don't have to tell me that his case is special."

Not even UBMs could match The Earth when it came to MP.

"Number. How much MP does Ignis Idea actually have?" Zeta asked, to change the subject.

"98 million. -on," La Crima said, again seemingly thinking nothing of it.

"...*What*?!" Not even Zeta could keep her composure upon hearing that.

There were high-level tian spellcasters with Superior Jobs that struggled to reach one million MP. Exceptions like The Earth aside, even Masters with MP growth boosted by Embryos would have only two or three times that, at most.

Yet Ignis Idea had *98 million MP* — clearly an insane number.

"Spell power isn't directly proportional to max MP, but there is a correlation. Besides that, I also gave him more arms he may use to release his spells. -spells."

Despite creating something so powerful, La Crima showed almost no excitement as they finished their explanation.

"Ignis is the most potent magic-output device besides The Earth. I am sure he will have no trouble burning down a castle. -tle."

Royal Capital, Altea, Castle

As she remembered that event, especially La Crima's last line, Zeta heaved a silent sigh. It truly did seem like the castle might be burned to the ground.

It's too early, she thought. Claudiah's request would be easier to fulfill if Zeta just let that happen, but it would ultimately get in the way of her own goal.

I'm here for the ten orbs that were brought into Altar. Specifically, the Treasurebeast Orbs brought here alongside Canglong by the Huang He diplomatic mission. They had been a gift to Altar as part of the marriage-alliance deal between the ruling families of those two countries.

When Huang He opened their treasury to select the ten orbs they would send as a gift, I was able to steal seven. Getting more than that was too hard even for me.

The treasury was full of magic traps left behind by the fabled Draconic Emperor who had created the orbs, so stealing from it was a challenge even for King of Thieves herself.

That's why I'll be retrieving the orbs that were removed from the treasury the normal way. Zeta had many uses for these UBM orbs and the MVP special rewards they contained. She could hand them to fellow I.F. members based on their abilities, and she could give them to Logan as sacrifices for his devil summoning skills.

The orbs could also be used to simply spread chaos, just like they were already doing in Caldina.

Somewhere in this castle, there were ten UBMs whose abilities were known and that had been weakened by centuries of being sealed away. Their value was immense, and no one in I.F. could ignore them — especially not King of Thieves.

There was a high chance that they would be at the guest house, but I couldn't find them there. That leaves two options: they're either with the prince, or they've already been handed over to Altar.

Whichever it was, Canglong was bound to know.

With the castle in chaos, the royalty must be taking shelter somewhere. I'll find where it is and find out the orbs' location by taking the prince or his fiancée hostage.

With that decided, she began searching for Canglong. There was a hallway here leading deeper into the castle, shrouded in darkness since the magic distribution system had been cut. She prepared to take a step forward into it...*only to jump to the side.*

A split-second later, something golden moved at supersonic speeds and pierced the space where she was standing only a moment ago.

This is... The golden object made a quick turn and chased after her.

Zeta got a better look at it as she evaded the object — it was an *extending prosthetic arm.*

She followed it with her eyes to its source...a humanoid silhouette at the other side of the long, dark hallway.

Though, perhaps "humanoid" didn't quite describe what she saw.

The figure was tall enough to touch the high ceilings of this castle, and that was only one of its unnatural features.

The silhouette continued to freely attack Zeta with its golden arm —though, it was questionable if it was actually *targeting* her.

Although the first attack seemed to be aimed directly at Zeta, the entity had lost sight of her right after, most likely due to Code III — Zeta's optical camouflage skill.

Still, the prosthetic covered an enormous area just by flailing about. It was entirely possible for the entity to land a hit on Zeta by accident.

Because of this, Zeta focused entirely on evasion, and had successfully dodged everything so far.

However, a number of *Fu tags* applied to the prosthetic arm suddenly blasted beams in every direction.

I can evade this too. But wait... This is...

Zeta evaded the fiery bolts — but the moment she did, she realized that they weren't meant to be an attack.

"There gOes your camouflAge. I can seE a bit of whAt ya can do nOw," the entity muttered, its voice distorted by some means.

Just like the figure had said, the skill that hid Zeta from view was expiring.

That was because the magical beams had lit the surroundings on fire and increased the temperature of the air.

Zeta's Embryo's abilities required extremely precise control, so she couldn't account for sudden changes in the environment fast enough. Code III actually required even more fine-tuning than any other skill, so perhaps it was inevitable that she wouldn't be able to keep up with the sharp increase in temperature.

Brought out by the flame, Zeta's outline became a visible distortion in the air.

I suppose she already has a good guess about my abilities, Zeta thought. The rumors surrounding her, as well as her fairly recent duel against Logan, had made it easy for this enemy to assume the nature of her Embryo.

Left with no real choice, she gave up and canceled the optical camouflage.

The entity also stepped into the light of the fire, making it obvious whom Zeta was facing.

"Master Jiangshi, Xunyu."

"And yoU're King of Thieves, Zeta, arEn't ya?" Zeta was now faced with the Huang He Superior that she recognized as the greatest threat among the Masters left at the capital.

Xunyu also recognized Zeta's face from the brief period when she had been the top duelist in Dryfe.

And both of them knew full well just how dangerous the other was.

In that hallway, bathed in flame, the two combatants stared directly at each other.

As they both stood on guard, each watching for any movements the other made, Xunyu said, "Since you'rE here, I guess this whole attAck's Dryfe's doing? Man, they'rE just doin' whatever they want nOw, huh?"

"Question. I won't tell you whether your assumption is correct, but I have a question of my own… How did you notice me?"

Zeta couldn't help but wonder how Xunyu spotted King of Thieves herself while she was hiding her physical form and even her very presence.

"Huh? I couldn't feEl or see ya, but yoU *are* mOvin' through space, arEn't ya? I'm sensitivE to stuff like thAt."

"…Understandable." Though limited, Xunyu's Superior Embryo had a skill that let it attack by teleporting through space itself. Because of that, Xunyu's Fu were imbued with space-scanning magic. Such spells were the specialty of Onmyoji, but Master Jiangshi could perform them as well.

Xunyu had searched the castle's interior and found Zeta exactly *because* she was moving at a slow pace — something you wouldn't expect from a person inside a building under siege.

"Unexpected. I didn't anticipate this. I thought you would go fight the Ideas."

"You mean thE things makin' a mess out frOnt? Did ya see what an entrAnce they made? You dOn't have to be as keen as me to tell that it's a distrAction. Well, no onE who's meant to protEct the castle would leave those things bE…but that's not my rOle." Someone meant to guard the castle wouldn't be so quick to set it on fire, after all, even if that was what it took to expose an enemy. "What I'm here fOr…is to protect Cang and thE others. Activate."

With that word, all the Fu that Xunyu spread throughout the hallway with her prosthetic arms suddenly fired beams towards Zeta.

"Understandable." Zeta saw this coming, though, and twisted her body quickly enough to evade the beams.

However, Xunyu reacted just as quickly to the evasion and moved her arms at supersonic speeds, tracing them across the sides of the hallway. Attached to the insides of her arms were countless offensive Fu, which joined the ones that she'd spread around the area to unleash a barrage of fiery blasts that became quite difficult to evade.

Unlike in the arena where she'd fought Figaro, the space here was limited. The net of beams she created left no space large enough for a person to slip through.

Zeta had nowhere to run…

"Code II: Shelter."

…so she simply *didn't*.

Half a second later, countless beams pierced into her.

They carried enough power to turn her into burnt Swiss cheese… yet that didn't happen.

The beams all stopped before they struck Zeta's body as though they had hit an invisible wall.

And after withstanding this attack, she went on the offensive.

"Code I: Forming. Code IV: Artillery."

"Ah…!" In the space of a moment, Xunyu wrapped herself in the left leg part of Tenaga-Ashinaga.

A split-second later, she was assaulted by attacks from every direction.

They all had enough power to pierce through steel, but not enough to damage a Superior Embryo like Tenaga-Ashinaga.

However, the lack of power wasn't the main issue…

…*I can't see them,* Xunyu thought. All the attacks aimed at her just now were completely transparent.

She could see *something,* but only if she strained her eyes. It seemed like a distortion in the air, something akin to a heat haze.

They're…projectiles made of air. There were Wind magic spells that compressed the air and fired pulverizing projectiles just like these.

But Zeta wasn't using magic — it was an Embryo skill.

That could only mean that her Embryo was…

"…, …?" Xunyu tried to say her guess out loud, only to realize she couldn't make a sound.

I'm in a vacuum… The flames that had lit up the hallway had vanished, as well.

This place was completely devoid of air, besides the projectiles Zeta was using.

There also seemed to be a difference in pressure that prevented any new air from flowing in.

A barrage, followed by a truly nasty trick. I'm undead, so I can deal with not breathing, but I imagine that it'd be over for most people by now. As Master Jiangshi, Xunyu had all the positives of being undead without the negatives, letting her function normally even in a situation like this. Ignoring the vacuum around her, she continued attacking with her prosthetic arms.

Zeta evaded or deflected them using invisible walls.

"Change." Realizing that the vacuum had done nothing, Zeta switched to another tactic.

That switch was obvious even to Xunyu — all the metal lights and door ornaments began to rust at an absurd rate.

She increased the oxygen concentration in the air... Pure oxygen was an extremely potent natural oxidizing agent. It reacted with countless types of matter, creating various other compounds. Xunyu quickly realized that her equipment was being affected as well.

Oxygen also had strong inflammatory properties, making it dangerous to use fire magic. If Zeta hadn't snuffed out the flames with her vacuum, this place would now be burning as brightly as the main gate.

She's not wearing the bandages just for fashion... On their inside, there's gear that acts like space or diving suits, protecting her from the changes in air pressure and atmospheric composition.

The nature of Zeta's Superior Embryo was more or less obvious by now.

"Optical camoUflage, invisible walls, air projEctiles, vacuum, oxygen concentration cOntrol... Your Embryo has powEr over the air itsElf, dOesn't it?" Xunyu said, continuing to attack with her arms, defend with her legs, and dodge using fire attacks. "You get optical camouflAge by distorting the air. You insulatE yourself by creating multiple lAyers of vacuum and air. Your bArriers are just cOmpressed air. The wind projEctiles are exactly thAt. Then the vacuUm, and the opposIte with oxygen overcOncentration. It's too damn obvioUs."

Zeta said nothing in response, but there was a hint of surprise on her hidden face.

"AnyOne would figure it oUt if you used as much stuff on thEm as you did on me. But it's nOt like it's a big deal thAt I know it now, right?"

If Xunyu was right about Zeta's Embryo's abilities, Xunyu's awareness of it wouldn't be much of a disadvantage. After all, no living creature could survive without air. It was the opposite of Gerbera's Alhazred, which lost half of its potential when the target merely knew of its existence.

Zeta's Embryo was as strong as ever, even if the enemy knew exactly what it did.

"This Embryo isn't limitEd to just basic control either. You can actually mess with the air's cOmposition. There's a whole lOt ya can do with somethin' like that. Even the skills yoU're using look the same, but are actUally pretty dAmn different."

Xunyu was referring to the barrier that protected Zeta from the beams and the wall that was blocking her prosthetic arm attacks — the barriers that deflected physical attacks much like Silver's compressed air walls. The barriers were actually so dense that they didn't even allow light to pass, but she camouflaged them by making them transparent using Code III. Zeta had a wide array of abilities at her disposal and always used the right one for any situation. It was second nature to her.

"And evEn though you mEss with the air and its compositiOn, you're not creating any poison gAs or anythin' like thAt. You're just cOntrolling the air thAt's already there, aren't yA?" Xunyu guessed that instead of "filling" the space with pure oxygen, Zeta had actually separated the oxygen from the other gases, which she was now using for her air barriers and projectiles.

That made Zeta's abilities seem weaker, but it was important to remember that she could use the air around her to do *whatever she wanted*.

Zeta was a Superior so versatile that she could fight just about anyone.

Xunyu herself had lots of versatility, but it seemed that Zeta outshone even her.

Another notable aspect was just how *well* Zeta controlled these powers of hers. When Xunyu presented her guess regarding her powers, Zeta was slightly shaken, but that hadn't affected her barriers or projectiles whatsoever. She was also constantly moving so that she wouldn't be an easy target for Xunyu's ultimate skill.

I guess I should be glad that she can't take me out with just this, Xunyu thought. Code IV — the skill Zeta used to fire the projectiles — wasn't strong enough to break through her defenses, while the air barriers weren't capable of completely deflecting her attacks.

Her versatility had come at the cost of output.

On top of that, the vacuum and corrosive air that would kill living creatures were powerless against an undead.

It seemed that Xunyu would win this damage race, but...

The Embryo is likely meant to support her actions and moves as a Thief. The outcome of this battle will be decided by something else.

It wouldn't be a true battle between Masters if it came down to their Embryos alone.

There's also King of Thieves' ultimate job skill...the one that lets her tear out the other guy's heart in that duel just by touching him. I can't let her get too close to me. Besides that, she has that Superior MVP reward I know nothing about.

Xunyu had read about King of Thieves' ultimate job skill. It was called "Absolute Steal," and it allowed the user to steal *anything* within the object they were touching.

If they used it on an inventory, they could take any item inside regardless of how steal-proof it was. If used on living creatures, it could easily remove their organs.

She can probably use her control over air to throw me off by creating a false image, then take advantage of that to close in and steal my heart. Hell, if I wasn't undead, she could've easily done that the moment she created the vacuum or made the air toxic.

That was exactly what had happened to Logan in their duel — Zeta had incapacitated him with toxic air and a localized vacuum before closing in and using Absolute Steal to take his heart.

She can easily create a pathway to a certain kill... Man, the more I think about it, the more it stuns me just how versatile this Embryo is. As usual, Xunyu speculated a little about what she could do against her enemies before crafting a strategy to corner and bring them down. She had stumbled against Figaro because she lacked information about his Embryo, but regardless, Xunyu no doubt had an eye for strategy and high adaptability. That was exactly what Xunyu was doing now — calmly analyzing what Zeta could do with her Embryo, and how she could be defeated.

Zeta actually noticed that Xunyu was doing everything she could to keep her distance, and she couldn't help but say something "... Question. I thought you were still a child. How are you so knowledgeable, with such a sense for battle?"

"Ha! I've been herE for years! You think I wouldn't leArn a thing or two over all this timE?"

"Obvious. I suppose that makes sense. Spending time here makes your mental age advance beyond your body's age."

Though Logan's mind seems to be as old as he is, Zeta added mentally. It was uncertain which one of them was developing in a healthier manner.

"Interesting. The subject of whether children should outgrow their bodies would make for an interesting discussion."

"FOrget about mY mental age and stOp talking like that. It's annOying."

Silence descended. Having one aspect of her identity denied like that made Zeta's expression change slightly under the bandages.

She was known as a calm and collected person even by her clan members, but that didn't mean that she was emotionless — as evidenced by her surprise at La Crima's explanations and her reactions in this fight.

In fact, if her visage hadn't been hidden by bandages, she wouldn't have been able to maintain her customary poker face.

"…Stop. If you feel that way, then try and stop me."

"ThAt's the plAn!" Xunyu's extending right arm flew towards Zeta, who tried to block it with an air barrier at first, only to switch to evasion.

A moment later, Xunyu's arm smashed through the air barrier, gleaming brightly as it did. The shine wasn't from her claws, but the dagger clutched in them — Yinglong's Fang, Suling Yi.

This weapon had a trait that made it stronger the more MP was placed into it, as well as a power that let it pierce defenses. With that combination, it finally broke through Zeta's air barrier.

Xunyu hadn't used Suling Yi at first because of its MP drain, but she'd now decided to finish this battle as quickly as possible. If she didn't, she feared Zeta would've eventually broken the stalemate and killed her using Absolute Steal.

Needless to say, Zeta reacted to this as well. For a Superior, she had relatively low HP and END. The blade that Xunyu was flailing around would take her Brooch with the first hit, then her life with the second.

However, Xunyu hadn't gone completely on the offensive. Instead of just extending her arms towards her enemy, she retracted them when necessary, giving her enough space to deal with whatever Zeta decided to throw at her.

King of Thieves was at a clear disadvantage now. Even though her ultimate job skill could instantly kill Xunyu, her opponent's reach advantage made this difficult. Her chances of victory were slim.

Realizing this, Zeta decided to use the ace up her sleeve.

"…Three types."

"Hm?"

"Three types. Solo combat type, wide-scale suppression type, and wide-scale extermination type. These are the three main fighting styles, and I am all of them at once."

"…I can tEll." Zeta's words had seemingly come out of nowhere and Xunyu responded with suspicion. This was both to get information about her opponent…and to buy her enough time to prepare her ultimate skill.

While attacking with both arms and defending with her left leg, she prepared her right leg to use The Limbs Reach for the Horizon — Tenaga-Ashinaga.

"I actually nEver saw an Embryo as vErsatile as yoUrs. It doesn't surprIse me that you cAn do any combat stYle."

Zeta's Embryo's control over air gave it immense utility. The very fact that she could hold her own against Xunyu made it clear that she was a capable solo fighter, and she could easily suppress and exterminate larger groups simply by manipulating the air around them.

"Shared sentiment. Even I have only seen two Embryos that are more versatile than mine."

"…That's twO more than I expected."

"Below. There is little point in trying to compete in versatility against people who are reckless and inexhaustible," Zeta said, picturing the two I.F. members she had in mind. "Question. Back to what I was saying, which of these three battle styles…" she continued as she raised three of her fingers, "…do you think is my *actual* one?"

"Ah…!" Zeta presented this like a question, and Xunyu instantly understood what she was getting at — there was one battle style that Zeta was the *most* lethal at.

Her question, therefore, was more like a statement: "I will kill you with my *true* battle style."

Combat, suppression, extermination…! She's so versatile that I can't even guess which one she'll use! Xunyu thought. However, it was clear that whatever was coming, it would no doubt spell her doom.

Should she go on the defensive? Or should she retreat? Xunyu did not have the answer.

She's probably a combat type if she comes close! And she's one of the other two if she keeps her distance to avoid getting caught up in her own attack! If she's a combat type, there's a high chance that she'll use her Absolute Steal! That was Zeta's ultimate job skill, able to rip out hearts. To Xunyu's knowledge, it was the most lethal skill she had, so she observed her enemy with all the caution she could muster.

A moment later, she noticed Zeta approaching her.

"SHaAH!" Xunyu tried to stop her, first by moving both hands as fast as possible, then blasting out her fire magic beams without concern for the high concentration of oxygen in the air.

However, the moment she fired them…she noticed something.

…The oxygen concentration is back to normal! It wasn't a vacuum, nor was the area flooded with oxygen — the air composition was close to standard.

That moment, several of the beams hit Zeta, *only to pass through her like she was a mirage.*

No, not "like" a mirage — that was exactly what she was.

It's a variation of her optical camouflage skill! That could only mean that Zeta herself was elsewhere.

As Xunyu prepared to use her spatial scan Fu, she felt a presence behind her.

"Gh…!" The moment she realized the presence behind her was Zeta, she released beams from the left leg that she had wrapped around herself.

Driven away by the blast, Zeta's presence made distance between the two of them.

Xunyu didn't feel like she had been touched or that she had lost any organs. By covering herself with Tenaga-Ashinaga, she was able to prevent Zeta from using Absolute Steal on her heart.

I blockEd it… I think. Despite that, Xunyu wasn't ready to relax just yet. Still wary of any follow-up attacks, Xunyu used her spatial scan Fu to search for Zeta…

"Where the hEll's she going?!"

…only to realize that she seemed to be heading *away* from Xunyu.

She had left Xunyu behind to focus on finding Canglong and Elizabeth.

"You goddAmn… I'll tear out your hEart!"

When she had initially used her spatial scan Fu and discovered Zeta's presence, Xunyu hadn't employed her ultimate skill because she wasn't sure if the presence was an enemy.

Things were different now. Xunyu *knew* that Zeta was an intruder — a foe to be taken down at any cost.

That meant that she could use her ultimate skill on Zeta, no matter where she was in the castle.

As she prepared to do just that, Xunyu noticed another change in the environment.

"Hm…?"

The air was different again. It wasn't a vacuum. Nor was it full of oxygen or some kind of poison gas.

Still, she could sense that something was different about it.

"It's…!" Another realization struck her.

She'd already considered it once. If Zeta made distance between them, it could only mean one thing.

"Activation. Absolute Dominion Over the Sky — Uranus."

Right after that voice echoed through the air, a part of the castle was drowned in dazzling light and temperatures reaching tens of thousands of degrees.

"Cremated. It *is* tradition in Huang He to burn corpses, is it not?" Zeta whispered, standing some distance away from the scorched area of the castle.

Zeta's Embryo — Cry of Air, Uranus — was, as Xunyu had assumed, an Embryo that controlled the atmosphere. By changing its density, concentration, and composition, she was able to create optical camouflage, vacuums, oxygen-filled spaces, defensive barriers, and even air cannons.

Back at Granvaloa, she even used Uranus's air barriers on submarines.

However, this versatility came at a cost of output. If you could do many things, you either needed more external Resources, or the things you could do were simply weaker than they would be in the hands of a more focused individual.

This was a rule that applied to all Embryos, and Uranus was a latter case.

However, there were ways to circumvent such flaws, however briefly.

In Uranus's case, it was its ultimate skill: Absolute Dominion Over the Sky — Uranus.

This ability briefly increased its output, letting Zeta surpass the limits of its atmosphere control.

In her battle against the SUBM, she'd used it to push seawater away with walls of air and open up a giant hole in the ocean.

The scale of what she did in her battle against Xunyu was far smaller, but the action was far more complex. Normally, her control over the air didn't go beyond merely manipulating its constituent parts, but now, she was actually able to create *new atoms* based on the existing elements in the air.

Zeta had used Uranus to create deuterium and tritium, then used them to cause a nuclear fusion reaction.

This reaction produced helium and *immense* amounts of energy — in other words, she had made a hydrogen bomb, without nuclear warheads or any materials, and in average ambient temperatures.

As far as such explosions went, it was unusually clean. Since Zeta had held back a little, it was a small-scale reaction, and she even controlled the radiation to prevent it from leaking to the surroundings.

However, that didn't limit the energy that had been released. It was more than enough to demolish the hallway they were in, and Xunyu was at the epicenter of the explosion.

"Answer. I am mostly a wide-scale extermination type," Zeta said to the empty air.

She was currently alone, with no one else in sight — a Superior who possessed the power of a hydrogen bomb...of nuclear fusion.

Powerful as she was, though, this had made her break out in a cold sweat.

It was obvious why — in order to create this fusion reaction with her ultimate skill, she had to control everything *manually.*

These "Codes" were skills in their own right, functioning like macros that limited and automated the control of her atmospheric manipulation, but her ultimate skill's fusion reaction had to be constructed manually. A single mistake could mean death by her own hands.

The fact that she used an ability that posed such a danger to herself just showed how cornered Zeta truly felt.

With Xunyu protecting herself against Absolute Steal and the environment being unsuitable for her Superior MVP reward, she had no choice but to use her ultimate skill.

"…Powerful. You are among the most powerful Masters I have ever fought, but it looks like not even *you* could withstand this."

Nothing remotely human could withstand the explosion of a hydrogen bomb and live.

On top of that, Zeta had taken Xunyu's only hope of survival. She had an accessory clutched tightly in her hand — a Lifesaving Brooch.

It belonged to Xunyu.

When Zeta had approached her, she used a particular skill. It was actually one of her most basic abilities as a Thief — Steal.

Its effect was simple — it gave her a chance to steal any item from an inventory or any piece of gear a target had equipped. As King of Thieves, Zeta's Steal skill level was EX, which gave a 100% chance for her to Steal *any* unprotected item.

This was one of the strategies she specialized in — taking the enemy's Brooch without their notice, then hitting them with a fatal attack.

With Xunyu not having any accessories that could protect her, her death penalty was all but certain.

"Confirmed. The Master Jiangshi job has high survivability, but I knew from her duel against Figaro that high heat can extinguish her without leaving a trace."

Because of that, Zeta had made the right choice in using the fusion reaction.

Or at least, so she thought.

"Hm…?"

Suddenly, she heard something shatter. Looking down at her hand, she saw that the Brooch there was still intact.

The brooch that shattered was *the one she was wearing.*

Belatedly, she turned and saw Yinglong's Fang, grasped by a metal arm and heading straight towards her spine.

"Gh…! Wait…!" Surprised, Zeta jumped away. But unlike before, the prosthetic arm didn't follow after her. As though rusty, it made a creaking sound before falling to the ground. It seemed as though the attack that shattered her Brooch was the most that arm could do at the moment.

"Hah…you finAlly…stopped talking…wEird…" Those words then reached Zeta's ears.

The speaker was none other than Xunyu — the very person who was supposed to have been burnt to ashes in the fusion reaction. But there she was, behind Zeta, in a state so awful that you couldn't tell where her clothes ended and her body began, extending only her right arm.

"You… How did you survive the explosion…?!"

"…I've alreAdy…been…evapOrated…once… I'd obviously…takE steps…to prevEnt it…hAppening again…" She'd learned from her loss against Figaro and had since weaved Fu of fire magic resistance into her clothes.

Thanks to this extra defense, she was able to avoid being completely annihilated.

Her defense obviously had not been perfect, though. She had been directly exposed to the heat of a small hydrogen bomb. It was more than enough to break through the fire resistance and scorch most of Xunyu's body.

The only reason she could even move was because Master Jiangshi were undead.

"Tch…thIs is it…fOr me…" And even the undead had their limits. Clicking her tongue, Xunyu began to literally fall apart.

"I leave thE rest…to…" Xunyu dissolved into motes of light before she could finish her sentence. Yinglong's Fang, which had almost killed Zeta, as well as the Tenaga-Ashinaga holding it, quickly followed their Master.

King of Thieves, Zeta and Master Jiangshi, Xunyu.

This conflict had ended in the former's victory.

"Hn..." Despite all of this, the face hidden by bandages didn't look pleased.

Her broach was destroyed right after she was certain she'd already won. Perhaps if this was a duel — where Brooches weren't allowed — Xunyu would've been victorious.

"You truly were a powerful enemy." Feeling both slightly defeated and impressed by Xunyu's incredible fighting, Zeta returned to her task.

About a certain knight…

There were rumors that a Paladin of the Royal Guard, Theodore Lindos, held a disdain for Masters.

This was because he disliked when Masters got involved in the kingdom's affairs, and he made no effort to hide it. Behind his back, some of the Altarian nobility called him petty and small-minded — especially compared to Liliana Grandria, who was willing to cooperate with Masters even after one of them killed her father.

Of course, some would take Theodore's side, but the real problem was that they had all misunderstood his stance on the matter.

He didn't hate Masters — he hated *himself.*

Some time ago, the knights had been the true protectors of Altar, and standing above them all were the Paladins of the Royal Guard — an elite group often called a cornerstone of the kingdom. Theodore had looked up to them since childhood and had spent much of his life training to become a worthy Paladin.

However, soon after he had finally achieved his dream, the world drastically changed. Countless Masters entered the stage, and the balance of power was warped beyond recognition.

Powerful monsters that had once required an entire order of knights to bring down could now be crushed by a single Master.

The world was changing so fast it made him dizzy, and what disgusted Theodore the most was…his own weakness.

He simply didn't have the talent he so desperately needed. This might sound like nothing more than an excuse to give up, but in Theodore's case, it was anything but.

Theodore had truly reached his limit — the point he could never grow beyond, no matter how much effort he exerted.

This fact was represented by several cold, hard numbers: one high-rank job and three low-rank jobs for a total level of 250. That was where he was, and it was the point beyond which he could go no further.

Theodore had reached maximum level.

Unlike Masters, tians had clear-cut individual differences in talent, represented by level limits that most of the time fell below the maximum of 500. Though he had managed to become a Paladin, his lack of innate talent made it impossible for him to grow any stronger.

At first, he refused to accept that this was the full extent of his ability.

More and more Masters were appearing in Altar, some of which were criminals like the princess-snatching Sechs Würfel.

Theodore had to grow stronger to protect his kingdom — but no matter how much blood, sweat, and tears he put into it, he just couldn't raise his level beyond 250.

It took some time for him to accept the level limit, but once he did, he began directing his efforts towards other ways of becoming stronger.

Since his base power was inadequate, he chose to make himself more versatile by taking low-rank jobs that gave him more utility skills. Through that process, he even managed to gain the Paladin's Purifying Silverlight and Grand Cross abilities.

On top of that, he learned how to "stack" his Grand Crosses — in other words, to use them at the exact same time as his fellow Paladins.

He did indeed grow stronger this way, and soon it was time to put his strength to the test.

Altar had entered a war against Dryfe. To him...no, to all living knights of the kingdom...this was the first major conflict with an outside force they had ever experienced.

Despite that, he stood ready to protect his homeland.

The knight's power was the kingdom's blade, while the knight's body was its shield.

Every knight was taught those words, and with that oath in his heart, he stood on the battlefield...only to fall without contributing whatsoever.

The devils of the Hell General's army dealt him a grave injury shortly after the battle began, quickly rendering him unconscious. And by the time he woke up in a church back at the capital...it was already over. He hadn't been able to protect the king, join his commander on his fatal charge, or even guard the backs of his brothers-in-arms.

The war had taken a heavy toll on the Royal Guard. In fact, it had more or less been annihilated. Many of those who survived went on to retire. One might assume that they did this to avoid the shame of defeat, but Theodore knew painfully well that his fellow knights had left because the battle had made them realize how powerless they really were.

After all...he himself wanted to quit being a knight for that very reason.

He was overcome with despair. In his mind, a knight who failed to contribute to a battle would be nothing but a burden, no matter how much effort he put in.

Thus, like some other knights, Theodore was going through the process of early retirement. In two weeks, he would return home as his viscount father's heir and inherit his land.

While waiting for that time to come, he was tasked with patrolling the castle, now far emptier than he recalled.

One day during his patrols, he walked into the indoor garden. He might have come here by mere chance, but perhaps there was a part of him that wanted to see this place one last time before he left forever.

"It hasn't changed at all…" he muttered, recalling the times he had stood guard over the king and his daughters as they held a tea party in this very garden.

The gardener must've still been working even though the castle had lost its king — the rose bushes were still blooming with well-shaped, youthful blossoms.

Perhaps this place will never change, even when the kingdom falls and the castle itself has a new master, Theodore thought, and the notion made his heart ache with sorrow — for his country, which he was certain would collapse, and for himself, a knight preparing to abandon his protection of this doomed country.

"…I would not be able to do anything even if I stayed." He lacked the talent and power to be of much help even if he remained a knight, so he tried to convince himself that he had made the correct choice.

While this conflict raged within him, Theodore heard a noise at the entrance to the rose garden.

Someone had walked in, prompting Theodore to hide.

Even he wasn't sure why he reacted this way. Perhaps he simply didn't want anyone to see him struggling to justify running away.

Regardless, the person who entered soon approached the garden table.

They…or rather, *she* sat down on a chair next to it and stared at the roses nearby.

Theodore recognized her well.

That is…Her Highness Elizabeth? The person was none other than the daughter of the late king and the second princess of Altar, Elizabeth S. Altar.

She had come here all by her lonesome, but that wasn't unusual. She was known to be a wild, carefree girl with a tendency to run off and do things on her own.

However, in most such cases, she would have a cheerful expression on her face…definitely not the gloomy look she bore now.

…*Perhaps I should call out to her.* As a naturally diligent person, Theodore considered tossing aside his inner struggle and presenting himself to her. However, he stopped when he noticed a change in her expression — a single tear running down her cheek.

She was still looking at the roses that bloomed around the garden.

He knew well the significance of this place — it was where the royal family and anyone close to them would gather to enjoy each other's company, and where Elizabeth had made many memories with her sisters and father.

The reason for her weeping did not need to be stated.

"Nh… Sniff…" Like a dam that had burst open, she began to cry without stopping.

The sight left Theodore completely frozen, and as he stood still… "Elizabeth…"

…the voice of another person reached his ears.

It was Theresia C. Altar — the third princess of the kingdom, as well as Elizabeth's little sister.

She wasn't riding the giant rodent right now, which was quite a rarity for her.

She had actually stood up on her own two feet to go and find her lost sister.

"Nh… Theresiaaa…" The younger sister instantly noticed the tears on Elizabeth's cheeks, which *made her change her expression.*

Perhaps due to her sickly constitution, Theresia wasn't the most expressive girl. In fact, her demeanor was almost doll-like.

Even she, however, couldn't remain unmoved while seeing her sister brought to tears by the memory of their father.

Theresia then approached Elizabeth and, without saying a word, gave her a hug.

Though there was still little emotion on her face, a tear could be seen running down the girl's cheek while Elizabeth simply continued crying as she had been.

They were both little children that had just lost their father. It was only natural for them to cry.

Upon seeing this, Theodore slowly and silently sneaked out of the garden through the entrance opposite the one the girls had used.

Not saying a word, he walked through the hallway, as though eager to put distance between himself and the garden.

And then, after making it to a place where he could be certain he was alone…he *bashed his head against the stone wall.*

A dull pain rang out through his body as blood flowed from the resulting gash in his skin, but that was far from enough to soothe his anger.

"You couldn't even protect their fragile little hearts! How *dare* you try to protect your own…?!" This anger was directed at himself, and it overwhelmed him.

After that, he rushed to retract his resignation.

He refused to run away just because of his own weakness, and instead resumed searching for ways he *could* contribute, with renewed intensity.

Even after Franklin's Game in Gideon, his resolution had not wavered. He knew his limits, acknowledged them — and yet he continued to move forward, certain that there were things he could do in spite of them.

And now, he had been caught up in the assault on Altea.

Once again, it was time for him to see if he truly could protect the kingdom — and the hearts of Altar's princesses.

Castle, Innermost Hall

Over ten minutes had passed since Ignis Idea had broken through the main gate.

Twelve knights of the Royal Guard — Theodore among them — were defending the innermost hall on the first floor. Beyond it, there were stairs leading down to a bulky gate forged of Mythical metal.

This was the entrance to the castle's emergency shelter, so in a way, the hallway where the knights now stood was the castle's last line of defense.

"Sir Lindos! Mr. Lazburn…King of Blaze still hasn't been stopped! He's still moving forward!"

"I see…"

The identity of the intruder was now known to everyone in the castle, and the knights and guards alike were using all of the castle's equipment to mount a defense against him.

However, that turned out to be less than ideal.

"The castle's defensive mechanisms are operating at just below thirty percent!"

"We suspect this is due to all the personnel we lost in the previous incidents…"

As he listened to these reports, Theodore's expression soured. The castle had countless defensive installations, both from the time of its original construction and added more recently by the Arch Sage. Theoretically, the place should be impenetrable.

However, many of the devices had been rendered unusable. This was partially due to deliberate sabotage of the castle's magic distribution system by one of the intruders, but mostly it came down to a sheer lack of people.

The countless devices installed in the castle — especially the ones designed by the Arch Sage — were meant to be used by people who had at least a little bit of magical skill.

However, most of the magic experts of the castle — the Arch Sage's disciples — had died to Gloria a little over a year ago.

It was difficult to find qualified replacements. Regardless of whether they hired unaffiliated casters or recruited people who were already working for the nobles, they needed even more personnel to run the necessary background checks. The castle's security couldn't be entrusted to an unreliable party, after all.

The same problem came up even with security installations that weren't magical. Thus, the castle's defenses were currently woefully unprepared for the current assault.

There simply weren't enough people to properly protect this place, and they knew that all too well.

"How are Her Highness and the others?" Theodore asked.

"According to a message from Marquis Findle, they're making their way into the shelter without any trouble." Elizabeth, Canglong, and Milianne were currently being escorted to the shelter. They were accompanied by six members of the Royal Guard, a group of maids, and Marquis Findle, who was the head of intelligence as well as a capable manipulator of magic equipment — a skill necessary to make it past the shelter's defenses.

"…Have you heard anything from Lady Grandria?"

"No… Not yet." However, Liliana and Theresia weren't part of the group heading to the shelter.

Normally, Liliana would be the one commanding the Royal Guard here, but she wasn't present at the moment.

While the other children were being taken to the shelter, Theresia had been nowhere in sight. Liliana had left the command of the knights to Theodore and headed out to search for her.

She likely assumed that I would make a better leader at the moment than she would, he thought.

One of the low-rank jobs Theodore had was "Leader," which gave a small boost to the stats of all members of his party. Being talentless himself, he had chosen to contribute to his order and the kingdom by strengthening his fellow knights.

The high-rank version of the job, Commander, would grant a greater boost and have a wider range, but it wasn't an option for him because he could only have one high-rank job.

Even so, he would do what he could.

"Where is King of Blaze right now?"

"First floor. The second hallway in the south."

"The magic distribution in that area should still be active. There should also be a barrier device that can be activated without caster abilities. Contact the guards there and tell them to seal off the second hallway."

"Understood!" The subordinate quickly used comms magic to pass on the order, and a few dozen seconds later...

"Your idea was a success! King of Blaze has been sealed off!" The subordinate sounded overjoyed, but Theodore wouldn't allow himself to feel too relieved.

He melted the front gate, he thought. *Not even the Arch Sage's barriers will hold him for long.*

Theodore estimated that Lazburn would stay contained for ten minutes at most.

"Sir Lindos, I must say — I'm very impressed with your knowledge of the castle's magic distribution system and equipment."

"...The best thing someone without talent can do is gather knowledge. I suggest you also learn as much as you can about all the defense mechanisms and escape routes you are authorized to know about."

"I-I will."

"Also, it's far too early to relax. The barrier bought us some breathing room, but it is only a matter of time until he breaks out. Some magic channels have been broken, as well. We were able to activate that barrier, but much of our security equipment in other areas does not have enough power to function. This includes the surveillance network. And let us not forget that Her Highness Theresia has not been taken to the shelter yet. I assume I've said enough for you to understand our role here?"

"Yes… We must protect the gate leading underground until the princess's safety is secured."

"Exactly," Theodore said with a nod.

A moment later, he glared at the only path leading to this final line of defense — the hallway that was closed off by a shutter.

"Sir Lindos?" the subordinate said, unsure why Theodore's expression changed.

"…*The box* is moving," he muttered with a stern look. "It is slow, though. It does not seem to be running away. That can only mean…"

"Fshh… fshh… fshh." A strange sound like someone breathing could be heard beyond the shutter… *which immediately melted.*

"What?!" a few subordinates exclaimed.

"Ready your weapons! The enemy is upon us!" Theodore exclaimed as he and the others prepared for a fight.

Something passed through what used to be a barricade, finally coming into full view of the knights.

It was a three-metel-tall figure with a form that was far from human.

"Fshh… Fshh… Oh my, what a strong-looking gate. Have I found it? Should I assume no, given how weak you all seem to be?"

The creature seemed to be an amalgam of spider and human, like a giant spider whose features had been twisted into a more humanoid appearance by having its four front legs replaced by a single set of human limbs. Needless to say, the result was sickening.

"Who are you?" Theodore asked the talking spider-monster.

"I am King of Venom, Allo Ulmill," the creature responded with a light bow. "I was once a member of The Death's leading assassin group, 'The Death's Thumb.' Now, I suppose I should go by 'Aranea Idea' — a supporting member of I.F., loyal to the clan and especially to La Crima."

The creature casually revealed information that surprised everyone listening.

"Ohh, and the reason I introduced myself in such detail is simple — everyone here is going to die. Fshfshfsh," Aranea said, his shoulders shaking. It was hard to tell, but it seemed that he was chuckling.

He was actually *laughing* as he declared that he was going to slaughter every member of the Royal Guard here.

"But all of that information is quite valuable by itself," Aranea said before pointing at the hallway behind him. "I am sure you would be doing a great service if you brought that information back."

"Sorry to disappoint you, but anyone who would crumble before a powerful foe has long left the order," Theodore said firmly, rejecting Aranea's invitation to flee.

All the knights who were afraid of facing formidable enemies or who feared their own weakness had run away from the order after the war. There were no potential deserters left in the Royal Guard, and you could tell just by looking at their expressions.

"How unfortunate," Aranea said, shaking his head. "I set all this up so that the cowards would die first."

A moment later, a purplish, burbling liquid flowed out of the hallway he had pointed towards.

"Poison…"

"Of course. What else would you expect from King of Venom? Fshfshfsh!" He laughed again after emphasizing the title of his Superior Job. "I must say, you are quite the bunch of weaklings. The highest level you could reach is only half of the maximum 500. The shields of Altar seem to be quite fragile, actually. I have two things I must do, so I wouldn't want to waste too much time on the likes of you."

"Two things?"

"Yes. I am quite a busy person. First on the agenda is sabotaging this castle."

Seemingly filled with joy for some unknown reason, Aranea readily revealed his first goal, but it wasn't anything surprising to the knights. Theodore could instantly tell that he was the same kind of opponent as King of Blaze who had destroyed the main gate.

"And my second task…is assassinating the second princess."

These words made most of the Royal Guard react with open rage and ready their blades, but Theodore was able to keep himself together, albeit barely, and wring out a single question. "…Why target Her Highness?"

"I have been conveyed to La Crima by The Death himself. However, back when I still served The Death, I was in charge of instructing a lower branch. The Death's Pinky, they were called. They were talentless, though, and were effectively the lowest group under The Death's command."

"Hm…?"

Theodore and his companions didn't know this, but that was the name of the assassin group that had attempted to take Elizabeth's life on the request of Marquis Borozel, only to be destroyed by the Superior Killer — Marie.

She had solved the problem all by herself. No one had even realized that Elizabeth's life had been in jeopardy, and the incident faded away into obscurity.

However, the story didn't end there.

"It seems they were destroyed in their attempt to assassinate the second princess, so I figured that as their instructor, I would shoulder their duties and kill her myself."

He declared that he would assassinate Elizabeth as casually as someone might state that they were going to take out the trash.

"If you tell me where she is, I will let you all go for the moment. What do you say? I'm being honest this time."

The Royal Guards who had Truth Discernment could see the sincerity of Aranea's words.

Before responding, Theodore fell silent for a moment. And then...

"I see. Here's your answer, then... *We refuse.*"

...he rejected the offer utterly.

They were standing against a talented monstrosity. In a world where humanoid...or at least tian powers were determined by the jobs they held, Aranea was a remarkable figure who had acquired a Superior Job.

Besides that, he had been modified by a Superior Embryo to become even more powerful.

Theodore, in contrast, could only acquire three low-rank and a single high-rank job — comparing them at all seemed like a foolish endeavor.

Despite outnumbering their foe, the knights' chances of victory were minuscule.

Theodore's decision would no doubt lead them all to their death.

Even so, he — *all of them* had chosen to defy the enemy before them.

"Our power…!" Theodore called.

"…Is the kingdom's blade!" the knights answered, brandishing their swords.

"Our bodies…!" Theodore called.

"…Are the kingdom's shields!" the knights answered as they raised their own shields.

"Royal Guard… Prepare for battle!"

"Sir, yes, sir!" They were fully prepared to fight Aranea.

Their will was one, and not one of them felt any fear.

They were the Royal Guard — those who *used* to be the true protectors of Altar.

"Fshfshfsh… You continue to struggle? Frail as you might be, you are still good prey. Fshfshfshfshfsh…" Aranea laughed, moving his spider-like mouth. "Do be careful, though. My poison is more fiendish than even that of your typical UBM. It will easily melt a limb or two. And this body of mine is far stronger than the one I possessed as a mere Superior Job and a member of The Death's Thumb. To be honest, this will barely qualify as a fight."

As much as these words were a threat, they were also the unvarnished truth.

Even so, they did nothing to shake the knights' resolve.

"Charge!" Theodore cried.

"As you command!" the knights answered. He didn't fall back, and neither did they.

And so, the Royal Guard faced down a foe that far outclassed them.

"Fshfsh… Fatal Mist."

"Everyone! Take an Elixir!" Aranea had used King of Venom's ultimate job skill right off the bat, prompting Theodore to order the Royal Guard to use the Elixirs they had been provided with.

This gave the Royal Guard the upper hand in this exchange.

Aranea's Fatal Mist was a skill that allowed him to pick several of his ten poisons that give disease-based debuffs, and then create a mist based on those poisons without worrying about any chemical interactions between them. And as King of Venom, he also possessed the Toxification skill at EX level, which doubled any disease-based status effects he inflicted.

Being exposed to a mist carrying such potent poisons would normally be fatal to anyone.

Aranea's Poison Resistance was also at EX level, allowing him to negate any and all disease-based debuffs. It wouldn't have been unusual if he was the only one still standing the moment after he used Fatal Mist.

The only way the Royal Guard could avoid this powerful poison attack was by using Elixirs. With the exception of those from diseases the imbibers had acquired by ordinary means, Elixirs negated all disease-based status debuffs, and then granted immunity to them for the next three minutes.

By drinking these elixirs, the Royal Guard avoided instant death and now took no damage from Aranea's greatest weapon.

It seemed as though King of Venom was rendered powerless now, but...

"Fshfsh! Elixirs! Excellent! I love this!"

...he actually reacted with *joy* when he saw the knights employ this defense.

It was no doubt eerie, but the Royal Guard still showed no fear.

"Three, two...Grand Cross!" Theodore called, giving a hand sign.

"GRAND CROSS!" the knights answered.

Grand Cross was the strongest attack in a Paladin's arsenal. As an ultimate job skill, it was difficult to acquire, so the only ones actually using it were Theodore and just three other members of the Royal Guard.

However, all of them had learned the art of stacking.

Following their defeat against Franklin back in Gideon, many Royal Guards had gone on to learn Grand Cross and do plenty of stacking practice, and you could see the fruits of their efforts in this four-stack strategy they used on Aranea.

Cross-shaped pillars of light rose up into the sky, delivering an immense blast of both holy and heat energy.

Not even Pure-Dragons could withstand this torrent of light.

"I see. Very impressive…though not very effective, I'm sorry to say," Aranea remarked.

Despite being the target of the pillar, Aranea still seemed perfectly fine.

"Fshfsh… This won't burn me. I have resistance to heat. If you saw my colleague, you should understand why."

Aranea was wearing multiple accessories that granted fire resistance. He'd originally equipped these to protect him from Ignis Idea's immense heat — but they proved effective against Grand Cross, as well.

"Exactly as I anticipated!" The moment the pillar of light vanished, all twelve of the Royal Guards charged Aranea in unison.

"Ohh?" Aranea voiced his surprise. He had expected them to be shaken by this, after all.

Theodore, however, had known all along that Grand Cross would have little effect on this creature.

One of the three low-rank jobs he had was Appraiser, which provided vision-based utility skills like Reveal, Identification, and See-Through Sight.

All of these were useful, but they often came as extras from other jobs, and their maximum skill level for Appraisers was below the generic low-rank limit of 5. Because of this, only a few people took the job.

Theodore was one of these few, because he had a strict job limit and Appraiser allowed him to acquire all of these useful perception skills using only one of his allotted jobs.

He'd already used Identification to find out that Aranea was wearing accessories that granted heat resistance, and their Grand Cross attack had been nothing but a distraction.

That was the true meaning of the hand sign he had given before the Grand Cross — he was directing the knights to attack while the light was still active.

"OAAGH!" The Paladins of the Royal Guard roared as they thrust their blades, imbued with Knight skills, into Aranea's body.

"…This won't work," the creature simply said. None of their swords could penetrate any further than the outer layer of Aranea's carapace.

"Gh…! Is he *this* resilient…?!" Theodore said, shocked that his blade, aimed right for the chest, could pierce no deeper.

"Fshfsh. Identification helped you see my equipment, but it looks like Reveal didn't let you see *all* of my stats. I suppose it must be due to the level difference… Oh, in case you're wondering, my total level is 980." Reveal was a skill that showed the target's stats, but if the target had skills or gear that interfered with it, then differences in level could make it impossible to get concrete values. "Not that my stats as King of Venom mean much now anyway," Aranea added.

"What…?"

"Perhaps you could've pierced the frail flesh I used to have… but you can barely scratch my new body."

King of Venom held the Venomancer Superior Job, which was part of the alchemist grouping. As such, it offered high MP and DEX, but not much else. Normally, the Paladins here would've been far stronger than him, and their joint attack would've spelled his doom.

However, this was no longer King of Venom, Allo Ulmill, but rather Aranea Idea — a human modified by a Superior Embryo.

"This isn't a fragile human body any longer." An upper-Pure-Dragon-tier spider monster had been used as material in the operation that had transformed him, merging their flesh. Such human-monster hybrids were commonly employed by La Crima because they allowed the creation of Ideas that were physically more powerful than the average vanguard, but still maintained their rear guard or crafting skills.

Aranea was no different — all of his stats were far above those of a common Paladin.

"I'm superior to all of you combined *and* I have these amazing skills," he said, looking down on them like a human would look down upon ants. "You have spirit…but do you really think you can stand up to me?"

"…Not yet!"

In spite of everything, the Royal Guards decided to keep on fighting.

Their perfect joint attack had only managed to wound Aranea lightly, *but he was wounded nonetheless.*

Even the Grand Cross stack they'd released earlier hadn't been completely negated — minor burns were visible on Aranea's skin, and the heat pouring off him was tangible.

Maybe the attack had done less damage than a typical low-rank fire spell, but it had still *done damage.*

That meant that Aranea wasn't an unbeatable monster. He could certainly be overcome.

"The possibility exists!" Theodore roared.

There was once a creature that had completely crushed the Royal Guard.

It had a barrier that negated physical attacks, as well as a complete resistance to holy damage. Designed to be the ultimate foe of all Paladins, this unmatched creature had almost completely wiped out the Royal Guard.

However, it was actually defeated by a Paladin...a Master.

He'd brought down the very creature created to defeat people like him.

Theodore and the other Royal Knights had all borne witness to this triumph. They had all seen him raise up his right hand in victory.

That was why they could never allow themselves to give up, for they too were Paladins sworn to protect Altar.

"Attack! Keep fighting as long as your limbs can move...or until this creature falls!" Theodore called.

"SIR, YES, SIR!" the knights answered. They kept on moving. They imbibed more Elixir and continued to fight.

Not a single man among them gave up. Every single knight relentlessly sliced at Aranea's body, striking as though they expected their shallow cuts to chop off all his limbs.

Clearly irritated, Aranea said, "Fshfsh... How annoying!" Right as Theodore's sword pierced his chest again, the creature swung his spider arms. Backed by Pure-Dragon-tier power, the four arms sent four of the knights flying, but the other eight continued fighting regardless.

...*An opening!* Theodore thought. Aranea was strong — perhaps ten times as strong as they were.

On account of his hardy spider exoskeleton, Aranea even outclassed them in the Paladin's speciality — END. This Idea had an edge over them in AGI, as well, but since non-mounted Paladins were slow to begin with, this didn't mean he was all that fast — not even close to supersonic speeds, in fact.

97

And even if that gap between their AGI stats was immense, there was little difference in their actual speeds, which meant that Aranea couldn't just choose to kill them in the blink of an eye.

"You impertinent little...!"

There was a reason why Aranea's AGI was lower than one might expect.

The spider monster fused to his flesh had been far faster than him, but that was because it had a mastery over its arachnid form.

Allo Ulmill was ultimately human, so it was hard for him to move as a spider. He could have been given a fully arachnid body, but no one knew how long it would take him to learn to move in such a form. In the end, it had been more efficient to give Aranea a mostly humanoid form, even if that resulted in a lower AGI overall.

This could be considered a flaw of human-monster hybrids — END could be maintained, but AGI couldn't.

Unlike someone using a Guardian fusion skill, Aranea had been physically merged with a monster. Since parts of him were still human, he could never fully utilize the monster's power.

However, that also meant that he kept all the *advantages* of being human.

"Don't underestimate me!" Aranea once again moved the spider-arms, this time releasing countless webs through their tips.

"Huh?!" The webs quickly stuck to the surrounding knights, pinning them to the walls.

"Kh-agh...!" The impact knocked the wind from Theodore's lungs. He quickly caught his breath and tried to move, but the Binding effect from the webs had immobilized him.

"This is…!"

"Fshfsh… A web, as you can surely guess. You did manage to give me a bit of trouble, but that's all over now," Aranea said, continuing to flood the area with spider silk.

Perhaps it was obvious that a spider-man would be able to use both poison and webs, but Aranea had not been granted these powers by his fusion with a spider monster. Rather, it was the other way around — Allo Ulmill had mastered both of these things, and that was why he had been merged with a spider in the first place.

"Fshfsh… I always liked doing this," Aranea mused. "Can't use Elixirs when you're all wrapped up, can you?"

That was the reason why King of Venom had become a skilled user of thread-based binding techniques.

As mentioned before, Elixirs were his bane. He naturally needed to devise a counter to them, and this was that counter — binding his enemies so they couldn't drink them in the first place.

Skills that used threads as weapons were dependent on DEX, so his build worked well for this kind of attack, even as the frail King of Venom.

"Fshfsh… Now, there's nothing you can do but wait in terror for your Elixir's three-minute timer to expire."

Aside from being effective, this strategy also suited Aranea's taste.

This was why he'd actually been glad they'd all used Elixirs.

Just as he said, they'd given him some trouble, but this was the end.

All that was left for him was to watch as the Royal Guards here died in fear before heading down to kill the second princess.

With that in mind, Aranea looked at their faces...

"Ah..."

...and saw something he could scarcely believe.

Throughout his life, he had dealt out death to many. He'd bound and poisoned thousands of people exactly like this.

All of his victims, without exception, had shown despair as their inevitable death approached.

To Aranea, seeing that despair was a reassurance that he was the one who dealt out death to others, and it always filled him with a sense of relief.

By gaining this body, he had become even more skilled at killing. His body was tough enough that swords barely scratched him. He was powerful and his life had been extended. He could clearly feel death becoming a distant concept to him, and Aranea could honestly say that his life had never been better.

He was the death dealer. In turn, death would never come for him.

Since that was his outlook, Aranea felt *absolute terror* when he noticed that his prey, bound and out of options...remained stoic, brave, and unfaltering.

"Ngh..." Aranea let out a noise of distress as he took a step back.

"Target — below yourselves... GRAND CROSS!" Still bound, Theodore and the others who were able to do so used Grand Cross on the floor below them.

The next moment, the Paladins burst into flame.

Embraced by searing heat, they lost great amounts of HP even with Paladin's Aegis protecting them. Still, they soldiered on through the pain.

The memory of one particular Paladin who had kept on using his flames even as they consumed him was still fresh in their minds.

He had been driven by his will to protect the people, and they would follow his example.

And as a reward for this self-destructive act...

"M-My webs... You burned them off...?!"

...the silk binding them was incinerated.

While Aranea himself had resistance to fire, that didn't apply to the webs he released. Like any organic material, the silk burned up in the searing light of Grand Cross.

"CHARGE!" Theodore called, and then he said something Aranea did not catch.

It mattered little, however. The more important fact was that the Royal Guard were still moving and attacking him.

"Y-Your struggle is futile!" Aranea swung his arms and sprayed out silk again, sending the knights flying once more.

However, there was something in the way this time — ten, or more, metallic steeds.

"What are these horses...?!" In fact, they were SMPS — Second Model Prism Steeds — the mass-produced units that had been given to the Royal Guard.

Mounted combat was impossible indoors, but since SMPS could create barriers, they were still useful as covers.

"Ghh... You're in the way!" Aranea destroyed the surrounding steeds with his webs and arms.

The steeds quickly shattered under the assault, but the knights thought nothing of it. They only needed the SMPS to buy time.

"Grand Cross!" two voices called.

"Hm...?!" Suddenly, a stacked Grand Cross manifested under Aranea.

This two-stack was weaker than the first four-stack, but it was still able to temporarily blind Aranea and burn away the webs he was releasing.

"Do you truly think this will be enough to defeat me...?!" Pressured by the torrent of light, he struggled to escape it. His accessories kept the damage low, so it would never actually kill him.

In his mind, this was just another desperate attempt at stalling from the Royal Guards, just like the horses.

And then, the pressure he felt from the flood of light was abruptly cut in half.

One of the users ran out of MP...! Aranea thought, based on his perception of the situation. Grand Cross was far from cheap to cast, so it wasn't surprising that it could quickly drain the user's MP reserves dry.

The pressure was now weak enough for him to easily escape.

"I'm ou—?!"

But as soon as he did so...

"OAAGH!"

...there was Theodore, lunging at him from close range with his sword.

Everything he had done so far was only a set-up for this one attack.

Theodore had deliberately stopped using Grand Cross so he could approach Aranea and thrust his sword straight through his chest.

He aimed for the same spot he'd attacked many times before. Worn down by the continuous assault of slashes and stabs, Aranea's tough skin finally gave way...and the blade sunk into his body.

Aranea made no sound. It was as though time had stopped.

Theodore, drained of both MP and SP, had delivered the strongest attack he could muster and seemed to be frozen in that position.

Aranea looked down at the sword that pierced his chest...

"Fshfsh… WHAT A SHAME!"

…and laughed before swinging his human arm to send Theodore flying.

"Ugh…" Theodore coughed up blood, likely from his shattered ribs piercing his internal organs.

"S-Sir Lindos!"

"Then we must fight without him…!" After their costly escape from the web and Aranea's many attacks, the knights were all heavily wounded. Many had even lost consciousness already.

They tried to keep fighting Aranea in spite of that…

"Cough… Th-This is…!"

…but then, they hit their time limit.

The effects of the second Elixir had begun to expire.

Most of the poison from the Fatal Mist had been neutralized by the many Grand Crosses, but the small amount that still remained began to affect the knights that still stood.

Now, hands were shaking too much for them to even take a third Elixir.

"Fsh, fsh, fsh… My, my…for such a frail bunch, you certainly gave me a lot of trouble. But as you can see, it was futile," Aranea said, pulling out the sword Theodore had stabbed into his chest. "You were probably aiming for my heart, but it's not there. Not like I would die if you actually did manage to pierce it anyway."

Except the brain, Aranea had multiples of every vital organ. He was designed to survive even if his insides were critically damaged.

"But your futile struggle really made an impression! I won't forget any of you! I'll even tell the second princess all about it when I kill her! She deserves to hear the tale of the weakling knights who gave everything they had just to stab me once! FSHFSHFSH!" Aranea laughed out loud and looked down at the knights, wounded and poisoned…when suddenly, he heard a strange noise *like a loud crack*.

"Hm...? What is that sound?" he asked, looking around.

Some seconds later, he was ready to assume that the sound had either been the knights' equipment breaking or the hall itself preparing to fall apart from the intense battle, but then...

"Yeah...stab you...just once."

...Theodore, still battered and lying against the wall, said those words.

"Oh? You can still speak? Aren't you more injured than anyone else here?"

"...I only gave you...a slight wound." His words seemed like incoherent muttering.

Perhaps Theodore's consciousness was simply wavering because of the poison and injuries, but for some reason, these seemingly meaningless words sent a chill down Aranea's spine.

"What about the woun— Hm?" Aranea tried to speak, but his words were cut off by that same crack-like sound. This time, it gave off an ominous feeling, like the noise that preceded a dam bursting.

"What is this sound...?"

"I...saw it... That is why...I kept...targeting it..."

"Speak, already! What were you targeting?!" Aranea shouted, clearly irritated by Theodore's mumbling.

"*The box,*" Theodore responded.

"What...?" The crack-like...no, the *cracking* sound reached Aranea again.

It wasn't reaching his ears through the outside air, but resonating within his very bones.

The Royal Guard had given everything they had, and then some, just to deliver a single stab wound.

Their target, however, was actually *inside the wound*.

Theodore had been focused on it even before Aranea had shown himself.

105

The Appraiser job possessed three utility skills: Reveal, Identification…and See-Through Sight.

This last skill gave the user a power similar to X-ray vision, or perhaps something more like the devices used in airport security checks. It was used to Identify items with special, multilayered structures or to detect dangerous objects.

Theodore normally used this skill in the course of his guard duties, and it had allowed him to see the object within Aranea's body before he even arrived.

"What are you talking ab— Ah?!"

Theodore had seen and targeted it from the start.

There was only one thing that could be making that sound — the *box-shaped inventory* inside Aranea's body, implanted to store the materials for his poisons and webs.

The cracking noise was now happening more and more frequently.

"Wait. Wait…!"

The existence of the inventory was only logical. Spreading poison and releasing webs required materials; despite that, Aranea was able to flood the hall with venom and turn the entire place into one giant spider web.

He couldn't possibly have fit all of that into his physical body, so he must have stored the materials somewhere.

However, Identification didn't show any inventories on him.

That was what made Theodore realize that the immense amount of material Aranea used had to have been kept within the box *inside* him, which he had spotted with See-Through Vision. Since the box was necessary for Aranea's survival, it had been implanted into him so that he could never lose it…but that came with one major flaw.

"Wait, wait, waitWAITWAITWAAIT!" The repeated cracking sounds made Aranea lose his cool, his voice rising to a desperate scream.

The prospect of being on the receiving end of that which he had so often dealt out to others terrified him.

He didn't fear the sounds themselves, but the event they foretold — a minor law of this world.

Inventories could be destroyed from the outside.

And when they were...*they released all their contents.*

"WaAiT... ABGHAH?!" Following one brief final cry...Aranea was torn apart.

The items that overflowed within his tough body instantly pulverized his organs, and a few moments later, the sheer volume of them, far greater than his body could fit, burst forth. Aranea's body was ripped to pieces.

No matter how modified and improved, his body could not withstand this. The Idea who firmly believed that the modifications he'd undergone had allowed him to escape death forever...died precisely *because* of those modifications.

Theodore, though badly wounded, calmly watched the end of this fearsome foe.

"Heh..." He smiled for the first time since the war...as the flood of materials — poison included — washed over him.

Fire

The Lazburn family was known to excel at fire magic.

Tian aptitudes and maximum levels differed from person to person, but the Lazburns were almost always adept at wielding fire spells and capable of reaching high levels. Though the most obvious examples of such talent inheritance were the inhabitants of Tenchi, the Lazburns were also an excellent demonstration of the principle.

Because of this, the Lazburns had devoted their lives to fire magic for generations.

In a world with jobs and levels, tians like the Lazburns, who clearly knew how to improve themselves, were fortunate indeed. He — Feuer Lazburn — was no different. He spent his years learning fire magic from his father — the previous King of Blaze.

One lesson that had been hammered into him went as such: "The three higher elemental Superior Jobs are The Atmos, The Earth, and The Ocean. They are only accessible to those with the aptitude for all the types of magic they employ. However vast their powers might be, though, they are shallow. We are a family of fire and fire alone, but that doesn't mean that we are inferior to those who command all aspects of the atmosphere. When it comes to fire, the Kings of Blaze — who have all been Lazburns for generations now — are superior to The Atmos. And fire magic is the most powerful magic of all."

108

What Feuer's father had meant by that was that the Lazburns were the strongest casters in the world, and Feuer couldn't help but feel that his father was absolutely right.

No one needed to command every kind of magic. You merely had to devote yourself to one thing and become the strongest at that. Since the Lazburn had mastered the arts of extreme heat, it was obvious what Feuer had to do.

From a young age, he had dedicated his mind and body to the study of fire magic. Even after his father died and he inherited the King of Blaze job, Feuer refused to stop. He gained the job's ultimate skill and even improved on it, always striving to grow stronger.

And when King of Blaze, Feuer Lazburn became a well-known name throughout the kingdom, he sent a challenge letter to a particular person.

The person's name was…unknown.

No one knew his name. Not even royalty, and not even people who could use Reveal. He was a true enigma.

Despite that, he was respected as a pillar of the country. When everyone spoke of him, they all referred to him only by his job:

"Arch Sage."

On that day four years ago, the central arena of Gideon the City of Duels was bustling with activity.

Almost every seat was taken, and among the guests of honor was King Eldor of Altar himself.

Since the first queen of the kingdom was an Over Gladiator born in Gideon, it was traditional for Altar's royalty to attend any important duels taking place in this city.

And what an important duel this was!

At the time, The Lynx, Tom Cat was still the duel champion and many newly arriving Masters were overtaking the rankings. The main event of this day, however, wasn't a duel between rankers at all.

It was a clash between legendary tians said to be the first and second strongest casters in the kingdom.

One was King of Blaze, Feuer Lazburn "of the Embers" — a well-known wielder of flame magic.

The other was an advisor to the king, the living legend who was the "Magical Apex" at the time — Arch Sage.

As the Masters were still growing in power, this was a battle between the most powerful casters in Altar.

"It has been a while since I stood on a stage like this. Do go easy on me, Sir Lazburn," said the Arch Sage with a smile.

"...Sure," Feuer replied, his face stern.

The reason why this duel was even happening was the letter of challenge he'd sent, and his goal here was the Arch Sage's title, "Magical Apex."

The Lazburns believed themselves to be the strongest casters of all, and they devoted their lives to making that a fact.

However, the title of "Magical Apex" currently belonged to the Arch Sage, so Feuer had challenged him to make it his own.

He broke all limits in his own training, and now — while he was still in his prime, before age would begin to take its toll — he had sent the letter that had led to this duel.

Feuer had also made the challenge public, making it clear that if he didn't accept, the Arch Sage would be viewed as a weak coward for running away from the challenge.

The reactions to his actions were mixed.

Some praised Feuer for his bravery in challenging a true legend, but most were put off by his flagrant disrespect towards someone the country so revered.

Even so, he refused to retract the challenge. The title of "Magical Apex" was the Lazburns' ultimate desire.

His father had wanted it as well, but he was struck down by sickness before he could challenge the Arch Sage. He had died with this one heavy regret in his heart.

Feuer had been by his father's side as he passed, so he had made a promise to defeat the Arch Sage and reclaim the title of strongest caster for the Lazburn family. This challenge was the culmination of a life dedicated to training.

"You look terrifying," said the Arch Sage. "Have I wronged you in some way?"

"…No. I have nothing against you personally," Feuer replied. If he *had* to name one thing that bothered him, it would be the fact that he was the "Magical Apex" while also being the Arch Sage.

The high-rank job Sage was directly opposed to the Lazburn family's line of thinking.

"Sage" was a job that could only be taken by those who had an aptitude for all three higher elements. They could wield magic of the atmos, earth, and ocean. Some Sages could even cast healing spells.

However, this versatility often made them less powerful than the specialists of the elements.

Sages were a prime example of what Feuer's father called "vast, but shallow," and if it wasn't obvious already, Arch Sage was the Superior Job of the grouping. Thus, the very existence of an Arch Sage who was the "Magical Apex" flew in the face of everything the Lazburn family stood for.

For Feuer, that alone was enough of a reason to issue this challenge.

Facing the Arch Sage, Feuer contemplated the past — specifically, the words of his bedridden father.

"From what I've heard, the Arch Sage can use Crimson Spheres. That means that he has access to the ultimate skills of the high-rank jobs under the three higher elements. That is impressive indeed, but it also means that he can't reach the true depths of the fire element like King of Blaze can. A Lazburn can surely defeat him."

Even if the Arch Sage had ultimate skills from high-rank jobs under the higher element of the ocean, which could include defensive magic that worked by dampening energy, the ultimate skill of King of Blaze would deliver more than enough energy to overcome that.

"Apparently, he's also able to use dark-based hybrid magic that exterminates living beings on a large scale. That's impressive too. But since it attacks such a large area, it can't be used in the confines of a duel arena. In a one-on-one battle, he has no means of delivering more power than King of Blaze's Fixed Star."

Fixed Star was the name of the job's ultimate skill, and as the name suggested, it created an orb of burning plasma not dissimilar to the one that shone down upon the earth from on high.

In terms of sheer extermination potential, the Arch Sage's Imaginary Meteo was stronger, but against a single unit, Fixed Star came out on top.

That was why Feuer's father was confident that he would win. "I could've beaten him if it wasn't for this damned illness," he cursed.

However, Feuer's outlook was a bit different than his father's.

...I think that the Arch Sage can use the ultimate job skills of not just high-rank, but Superior Jobs as well, he thought. They were dealing with a prodigy who had lived for over a century and spent all that time honing his magic skills.

It would not be surprising for someone so talented to have reached that level.

Feuer fully believed that the power carried by his family was the strongest in all the world, but he didn't underestimate his enemy either.

And if the Arch Sage could use all the ultimate job skills of all elements, Feuer resolved to defeat him with something even greater than the Fixed Star spell he worked so hard to learn.

I will use something even more powerful than Fixed Star and bring home the title of Magical Apex. He had far fewer cards in his proverbial deck than the Arch Sage, so he planned to make the battle a quick one. He believed he had to channel his strongest magic from the moment the battle began and use it to instantly overwhelm his opponent.

Feuer would give his all — his entire family's many years of training — into his very first attack.

While Feuer was extremely serious about the upcoming battle, the Arch Sage seemed wholly composed.

He didn't even have to accept this challenge to begin with. He was one of the pillars of Altar, and no one would ever doubt someone who had been providing such a great service to the country for over a century. No one would call him a coward for refusing Lazburn's challenge. In fact, the general opinion would be that Lazburn simply wasn't worth his time.

Despite that, the Arch Sage had accepted. He even spoke to Count Gideon, convincing him to turn this battle into a major event held in the central arena.

"We both are powerful casters," he told him. "It is necessary for us to use Gideon's barrier equipment, just in case, and it would certainly draw a crowd you could profit from."

Though, with a depth and foresight that was too great for anyone but him to truly understand, it was hard to tell if his words expressed the true nature of his intentions.

Regardless, this duel had been set up with agreement from both combatants, and the time had come to commence the battle.

"BEGIN!" the moderator cried, instantly spurring Feuer into action.

"Burn! Burn! Burn! Mimic of heavenly light and scorcher of earth! Shining star that fits in the palm of my hand!" Channeling his magic into the spell, Feuer intoned the most intense Chant he had ever used.

"Chant" was a supplementary skill that increased the effectiveness of spells if the caster said something while casting them. The words differed from person to person, and his was one that was meant to light his very own soul on fire.

"You are the twins of ruination! The incarnation of binary stars!" As he spoke, Fixed Stars appeared in *both* of his hands.

This was the technique he'd developed — double-casting his ultimate job skill.

This was what lay beyond singular Fixed Stars, and it was the technique that Feuer alone had perfected. He wasn't the first who had tried, however. The technique was just so dangerous that all the past Kings of Blaze who had attempted it had lost control and burnt themselves to ash.

But Feuer had poured enough blood and sweat into his training to finally achieve it.

Not even a Superior Job's ultimate ocean-element skill could stand against this. Such a defensive skill's energy-damping effect would cancel-out one Fixed Star, but the other would still be more than enough to destroy his opponent. That was the very simple reason that Feuer had decided to use *two*.

With this, he would surely win this fight.

These stars will guide the Lazburn family to vict— he thought, before he saw something that shocked him.

The Arch Sage, who was standing on the ground until but a moment ago, was now floating in midair.

And surrounding him…there were *four* Fixed Stars.

"…Ahh… AHHH!" Feuer screamed as he realized that the Arch Sage had easily surpassed the pinnacle he'd worked so hard to reach.

A single Fixed Star cost over 300,000 MP. Using four would drain even Feuer's reserves — yet the Arch Sage seemed to be able to do this without breaking a sweat.

But more important than that was the fact that the Arch Sage had chosen to use Fixed Stars *after* seeing that Feuer was going to cast them.

That meant that, despite starting to cast them after he'd already begun, the Arch Sage had managed to prepare these four Fixed Stars before Feuer had even finished casting two.

That was proof that the Arch Sage's fire magic was superior to his, not just in pure volume, but in proficiency and speed.

If Feuer was an incapable fool, he could have chosen to blindly believe that his Fixed Stars were more powerful, or that the Arch Sage's four only *looked* menacing and that this was all nothing but a bluff.

Alas, he was a born genius of fire magic who'd dedicated his life to learning the ins and outs of the art.

That was why a single glance at Arch Sage's Fixed Stars was enough for him to know that they were equal to…no, *even greater* than his own.

But despite knowing that, he couldn't back down.

"FIXED STAAAAR!" he roared, releasing his orbs of plasma. "…Fixed Star," the Arch Sage responded. The outcome of this clash was already *clear as daylight*. Feuer understood that painfully well, but he couldn't let himself run from the conclusion of his many years of training.

The six Fixed Stars flew towards their targets.

The two launched by Feuer were consumed by two of the four launched by the Arch Sage, while the other two went on to incinerate him.

So ended the battle between the strongest tian casters — all in less than a minute.

An old man sat on a tree stump in the mountains. His eyes were closed. Some would assume he was meditating, some would think he was sleeping, and still others would believe he was actually dead.

Three and a half years had passed since his — King of Blaze, Feuer Lazburn's — duel against the Arch Sage, and he had retreated to a location in the mountains southwest of Altar.

He had previously lived in an urban mansion, but he had burned it down with his own hands before moving here.

Following the duel, the people's opinion of him had sunk appallingly low. To those who understood what had happened, Feuer was no doubt a remarkable caster. They knew that they'd witnessed an exchange of extremely potent magic.

But in the eyes of a layman, he had been crushed like an insect by magic twice as powerful as his own. They didn't even consider that he was the first King of Blaze to use multiple Fixed Stars at once — all they knew was that he was nothing before the Arch Sage.

Therefore, most people believed that he vanished to escape the shame.

In truth, he didn't care about their opinions one bit.

His mind had no room for such noise, for it was overwhelmed by the truth that he had been utterly defeated by his target.

He'd challenged the most well-versed caster in the world with the element that he'd dedicated his life to, and yet the Arch Sage had crushed him with that very same element.

All the training he'd gone through to prove himself the strongest — to surpass the Arch Sage — turned out to be for naught.

It was as though his entire life had been negated.

Ever since then, he'd been living as a hermit in the mountains.

He'd dedicated his existence to fire magic and fire magic alone. There was no one to care if he disappeared.

As he meditated, he was silent, but his surroundings certainly weren't.

They were filled with the crackling sound of flame, caused by the sixty-four balls of fire floating around him.

They were not Fixed Stars, of course, but low-rank Fireballs. Even so, very few were capable of controlling so many of them at the same time.

After losing to the Arch Sage in breadth, power, and speed, he took to honing his skills yet further and had achieved greater control and speed than he'd possessed during their duel.

By striving to improve himself even further, he was able to break more limits and achieve the result before him.

However, he knew that this was as far as he could possibly go.

"It's still not enough..." he whispered to himself, and the orbs vanished.

His goal was the same as ever — simultaneous control of multiple Fixed Stars. Currently, he might've been able to maintain as many as the Arch Sage had in their duel, if not more.

However, there was something that made it fundamentally impossible for him.

"I don't have enough magic..."

He simply didn't have the MP to release four Fixed Stars at once. Even when he drained his reserves dry, he could only call forth three of them at once.

Maximum MP could be increased by gaining more levels, but even those with Superior Jobs had limits to how high they could go.

The Arch Sage had lived and leveled for over a century. To match him, Feuer would need at least several decades more.

It wasn't certain if Feuer would even live long enough to catch up to the Arch Sage, and he would never overcome him even if he did.

The Arch Sage had chosen to use Feuer's own speciality against him, but he actually had access to spells of all elements. If he'd chosen to use magic that fire was weak against, not even having the same amount of MP or control would help him.

To defeat him with only a single element, merely equaling the Arch Sage wasn't enough — he had to surpass him.

That was exactly why he'd crafted the double Fixed Star technique.

"Tch…" Feuer immediately thought back to the day of the duel. Specifically, he remembered how the Arch Sage looked as he completely destroyed him.

His eyes were like those of a kindly adult looking at a child showing off a curious hunk of garbage he found.

To the Arch Sage, the power Feuer had given his whole life to earn was nothing but that — a child's worthless nonsense.

"…A child, eh?" Feuer understood that the Arch Sage was known mostly for his Imaginary Meteo because he'd washed his hands of Fixed Star many decades ago.

He'd stopped using it because he deemed it unfit for his purpose.

And Feuer had challenged him with a lesser version of this "unfit for his purpose" technique. *Of course he would be disappointed and look at me like I'm a child,* he thought in self-derision.

That was why he had to surpass the Arch Sage's fire magic.

Indeed — Feuer had *not* given up.

He became a hermit, meditated, and trained so he could challenge the Arch Sage once again.

He'd been completely defeated, but he was also so set in his ways that from now on, all he could do was dedicate himself to acquiring the "Magical Apex" title — or rather, to defeating the Arch Sage.

That was why he'd continued training even after the staggering defeat.

He didn't know that the title of "Magical Apex" now belonged to a Master known as "Fatoum," nor did he know that the Arch Sage had died in a war.

He'd isolated himself from society and focused solely on training.

Some would consider him insane, but he was of sound mind.

It was simply that his personal perspective and the world he lived in didn't allow for any other course of action.

However, one day, this life of his came to an end.

"…Who are you?" Feuer asked, his eyes still closed.

He wasn't speaking to himself or to any memory — he actually had a visitor.

"A pleasure to meet you. Feuer Lazburn, I assume? -sume?"

Two people stood among the trees and shrubs of the mountain grove.

Their voices were like a paired chorus. One was a pale woman in a wheelchair, while the other was a robust man in black pushing it.

Together, they were Soul Trader, La Crima.

"I am La Crima. A Master and the current Soul Trader. -der."

"A Master? I have heard of your kind. What do you want from me?"

"I came with an invitation. Would you like to join our clan as a supporting member? -ber?"

"Clan?"

"A clan known as 'I.F.,' which only allows the wanted. -ted."

"Criminals, eh? I don't recall being on any wanted list."

"…But you killed many, did you not? -not?" La Crima asked with certainty. "This mountain is very quiet. I sense no monsters or people here, yet I hear that this area is inhabited by high-level beings, making it an excellent spot for training. -ning."

"…What are you trying to say?"

"How many levels did you gain? -gain?" They were basically asking how many monsters *and tians* he had murdered to raise his level.

As certain people were aware, a portion of the Resources from dead monsters was used to create loot, so if one wanted only experience, tians were the better targets.

"It was wise of you to attack tians who hunt here instead of attacking settlements. -ments. No one would be surprised if they didn't return, and high-level tians give a lot of experience. -ence."

"…Heh." Feuer chuckled — not because of some sick joy, but because he was simply amused.

He actually agreed with what they said.

"You're not wrong. I didn't keep count, but I killed all of them to gain more magic," he said as though this was a normal thing to do.

It seemed insane, but again, he was of sound mind.

It was simply that his personal perspective and the world he lived in didn't allow for any other course of action.

His entire mindset was focused on becoming the world's greatest wielder of fire magic and proving that he was.

And the world he lived in was the microcosm of the Lazburn family. His goal was merely to become strong. The idea of using his power for the sake of others had never even crossed his mind.

That was why he thought nothing of killing actual people to gain levels.

"If what I hear about Tenchi inhabitants is true, you are much like them. -them."

"I can understand why you might think that. Anyway, you said something about me joining a criminal clan? Sorry, but since I must keep improving myself, I have no time to dedicate to anything else." He refused the strangers' offer, creating orbs of fire in each hand.

They weren't his earlier Fireballs, but the double Fixed Stars — his ultimate technique, surpassed by no one but the Arch Sage.

The one eye of the black La Crima — the only one between the two that was exposed — watched the blazing orbs as they spoke. "In exchange for joining, I will grant you a stronger self. -self."

"A stronger...self...?" Feuer said as he raised an eyebrow.

"If you accept my proposal, you can be certain that you will receive that. -that," they said as the white La Crima stuck out her hand like a devil looking to seal a pact.

In response...

"If you claim you can give me more power than I currently have, I want to see some proof first!"

...Feuer released his Fixed Stars.

This was the deadly magic that had evaporated any humans and monsters he'd encountered on this mountain.

However, La Crima just let it hit them.

The aftershocks alone were enough to scorch the surrounding trees and even Feuer's own small shelter.

La Crima was right at the center of this intense heat, and the two Fixed Stars...were now clutched tight in the hands of the dark man.

"...I see. I haven't been this shocked since my fight against the Arch Sage..." The strange man had let go of the wheelchair, stuck out his hands, and caught both Fixed Stars like they were nothing but rubber balls. The spell could melt even Mythical Metal, yet the man's hands were not incinerated — in fact, they didn't even seem damaged.

At some point, he'd also stopped looking human.

He was now larger, more warped, and covered in a luster like that of gold or silver.

On his metallic chest was emblazoned the name "Ferrum Idea."

"This is a sample of the stronger self I can grant you," the white La Crima said, with her voice alone. Following the transformation, the dark figure had become silent.

The white La Crima hadn't changed at all, and not even her clothes or skin seemed to have been affected by the intense heat.

For all anyone knew, perhaps the white La Crima wasn't the "real one" either.

"...I see you weren't lying," Feuer said as he looked at the dark La Crima, who had been completely unaffected by his greatest attack.

If they had made this power for themselves, then he could indeed trust them to make him stronger than he was.

"Allow me to introduce myself again," said the white La Crima, in a melodic voice. "I am La Crima, a Superior and an improver of people. Allow me to turn your tears into ones of joy. If you wish for power, I will make you far stronger than you are now. Is there anything specific you request?"

In response to the stranger's playful presentation...

"...Magic. I need enough magic to surpass the Arch Sage."

...Feuer found himself speaking as if he had already agreed.

This likely meant abandoning his humanity, but he did not care about that. To him, the most important thing was using fire magic to defeat the Arch Sage and proving that he was the strongest.

"Very well. I will make that part of the procedure," the white La Crima said, casually accepting Feuer's seemingly outrageous request.

He looked at her in silence. This person, he thought, could easily shatter the wall he was facing now.

Was this grace from above…

"…Are you some sort of demon?"

…or an unholy creature seducing him to the depths of hell?

In response to his honest question, La Crima said, with no jest in her tone, "Not at all. I believe I should be called 'a merchant of life.'"

Chapter Twenty-Two What Was Sought

Royal Castle, Second Floor, Hallway

"Your Highness! Your Highness Theresia! Where are you?!" Liliana, the vice-commander of the Royal Guard, was riding her SMPS through the castle's hallways, looking for the princess who'd gone missing shortly after the assault began.

So far, she had found not a trace of Theresia or the hamster she always rode.

Explosions were ringing out all over the castle, and Liliana was starting to fear that Theresia might be lost forever.

It's like this again... she thought, overcome by her own powerlessness. *I'm completely useless again...!*

This wasn't the first time she'd felt this way.

Liliana was close friends with Altimia and Integra.

Altimia was the first princess of Altar, the one chosen by The Primeval Blade to bear the title of Sacred Princess. Despite being younger than her, the girl also surpassed Liliana in swordfighting skill.

Integra was the Arch Sage's favorite disciple, and she possessed magical talents that were said to be even greater than his had been, as well as intellect that allowed her to instantly untangle difficult dilemmas that left Liliana stumped.

They were immensely talented...unlike her.

Liliana was the daughter of the Celestial Knight and had some talents of her own, but she wasn't nearly as special as her two friends.

She'd lost count of the number of times she'd wished to be as powerful as they were, and even becoming a Paladin had not changed that.

She'd joined the Royal Guard and proved she was more than worthy of that honor, but she still had yet to catch up to the achievements of her father and the more experienced knights. Even so, she'd continued striving onwards, hoping to one day gain enough power that she was satisfied.

However, the war had shown her just how far she still was from her goal. Her father and the other Paladins she looked up to, as well as many of the younger new recruits, had died while battling the devil army.

And after that, Liliana had become the vice-commander of the Royal Guard.

The position of commander was reserved for the Celestial Knight, and she was chosen for vice-commander because all of the Paladins stronger than her were gone.

She knew in her heart that she was unworthy of it, yet she had no choice but to take the post and lead the Royal Guard.

Her father and many of her comrades had died, leaving her with a heavy burden to bear. It was almost too much for her, but she refused to break under the strain.

She still had a now-fatherless little sister to look after.

She still had her comrades who had survived and were now overcome by immense grief.

She still had Altimia, a friend who knew the pain of losing a father just as well as she did.

And finally, she had the people of Altar, terrified of the prospect that the kingdom might fall.

As a knight, she *couldn't* allow herself to break.

To protect what she had to protect, she took on the role of vice-commander and tried her utmost to fulfill her duty.

But though her heart was ready, reality reminded her time and again that the power she possessed simply wasn't enough.

Liliana had been involved in many dangerous events since she became the leader of the Royal Guard — most notably the incident where her sister had almost been killed by countless worms and the now-infamous terrorist strike in Gideon.

Even the would-be tragedies happening right before her eyes were too much for her to handle alone.

As much as she wanted to protect what was dear to her, she was just not powerful enough to do it. This current assault was no different.

She had no means of defeating the attackers, nor could she easily locate the princess she had to protect.

Liliana dearly wished she had the power to at least do that much.

"If only Integra were here…" Her childhood friend was perhaps the smartest person in the kingdom. It was entirely possible that she could provide Liliana with some path to improvement.

"…No! I need to focus on what I can do right *now*…!" Liliana said, shaking her head. This was no time to be wishing for something that could never happen. Doing so would be nothing but escapism.

Liliana did her best to shake off those negative thoughts and give her all to the search.

As she galloped away, *one of the paintings in the hallway was watching her.*

Royal Castle, Fourth Floor, Hallway
The fourth floor of the castle was the royal family's living quarters. Because of this, its hallway was decorated with fancy furniture, paintings, plants, and well-made suits of armor.

Standing among them, there was a single Idea.

That's thirteen. I'd say I took out most of the wiring, he thought.

He had blue-black skin and leathery wings, making him look like a hybrid of human and bat. He was Vespertilio Idea, otherwise known as King of Raids, Morter.

Having finished his job of disrupting the magic distribution network in order to sabotage the castle's defenses, he pulled his winged hands out of the wall. La Crima had given him the ability to sense magic, allowing him to easily find magic-based wiring even with his eyes closed.

With those old farts distracting the guards, this was a real piece of cake... Though, man — the security in this place isn't working properly, but it'd sure be excessive if it actually did. It's a good match for the ruins I worked in, he thought, reminiscing about the past.

Up until a few months ago, Morter had been pursuing treasure hunters in one of the ruins in Caldina. He actually made a living out of ambushing those who found any success there and taking their finds.

Morter always took his targets' lives and treasures before they even realized he was there, making it a more lucrative "career" choice than one might expect.

However, those days ended when one treasure hunter he targeted turned out to be the sub-leader of I.F.

The man incapacitated Morter as though he was no more threatening than a baby, and as he was cowering in fear, the sub-leader told him, "Choose: die right here and now, or give up your humanity. I recommend the former."

In spite of his advice, Morter picked the latter.

In Morter's mind, living was always better than not. Even if he became a lowly slave, there might still come an opportunity for escape.

The man then treated Morter's wounds before handing him off to La Crima. She turned him into Vespertilio Idea, and now he was attacking the Altarian royal castle.

These powers I've got aren't even half bad, he thought. *I'm even more satisfied than I was back when I was just King of Raids.*

Actually using his powers in this castle showed him that he'd made the right choice back then.

He had been freed from his limiting human shell, and now he had been granted a form that made him feel all-powerful. He saw things he couldn't see before and did things that used to be beyond him. The feeling of emancipation he derived from that was exquisite.

But what are those *things, anyway…?*

However, his new sight also showed him questions he would never have known to ask before.

Morter could sense three major sources of magic in this castle.

One was obviously a fellow Idea — Ignis — but he had no clue what the others were.

One was weaker than Ignis, but more intense than a standard Superior Job, and it was simply standing in one place in the castle.

The other magical signal was fluctuating between strong and weak, and it was slowly moving through the castle's fourth floor — the one Morter was on.

He'd informed Zeta about these signals before they assaulted the castle, and she'd told him to go towards the fluctuating one while dealing with the security systems.

"Hm…?" Morter's train of thought stopped short as he looked down towards the first floor.

The spider guy is dead, huh? There's weak magic signals all around him… I guess someone broke the inventory inside his body. Well, that's what I would've done if I had to kill him.

Fully grasping the nature of Aranea's death, Morter didn't show much of a reaction.

He also knew that Ignis was trapped, but he had no intention of going to help him.

Since he hadn't been discovered yet and wasn't actually ordered to help his fellow Ideas, such things were no skin off his nose.

And besides, Morter's top priority was survival, followed by freedom. If he saw a way to seize that freedom, he would ignore his orders to seek it.

Though right now, he was on a leash of swords. Becoming truly free seemed impossible at the moment.

Well, we're experimental animals, after all. There are flaws in our designs. This doesn't really apply to the dumb bee, but the flame guy... He's stronger than the rest of us, but with all the MP Boosters in him, he'll die in no time.

As someone who used to "work" at some ruins, Morter was very familiar with the equipment implanted in Ignis.

MP Boosters were pre-ancient civilization items that greatly increased magic at the cost of life span, and since Ignis...or rather, Feuer Lazburn cared about nothing but magic, he had several of them implanted into him.

Morter guessed that he didn't even have a year left — maybe a month, if he was lucky.

The item wasn't the only problem, after all.

That psycho La Crima can modify people however she wants, but she knows almost nothing about biology or medicine. She only uses her Embryo's powers to mix people with monsters and items. That's why there are limits to what she can do.

Idea, La Crima's Superior Embryo, allowed her to freely modify people as long as she had the materials. La Crima had no knowledge of the processes and techniques involved, but Idea did, and that allowed it to mass produce its hybrid monsters.

The Embryo could make La Crima's designs work even if they were flawed, which was both a positive and a negative.

The stronger the Idea...the more combat-capable they are... the greater the risk of them destroying themselves.

Because of that, Morter was very satisfied with his modifications.

The three main things he had been given were the magic-sensing ability, the power to create an unperceivable space, and a low-tier flying ability.

His modifications were minor compared to what the others had received, and because of this, he had yet to find a flaw in them.

I guess the only successes are me, the Ferrum that's with La Crima all the time, and Cantus, I guess...? Wait, can you really call them successes when — hm...?

Morter looked down once again.

What's that fiery old fart planning? He had noticed a change in King of Blaze's magic signal. Feuer Lazburn was doing something, despite being trapped in a barrier.

As Morter tried to guess what it was, the castle began to shake.

"...Tch." He clicked his tongue, making a sound for the first time since he had begun his job here.

Seriously, what the hell is he doing? Quiet though the click was, a moment after he did it, a sword was swung down at him.

"Hh...!" Morter jumped to dodge it, but he couldn't evade his own confusion.

What? There was nothing here. I didn't sense magic or see any knights. Is this like Zeta's optical camouflage? But I — what is that?

His high-speed questions and thoughts were cut off by what he saw in front of him.

It was something that he knew was there. He'd seen it even before the attack, which made him even more confused.

He was facing the *suit of armor decorating the hallway.*

The armor had moved on its own to swing its sword at Morter.

...Is it a golem? No way — it wasn't showing a single bit of magic. The armor had not only moved, it had also changed shape and increased in size.

And eventually, above its head appeared the words "Massacre Armor" — a monster name.

It was a phenomenon that Morter — no, *most of mankind* — had never seen before.

"...What the hell is this?!" Morter blurted out as he reflexively jumped away again.

A moment later, the *wall behind him* bit the empty space where he had just been standing.

The wall, its open maw filled with fangs, was now marked with the name "Bigmouth Wall."

The changes didn't end there.

The decorative plants transformed into twisted torture devices and received the title "Torture Plants."

The framed paintings began to laugh and were named "Screaming Pictures."

Mere objects that were never human or monster were transforming into malicious monsters and attacking him right before his eyes.

"...Man, this place is haunted as hell." *This security feature is in really bad taste. Or is this some Embryo's doing?* Morter thought as he prepared to battle the monsters.

It was a clash between unnatural beings, and a hidden lens on the ceiling was watching it all.

◇◇◇

Royal Castle, Underground Shelter

Beyond the last line of defense guarded by the Royal Guard, there lay the castle's underground shelter.

Elizabeth and the others were heading deeper into it.

There were more than ten people in all, counting the bodyguards and maids, but that didn't slow them down one bit. The passage was wide and tall enough to even let Magingears pass through without a problem.

In the lead was Marquis Findle — Altimia's loyal confidant and the head of Altar's intelligence department. Six of those with them were Royal Guards, who surrounded Elizabeth, Canglong, Milianne, and the maids to protect them.

"We've arrived," said Findle. "For now, let us stay here and wait for our enemies to leave."

He approached the large door at the end of the passage and operated the touch panel on the wall, causing the door to open up and reveal the deepest area of the palace...the royal shelter.

"This construction is quite durable," Canglong noted, and rightfully so.

The place had been made by expanding a natural cavern, covering it in a thick layer of metal, and completely cutting it off from the surface. It also drew water from a source far beneath the castle and was equipped with a storage facility filled with a wealth of foods, all held in inventories that negated the effects of spoilage. Anyone in the shelter could survive for a very long time while waiting for rescue to finally arrive.

This was no doubt the safest place in the castle right now.

"I have never been here before," said Elizabeth.

"That is because it's only meant to be used in situations like this," said Findle. "The attackers are few in number, so I believe the Masters from the city will be able to take care of them. There is a chance, though, that we might have to wait here until those who went to the peace conference return."

Upon hearing his words, Elizabeth became downcast.

"A shelter… Where could Theresia be…?"

"Lady Grandria is looking for her right now. This shelter has observation equipment, so we will know when she brings Her Highness here and open the door for them."

"Will Liliana be okay…?" asked Milianne.

"Lady Grandria is the strongest knight in Altar. There is no need to worry about her." Despite his reassuring words, Marquis Findle was overcome with anxiety. The situation wasn't remotely favorable for them.

He had already been informed that one of the attackers was none other than King of Blaze himself. It was hard to be optimistic when dealing with a Superior Job, and Feuer had been given abilities that made him even more powerful than he had been before.

The Superiors and most of the rankers aren't around, he thought. *Mr. Figaro did not attend the peace conference, but neither has he returned yet. Lei-Lei and the new one, Hannya, haven't been sighted either… I suppose we should be grateful that we at least have Xunyu.*

Xunyu had separated herself from the children being escorted to the shelter so she could confront the intruders back on the surface.

At this very point in time, she was fighting her deadly battle against Zeta.

If only I had seen this coming… The fact that I did not merely highlights my shortcomings as head of intelligence. I will have to take responsibility for this once everything is over…

Findle's expression as he pondered this was stern. This assault had caught him off-guard, and now the princesses and an honored guest were exposed to danger while the lady of the castle, Altimia, was away. This filled him with immense guilt.

I will truly have to think about letting Masters into the intelligence department. Though, that may be my last action as head of that department... But for now, I must protect Her Highness and Prince Canglong, he thought as he approached the control panel and activated the climate control, among other things.

Canglong watched him work as he realized something.

"Did this place exist before the castle was built?" he asked.

"You can tell?" Findle replied.

"Yes. The castle's design has a focus on everyday convenience and aesthetics, while this place looks very unrefined. Also, for an Altarian facility that seems to be centuries old, this place has a lot of technology."

"Well observed. This underground area has been here before the first king even built the capital, and we have been using it since his time."

Hoping that some conversation might put the children at ease, Marquis Findle began to explain the history of this place.

"This land once belonged to a different country. Instead of Altea, there was an industrial city here which served as the capital of Adrasta — the expansionist nation led by Rockfell Adrasta."

That was the name of perhaps the most well-known conqueror in history. Bearing the job of King of Kings, he was the strongest tian ever recorded, and it was said that he commanded enough power to conquer the west side of the continent with ease.

"It is thought that this underground facility was built as part of the capital's fortifications in case of an attack, and since it was too difficult to dismantle, the first king of Altar chose to repurpose it instead, and he built a castle over it."

"So that is why there is so much technology here." With the exception of Legendaria, who were Adrasta's allies, the King of Kings had conquered the entire west side of the continent. Due to this, he had access to many ruins containing the kind of technology that Dryfe was famous for in the current time.

"A few years after building his capital, the King of Kings vanished from history. However, the city remained, and after Adrasta split into many countries again, it became a highly sought-after piece of land, making it the center of many conflicts."

The time of the King of Kings, the Draconic Emperor, and The Lynx would later be known as The Era of the Peerless Three.

It was believed that after the King of Kings' disappearance and the end of the Draconic Emperor's long life, the world would finally know peace, but that turned out to be absurdly wrong — the grand war that split the continent in two was merely replaced by many smaller wars.

Following the Draconic Emperor's death, Huang He to the east was thrown into a civil conflict over who would take the throne. The remnants of Adrasta to the west who had served the King of Kings went on to fight among themselves for every scrap of authority they could get their hands on.

To those who knew their Earth history, the situation might've reminded them of what happened after the death of Alexander the Great.

The civil war in the east had weakened Huang He quite a bit, while the chaos in the west split that area into many countries.

Many nations that existed in the current day — such as Granvaloa — were forged during this time, and many more had been founded and vanished from history.

And as though they believed that taking Adrasta's capital would make them the true successors to the King of Kings, the leaders of that time had relentlessly attacked it, all of them looking to claim it as their own. Eventually, everything but the underground area lay in ruins.

"However, after many battles...this land was eventually taken and secured by a certain individual."

"You mean…?"

"*The Evil*. This place was the final home of The Evil, who was defeated by the first king of Altar and his allies."

Near the end of the conflicts that ravaged the land now called Altar, two new people appeared on the world stage.

One was Azurite — a young shepherd who happened to unearth The Primeval Blade and be compatible with it, allowing him to rise as the Sacred King.

The other was The Evil. Born with that job, it was a mysterious being that history barely remembered.

While the Sacred King was having adventures all over the continent, The Evil was also growing stronger.

It was a living disaster, creating otherworldly monsters which struck fear into the hearts of all who encountered them.

Ultimately, The Evil took control of this city and was challenged by the Sacred King and his party. The battle took a heavy toll, but Azurite emerged victorious. That was the most famous story in Altar — the story of how their founding king defeated The Evil.

"After defeating The Evil, the founding king created his country and set this city as its capital," Findle continued. "It's said that there were various political and geopolitical reasons behind the decision to found a country in a place with such an ominous history. By the time he defeated The Evil, the first king already held power over multiple city-states, such as his queen's hometown of Gideon and — if you don't mind me inserting some family history here — the land owned by my ancestors. Presumably, they discussed what location would be best for the capital, but the founding king left behind a single sentence that seems to be relevant to this."

"A…sentence?" Canglong asked.

After a brief silence, the marquis said, "'The bearers must not abandon the *god's remains*.'"

"God's remains…?" Canglong echoed as he tilted his head. "Does that have anything to do with The Evil?" he asked. He was referring to the fact that the Superior Job grouping "The One," which The Evil belonged to, was sometimes viewed as having god-like properties.

"What he meant by those words isn't fully understood. That wasn't passed down to us. However, there are records saying that the Tomb Labyrinth was created shortly after The Evil was defeated, so perhaps…"

"If 'the bearers' refers to the Altar bloodline — as in, the bearers of The Primeval Blade that defeated The Evil — then the old king's proclamation would imply that Altea was built so that they would keep watch over The Evil's grave… Is that what you wanted to say?"

"Yes. That is one of the theories."

"A grave…? That's terrifying…" said Milianne despite understanding them only partially.

"No need to worry," said Marquis Findle. "If The Evil's remains are in Altea, they would certainly not be here in this shelter. This place has been examined countless times, and no one has ever found a single trace of any curse or grudge. We are completely safe here."

"Really? Phew…" Milianne said, thoroughly relieved.

"This is too complicated for me… You seem to understand it, though," said Elizabeth, glancing at Canglong.

"Umm, this story brings to mind a few things. And hailing from Huang He as I do, I cannot help but be intrigued by a place that is related to the King of Kings."

The Huang He Empire was the superpower that had stopped Adrasta's advance.

It had lost a lot of land during the civil war that followed The Era of the Peerless Three, but it was still an empire that had existed long before the era had even begun. Of all the current major countries, only Legendaria was more ancient than Huang He.

"The opposition between the Draconic Emperor and the King of Kings is an incredibly important part of history," Canglong said. The King of Kings from the west and the Draconic Emperor from the east... it was almost impossible to talk about one without mentioning the other.

"...That makes it all seem strange," Elizabeth commented.

"Makes *what* seem strange?"

"That you, a person from Huang He, and I, who lives where the King of Kings did, would ever be married." Canglong fell silent. Back when Elizabeth tried to address this during the Love-Duel Festival, he had chosen to avoid the question.

She'd thought of bringing it up during today's tea party, but the attack had interfered, so she'd decided to do it now.

"Cang...I've made my decision," she said. "I... I will become your wife."

Despite the current situation, Elizabeth made her intentions known.

Or perhaps she did it *because* of the situation — for all they knew, this could be her last chance.

"Your Highness..."

"But I still do not know you nearly well enough."

"...That is true."

"I never even loved anyone before..." Elizabeth wasn't yet ten years old. She was too young to have experienced anything like that. She got along very well with Canglong, but she never once felt anything "sweeter" for him. "But I still like having you as a friend. And since I do not dislike being with you, everything should turn out okay. I will eventually learn the things I do not know."

Since she felt no hate for him, she could stay by his side. That should have made it possible for them to learn everything they needed.

Elizabeth's sincere words filled Canglong's heart with warmth *as well as pain.*

That was due to the profoundly heavy truth he was hiding from her.

Since it was something she would come to know the moment they arrived at the palace in Huang He, he thought that it would be best if he revealed it himself.

"…Your Highness, I…"

"Cang?"

"I am not actually hu…*not a prin—*" Before he could finish his sentence, though…

"Umm… Move away from the middle of the room. It's dangerous."

…Milianne cut him off.

"Hm? Milia? What do you mean? What's dangerous?" Elizabeth asked.

"Umm… I don't know. I just feel that it is. The middle of the room is dangerous."

Her words made no apparent sense. She said it was dangerous, but nothing in the shelter seemed out of the ordinary.

However, they couldn't bring themselves to ignore her warning, so they all walked to Milia's side.

Canglong seemed to have something on his mind now.

Being interrupted didn't bother him, but he couldn't shake that there was something about Milia.

"Your Highness, who is this…?"

"I introduced her to you before the tea party. She is Liliana's little sister and one of my friends."

"Lady Grandria's sister… Then she is… Could she be…?"

Canglong's thoughts were cut off by a premonition of danger. He rushed to look at the middle of the room — specifically, the ceiling.

It had changed color, becoming visibly redder.

"An enemy!" A moment after Canglong cried out, the ceiling collapsed, and through the open hole rushed a flood of molten metal.

The maids yelped in fright, and the six Royal Guards stepped in the front to protect the rest.

As the sound and heat of boiling metal filled the shelter, a four-armed aberration descended through the hole.

"...Is this the place?" it muttered as it looked around. The creature was none other than Ignis Idea, otherwise known as King of Blaze, Feuer Lazburn.

"I-Is that King of Blaze?! But he was supposed to be trapped in a separation barrier...!" Marquis Findle began to panic, and for good reason.

The four-sided magical barrier should've been a major obstacle even to Superior Jobs, and it should've kept Ignis sealed for a good while.

Why was he here, then?

The answer was simple — the barrier was *only* four-sided.

"A hole in the ceiling... Did he melt everything under the surface?!" Between the surface and this shelter, there was a thirty-metel-thick layer of a metal not quite as strong as Mythical, but strong nonetheless. Made by the King of Kings — or, more specifically, the designers and followers who feared him — this shelter was the finest work of an era rife with war.

However, Ignis was able to melt through all of that merely by concentrating his firepower.

This completely unexpected break-in instantly transformed the shelter into a deadly prison.

This is bad...! Findle thought with a stern expression on his face. *I need to make sure Her Highness, the prince, and Lady Grandria's sister can escape!* Ignis was surrounded by the Royal Guards, but he barely seemed to care about that. Instead, he looked around once again and said, "Where is the Arch Sage?"

It was a question that no one present would have expected to hear.

"What...?" Findle asked, thoroughly confused.

"Where is the Arch Sage?" Ignis repeated himself as though that was the only thing on his mind.

That was exactly the case, in fact — he had attacked the castle in search of the Arch Sage in the first place. The only reason he was even here in this shelter was because he'd sensed its presence and thought he might have finally found his target.

"You are well aware that he is already dead!" Findle angrily shouted. *If the Arch Sage was alive, things wouldn't have gotten this bad!* he added, silently.

Despite Findle's words, Ignis didn't back down.

"I know. I heard of his supposed death even before I got this body. And I also heard that someone else now holds the title of 'Magical Apex.'"

He hadn't known that back when he'd met La Crima as a hermit, but once he'd returned to human civilization, the information was unavoidable.

As he was now, Ignis was fully aware of what happened in the world while he was away.

"But none of that matters."

Even so, the flame remained unfazed.

"The Arch Sage *is* here. Defeating him will be proof that I am the 'Magical Apex.' I have no interest in Masters with that title. His death and succession is faked. I know he would go that far. He is alive somewhere. He is here. Thus, I will find him, defeat him, and prove what I must."

He had no intention of listening to them. In his mind, the Arch Sage still being alive was pure fact — and even if it wasn't, Feuer would not stop until he found his target despite that.

It seemed like madness, but it was not. This was simply the logical end point of the thought processes of someone who'd dedicated his entire life to defeating and surpassing the Arch Sage.

He'd decided upon his reason for existence, and for the sake of that reason, he wouldn't bend, change, or limit himself.

He was a man who'd killed people just to gain the levels he needed to be that much closer to the Arch Sage.

He was a man who'd abandoned his humanity just to gain vast reserves of magic.

That was normal for him, and his entire system of values revolved around it.

At this point, he wasn't able to stop until he defeated the Arch Sage.

"...Is that one of Altar's princesses?" For the first time, Ignis said something that had nothing to do with the Arch Sage.

He was obviously pointing at Elizabeth.

"The Arch Sage is the kingdom's chief adviser. If I kill her, that should bring him here, shouldn't it? I feel like someone told me that. Was it Zeta? La Crima? Or...who was it, again?"

"You wretch...!" Findle shouted, overcome by rage. "I won't let you touch her! With the ruler absent, it is our duty to protect the princesses of Altar!"

"Then *call the Arch Sage.*"

"I cannot call the deceased! But I will call something that can defeat you!" Marquis Findle declared as he manipulated the control panel on the wall. "I will show you why I accompanied everyone to this shelter and why this place is called the safest in the castle!"

With those words, he pressed the "activate" button on the keyboard.

A moment later, a coffin rose up from a part of the floor.

Nearly ten metels tall, it almost reached the ceiling of the shelter, and when it opened up, a metallic leg colored red and gold stepped out of it.

It belonged to a giant golem.

"O creation of my ancestor, King of Colossi, Emet Findle I! O guardian idol of the royal family! The time has come for you to awaken! Stand tall and protect your princess and your kingdom!" This creature was security "equipment" installed into this shelter. Dating back to before the city was known as Altea, this weapon had even been deployed during the battle in which the Sacred King defeated The Evil.

Created by the first Azurite's brother-in-arms, King of Colossi, this was a legendary golem that had pulverized many monsters and weathered many blows as the primary tank in the Sacred King's party.

Made of the Mythical metal, Hihi'irokane, this was the Golem Bellcross.

It was the kingdom's strongest magic weapon, entrusted to the descendants of Emet Findle I and permitted to be used only when the castle was under attack. This golem could easily be called the castle's final defender.

Not saying a word, Ignis briefly glanced at the majestic construct.

"Target set! Bellcross, attack!" Findle ordered, and the metal giant charged.

When it came close to Ignis, Bellcross swung its enormous, hammer-like fist. A moment later, there was the sound of a fluid landing on the surface of the shelter.

It sounded as though Ignis had been crushed and pulverized, his blood splattering the walls...

"Piece of scrap. Don't get in my way."

...but that wasn't the case at all.

The splattering sound was actually the sound of *the drops of Bellcross's molten arm falling down to the floor.*

Ignis was holding up one of his four arms.

And on each of its fingers, there was an orb of light.

These five balls of immense flame created enough heat to melt the Mythical metal.

"Wh... What...?!" Seeing the arm of the strongest golem in the world — his heritage — be melted away with such ease left Findle dumbfounded, but it didn't end there.

After making the orbs on his fingers vanish, Ignis raised all four of his arms to the sky.

His pose made it look like he was going to begin some kind of juggling act, but instead, new orbs of light began to coalesce in his hands.

They appeared, then multiplied — from one to two to four to eight...

"A-Are those...? They cannot be!" The orbs, each of which carried unfathomable amounts of heat, were *all* the ultimate skill of King of Blaze — Fixed Star.

It was the same skill that had completely failed him back when he used it against the Arch Sage.

However, he had been able to summon far, far fewer back then.

A grand total of *sixty-four* Fixed Stars now floated around Ignis, and this absurd number didn't even make a dent in his total power.

Following his crushing defeat, Feuer had polished his ability to control many of these Fixed Stars at the same time. The only thing he'd needed to achieve this was greater magic reserves, and he now had more than any tian could dream of.

Because of that, the number and power of his Fixed Stars far exceeded what he had been capable of before. It was almost not worth comparing.

"Fixed Star Rain." The miniature suns fell like a meteor shower.

The surrounding space was drowned in white light, the air itself warped, and after a momentary flash, Bellcross disappeared without a trace.

Altar's ultimate guardian, older than the country itself, had vanished, and its enemy had barely even exerted any effort.

"I'll ask again." Ignis thought nothing of the immense power he just displayed or the object he just melted into nothing. "Where is the Arch Sage?" The strongest wielder of fire magic just repeated his desire once more.

"Marquis Findle! Take the young ones!"

"We will buy time!" The moment Bellcross melted, the six Royal Guards rushed to action.

They faced Ignis to protect Elizabeth and the others, knowing full well that they had no chance against a creature that had melted a golem made of Mythical metal.

Still, they believed that they could give the others more time to run away, even if it was just for a moment.

"Noble knights...forgive me." With these words, Findle overcame the shock of seeing Bellcross destroyed and rushed to the panel to open up the shelter's door. They had fled here for safety, but now, this chamber held nothing but death. Their only hope was to return to the surface.

But if the defense on the surface fell... No, you cannot think about that! No matter what state the surface was in, it was better than staying here and burning to death.

The heavy door of the shelter began to open, but Ignis noticed that they were trying to escape and pointed his four arms straight at Findle.

"We will not allow that!" a Royal Guard shouted, rushing to prevent his attack by slicing at Ignis' arms.

The blades didn't penetrate past the tough skin, but they did leave shallow cuts.

We aren't powerless against him! If he can be hurt, then... the knights thought, believing that they actually had a chance, however slim.

In that way, they were like their fellow Royal Guards who faced Aranea on the surface.

However, there was a major difference between Aranea and Ignis.

"Prominence Aura," Ignis said, causing the air surrounding him to heat up rapidly.

At that moment, the Paladins who were close to Ignis saw their blades melt away before their eyes. Their armor liquefied on their bodies, fusing with their skin.

"GHAAAAAGHHH!" Even if they tried to continue fighting, any weapons they brought close to Ignis melted away like snow.

Prominence Aura was a skill that created a superheated territory around the caster that acted as defensive-offensive armor strong enough to melt metal, but dealt no damage to the caster himself. For someone who could control sixty-four Fixed Stars at once, managing this much heat was no challenge whatsoever.

While Aranea's poison could be negated with Elixirs, merely approaching Ignis meant death. Even fighting from a distance wasn't an option since the immense heat would vaporize any projectiles and magics coming towards him.

A walking Sun that matched Superiors, a being that moved towards his objective and burned everything in his wake.

This was Ignis Idea.

"Your Highness...please run!"

"Marquis Findle! Forget about us! Please flee this place!"

"...Very well!" As the shelter's door opened up, Marquis Findle pressed something on the control panel.

He activated the sprinkler system. It had been installed in case of fires caused by cooking and other such activities.

Once it was on, its programming quickly reacted to the immense heat.

Nozzles emerged all over the shelter and sprayed at Ignis, causing a loud, roaring steam explosion.

All the water instantly vaporized and spread at a rapid rate, blowing everything away.

Neither Ignis nor the knights could possibly remain unscathed by the searing water vapor. The pressure of the explosion limited their movements, while the steam flooding the air made it difficult to see.

"Your Highness! Prince Canglong! Hurry...!" Findle used the opportunity to rush the children through the door.

But when they tried to go...

"Elizabeth!"

...Canglong called his fiancée by name for the first time ever, and then shoved her away with a desperate look on his face.

A split second later, a beam fired out of the wall of ste and pierced his chest.

The sound of flesh evaporating echoed throughout the shelter, followed by the thud of the young boy collapsing to the floor.

"Cang...?" His fiancée's voice was drowned out by the roar of flames.

This tragedy was observed by a device hidden among the sprinklers.

A letter

To the one who reads this:

I do not know your name. I will never see your face.

You will never see mine either.

But that is simply how we are.

As long as I exist, you cannot, and by the time you come into being, I will be gone.

And because this is how we are, I write down these words to be imparted to you in this letter.

If the current or succeeding emperor considers my will, it should eventually arrive in your hands.

There are two things you must know.

We are not human. We *cannot* be human.

This is an important truth.

This world is dominated by the relation between humans, jobs, and monsters, but we are an exception in this system.

We are the incarnation of an abnormality our ancestors etched onto the world in the distant past.

Because of this, we might eventually disappear due to the world's autopurification activity.

However, if you are reading this, it did not happen in either of our generations.

You might be at a loss of what to make of the power you were born with.

I once felt the same way as you.

Perhaps, though, that was only because I was born at an inopportune time and was frequently compared to my predecessor.

My predecessor likely utilized this power better than any one of us so far.

I was unable to match him. Perhaps you will. Regardless, know that there is no need to strive for that.

Our power is vast. We receive it by merely being chosen, without any effort on our part. We have exceptional power without ever having to gather it like others do.

Because of this, you might make grave mistakes in your youth.

You might have been born bathed in blood.

That would be a harsh reality that cannot be changed. Our power might be vast, but we have no means of bringing back those who are lost. Not even my predecessor was capable of that.

That is why I hope that you who are reading this will possess both power and will.

Do not be bound by sins hailing from a time before you.

Be aware of your power and carry a will of your own.

Our nature is affirmed when we use our power according to our own will.

It does not have to be for the protection of this country.

That is a choice we can make, but are not forced to.

Perhaps someone told you that you are a hero who will dedicate his life to protecting the country, but know that that is wrong.

I dedicated my life to protecting the country because I wished to make up for the civil war that I caused, and because I myself could not abandon the nation.

Thus, there is no need for you to follow this same path.

You are not obligated to do as you are ordered.

You should live the way you find suitable.

We are not human. We cannot be human.

Therefore, you cannot be bound.

Protect what you wish to protect.

Accomplish what you believe you must.

Do not be afraid to do as you will.

No one can ever bind you.

The power and talent you have exists only for the future you desire.

Royal Castle, Underground Shelter

There was a large hole in the prince's chest.

Burned by unfathomable heat, the wound had instantly cauterized. However, it was clear that the beam had taken his heart, making his fate obvious.

"Cang... CANG!" With tears in her eyes, Elizabeth shook Canglong's body, but the boy wasn't even bleeding, let alone breathing.

It seemed like all signs of life had left him.

"Did I hit something? I can't see," said a faint voice from within the steam. "I'll just keep doing this."

Like a moment earlier, beams fired in all directions, devastating the shelter and scattering people and objects alike, nozzles included.

Screams echoed throughout the premises as Ignis continued firing his searing beams indiscriminately. The sounds of melting, sounds of evaporation, sounds of flesh being burned, and the shrieks of the maids overwhelmed the soundscape.

Eventually, most of the nozzles were destroyed, freeing Ignis from his cage of steam explosions. It didn't seem like he had been hurt all that much.

"Such destruction... You wretch!" Findle barked as he glared at Ignis. A beam had taken his right arm.

Only two people remained unhurt — Elizabeth, who was clinging to Canglong's body, and Milianne, who just happened to be in the right spot to avoid the beams.

Everyone else was injured to various extents. Many were no longer even capable of movement.

As things were, Findle couldn't even take Elizabeth and escape.

"Where is the Arch Sage?" asked Ignis. His words hadn't changed even after causing all this devastation.

He was seeking the Arch Sage like a broken machine, making him seem barely human.

He began to approach Elizabeth.

"Your Highness! Please run! Save yourself at least...!" someone shouted, but Elizabeth remained by Canglong's side.

Eventually, Ignis was right in front of her.

"Where is the Arch Sage? If he doesn't show himself, I will kill the princess." Voicing his warped, yet unbending desire, the Idea reached towards Elizabeth with his hand, hot as a soldering iron.

Shrieks and roars of anger filled the crumbling room, but there was no one left to stop him.

The moment Ignis touched Elizabeth...*never came, for another hand grabbed his.*

"Hm...?" For the first time since he gained this inhuman form, Ignis displayed something that seemed to be confusion.

The hand that had grabbed his arm was burning. Ignis was clad in searing armor, and it set the offending limb on fire.

Despite that, it didn't let go. Just how much power was held within this tiny hand? It was tearing through his hardened skin, his wounds leaking blood which was promptly evaporated by his own heat.

Faced with this strange sight, Ignis asked, "...What are you?"

"...Cang?" Elizabeth opened her mouth at the same time.

The owner of the small hand was none other than Canglong himself — the boy who should've been killed by the hole in his chest.

Still lying down, he had raised his right hand and grabbed Ignis by the arm before it could reach Elizabeth.

But there was another thing that confused Ignis.

What is happening to his magic? It's as vast as the Arch Sage's... No... It might rival even mine... Ignis had dedicated all his power and talent to fire magic, rendering him unable to use Reveal, but as an experienced caster, he could sense Canglong's power nonetheless.

However, if he did have Reveal, he would have seen a truly bizarre sight — the boy's level and stats growing at a terrifying rate.

And the changes weren't just limited to the numbers.

"...Don't you dare touch Elizabeth." The boy who was presumed dead said these words as he rose to his feet.

He was now between Ignis and Elizabeth, ready to protect her.

There was still a hole in his chest, but it seemed to have mostly closed.

His evaporated heart and lungs were regenerating at an extreme speed. The hand that was holding Ignis's arm was also restoring itself as it burned, letting it maintain its form.

However, the black bandages that had been tied on him had been reduced to ashes.

"…My Self-Sealing Wraps have burned away. I suppose I will not be able to seal this away until they regenerate," he whispered as he looked down at the burning black bandages. They were an MVP special reward that he had picked from Huang He's treasury, and when worn, they *limited the wearer's own stats and skills.*

The item that he had worn to hide his true identity from the locals and Caldinians while in Altar…was now broken.

"No… I will not seal it away." Right now, he didn't actually mind that. What he needed now was not to hide it, but to *use* it.

"It" being the power he possessed…and his true self.

"Cang…are you okay?" Elizabeth asked. Rather than being confused by the oddity of the situation, she seemed to merely be happy that a friend she thought was dead was actually alive.

Canglong looked back at her and smiled before turning back to Ignis.

"Elizabeth… Let me finish what I wanted to say earlier."

With his back to her so she couldn't see his expression, Canglong spoke.

"I am not a prince. I do not have the right to inherit the throne of Huang He. I do not qualify for that." He continued his statement from before. "And…*I am not even human.*"

He revealed to her the secret that he had been keeping hidden for so long.

A moment later, his bones creaked and his limbs grew.

His height and width…his entire frame transformed into something that was entirely unlike a young boy.

Muscles grew under his skin, while scales sprouted over it.

Ultimately, he was transformed into a creature that seemed to be a mix of dragon and man.

"Cang...?" He did not reply to her. Canglong now looked more like the Idea he was facing. His appearance could easily be called "monstrous," and it was one he didn't want to show anyone...especially not Elizabeth.

Before he had left Huang He, his father — the emperor — had strictly forbidden him from showing this true form.

Despite that, he chose to reveal it now.

By his own will, he chose to do this so he could protect those whom he wanted to protect.

"You're—" Just as Ignis opened his mouth to speak, the dragon-man swung his arm, flinging Ignis's body into the wall opposite Elizabeth.

"Gh-ogh..." Overcome by shock far greater than the one from the steam explosions, Ignis coughed blood.

Looking at him, the thing that was Canglong began walking to a particular place — the spot where Golem Bellcross was destroyed. There, he reached for the floor and touched the metal giant's molten Mythical metal remains.

In his hand, it quickly changed shape to form a mask.

"Zifu Longmian," he said in a voice quite unlike the one he had spoken with before his transformation.

Meaning "word-hiding dragon mask," this was the name of a mask that a certain Special Superior Job would wear for important occasions.

As the person who knew what that meant better than anyone else, he placed the mask upon his own warped face.

"What *are* you...?" Most of those present here also wanted to hear the answer to Ignis's question.

The being standing before them was by no means a human boy.

He was not the slender young prince of Huang He.

He was a creature with a robust, draconic body and a mask over his monstrous face.

However, if anyone here was from Huang He, they would recognize him at a single glance.

Over there, this creature was akin to a god.

Indeed, he was the strongest gulong ren — the ancient dragon kin.

"Draconic Emperor, Canglong Renyue."

With a name that meant "blue dragon, beyond mankind," he was the humanoid Irregularity — the Draconic Emperor.

Ignis was quick to action. It wasn't clear how well Ignis understood the gravity of Canglong's declaration, but the power behind it was more than enough for him.

For the first time since coming to the shelter — no, since arriving at the castle — Ignis truly prepared for battle.

He judged that the entity before him was far above Bellcross and everyone else that stood in his way along the path to the Arch Sage. Canglong was not merely an obstruction for him, but an *enemy* that matched, if not surpassed, his target.

"Crimson Sphere!" Ignis started out with a *distraction* that took the form of over ten high-rank ultimate job skills.

Ignis had witnessed Canglong regenerate even his heart, but no matter how powerful his regeneration was, it should've been impossible for him to do so with his entire body reduced to nothing. This distraction wasn't something Canglong could ignore or evade.

The Crimson Spheres sped towards Elizabeth and the rest of their immobilized entourage. If Canglong wanted to protect them, he had no choice but to use himself as a shield.

And while he was busy doing that or regenerating the damage he sustained from it, Ignis would shower him in another Fixed Star Rain, leaving nothing behind.

However, faced with the Crimson Spheres, Canglong merely set his feet wider, assumed a strong stance, and *repeatedly punched the air, creating shock waves that dispersed every single ball of flame.*

That was over double the amount of Crimson Spheres that had melted the castle's main gate, yet they had just been snuffed out like the fires on a match.

The absurd sight left Marquis Findle and the royal knights speechless, but Ignis understood what had happened.

He released magic along with his punches... Ignis thought. Indeed — Canglong had extinguished the flames using his MP.

The punches were imbued with an amount of magic several times greater than in the Crimson Spheres, forcefully pulverizing the magical structure that composed them.

A means to release magic that doesn't involve spells... I did hear that Huang He possessed something like that... There existed a skill grouping called "Fa jin." The strikes of this skill grouping were normally used to drive magic *into* the target, creating shock waves that pulverized the insides regardless of how tough the outsides were.

However, that wasn't what Canglong had done — he had instead pulverized the airborne spells directly using his vast magical power.

That was a fundamentally different action, even if the movements he used to do it were similar.

No normal person would be able to release that much magic at once. In fact, even caster Superior Jobs would struggle with it.

This absurd amount of magical power rivals even mine... Is this the strength of the Draconic Emperor? Wait...the magic he released isn't quite like normal magic...

Ignis did not understand the true nature of Draconic Emperor as a job.

He had no idea if it was focused on stats, or what kind of skills it had.

In Huang He, the Draconic Emperor was considered a mystical entity akin to a living god, and even an experienced caster like Ignis knew next to nothing about him. The Draconic Emperor was the top of the duel rankings there, but the means by which he reached and kept the throne were a mystery.

Without saying a word, Canglong walked towards Ignis.

His movements were flawlessly graceful and his center of gravity was perfectly stable, making it clear that he had mastered the martial arts.

Why is he not running? Is his AGI low? Or is he moving in a way that will let him protect the princess and the others however he needs? Ignis tried to guess Canglong's intentions while weaving a spell in preparation, but before he could finish, Canglong's massive frame loomed right in front of him.

Supersonic speed?! The difference in speed between his walking and his movement just now was too great for any ordinary person to perceive, let alone counter.

But despite his shock, Ignis was able to react to it by reflex.

Battle casters who fought solo had to have the ability to stand their own against vanguards, who were generally faster than them; as one who'd walked that path for decades, Feuer Lazburn was able to weave a spell against Canglong as easily as he breathed.

He supplemented his Prominence Aura with Fixed Stars maintained on the tips of his fingers — the same technique he'd used to melt Bellcross's arm.

Canglong swung with his left fist, but entering Prominence Aura caused his entire body to catch fire.

That wasn't all — his fist flew right into Ignis's Fixed Stars like a moth to the flame.

158

Unlike before, he couldn't disperse it with magic, so his hand evaporated in an instant.

However, the hand was restored in a *split second* and immediately crushed the limb that held the Fixed Stars.

"Ghuh! Hhuh?!" Having lost one of his arms, Ignis let out a cry of pain and shock.

The impossibility of what was happening before his eyes made it difficult to to even speak coherently.

The Draconic Emperor had tried to punch him and had his arm evaporated — only to instantly regenerate it and use that momentum to finish the strike.

It seemed simple, but it was clearly impossible.

Absurdly fast regeneration…? No, it simply cannot *be this fast! It matches the Hierophant's Mercy of the Holy! How can he regenerate this quickly without even calling out a skill…?!* Ignis hastily backed away and began to shoot countless balls of fire in every direction. It wasn't an attack on Canglong or an act of desperation — he was actually trying to finish off the immobilized Altarians.

Canglong said nothing, his expression hidden by the mask, but his very aura made it obvious that his face had twisted with emotion.

Instead of following Ignis, he rushed to protect the others, just as he had before.

Ignis had done all of this solely to limit Canglong's actions and prepare for another assault.

The self-restoration function La Crima gave me can fix my arm to a certain extent…but the result will not be as good and will not come as quickly. Clearly, he is the outlier here.

Ignis was even more confused about the nature of the Draconic Emperor job than before. He could cancel magic, move at supersonic speeds, and regenerate just as fast, and his frame was rippling with muscles that let him easily pulverize even Ignis's enhanced body.

159

It was so well-rounded that it was impossible to guess what, exactly, the job was focused on.

…No, wait. Could it be?

Ignis's many years of combat experience and honed senses led him to believe that he *did* have an answer.

…I know something like this, do I not…?

The train of thought moved…

The power to neutralize magic…to negate attacks. Draconic Emperor… Draconic… Dragon?

It led him to a certain guess…

…Dragon King Aura?

A power possessed by a certain kind of monster.

Is the Draconic Emperor actually…? Treating this guess as a definite answer, Ignis's brain connected the dots.

The power to negate weak attacks, stats that could not be achieved by humans, extreme regeneration…

These features would remind some of certain entities faced by a select few champions. The strongest warriors of Altar might recall the great three-headed dragon.

Indeed, Draconic Emperor could only be…

"A human bearing the power of dragons and their kings?" Ignis guessed that Canglong was a humanoid with the abilities of the strongest monsters.

Canglong said nothing in response, focused on protecting the Altarians.

However, in his mind, he gave an answer.

Close, but not quite.

The Draconic Emperors were the descendant of gulong — ancient dragons — as well as gulong themselves. "Gulong" was another name for the strongest Pure-Dragons on the eastern side of the continent.

While the Border Mountain Belt in the west was inhabited by western-style skydragons, the ancient dragons of the east were more like the serpentine beasts from Chinese mythology in the real world.

Dragons with a similar appearance still lived in Tenchi, but the gulong were on an entirely different level. They were extremely intelligent and well-versed in the arts, and had lived alongside humans since ancient times as guardians or rulers. The gulong ren — ancient dragon kin — that still existed to this day were the descendants of gulong-human hybrids; back then, the gulong used them as representatives of their rule.

The gulong were monsters that had existed since the very first stages of the world. Thus the name *ancient* dragons, which they used to refer to themselves as well as being called this by others.

You could say that the previous observers had put them on this world to act as part of the world's system — as both tyrants and refiners of mankind. They understood the truth behind this world and were aware of multiple ways of managing this *game*.

As a result of all this, the people of the east saw them as wise and fearsome sovereigns of the land.

However, things had changed two thousand years ago, when the Incarnations attacked.

Back then, it quickly became clear that the gulong *knew things too well*.

The Incarnations had abilities far outside the norm for the world, as well as vast amounts of Resources to support them. The dragons immediately understood that they could not win against the men.

That was why they chose to take their leave *without* fighting.

They ran away, fearing the ultimate end they would face if they stood up to the Incarnations, and began searching for a way to survive into the future — to continue to exist.

What they arrived upon was one of the ways to control the very world — the ability to influence the job-managing Archetype System.

They quickly manipulated the Archetype System and disappeared, leaving behind only the gulong ren born from the union of dragons and humans — and the being known as the "Draconic Emperor."

This was a job that appeared only after the gulong vanished, which was because *the Draconic Emperor job and the gulong were one and the same.*

The gulong had turned their very existence into a job and left it to their future descendants.

Jobs couldn't be destroyed — they would exist for as long as this world did.

What mattered to the gulong wasn't their awareness or life, but their mere *existence.*

The Draconic Emperor was the aggregation of everything that made up the monsters known as gulong. It was their remains, their continued existence, taking the *shape* of a job.

And those born with this job had two special skills.

The first was "Gulong Cells." It gave the bearer of the job an ancient dragon body said to be tougher than even that of dragon kings.

Being the aggregate of all the gulong, the Draconic Emperor had life force that matched them…if not surpassed them.

Because of this, the Draconic Emperor was nigh-invulnerable. Wounds that would be fatal to anyone else were mere scratches to them. If a crushed heart or a burnt body was enough to kill the Draconic Emperor, then first in Huang He's duel rankings would've been Xunyu, not Canglong.

This immortality had been demonstrated even in this battle against Ignis.

Additionally, as a side-effect of Gulong Cells, the bearer's body was "dragonized," turning him into a Dragon King.

With their genetic makeup and resistances rivaling those of the highest-tier dragons, they were able to turn their magic into the defensive aura characteristic of Dragon Kings, simply called "Dragon King Aura."

The nigh-immortal Draconic Emperor himself scarcely needed it, but as Canglong had demonstrated with Elizabeth and the other Altarians here, it could be used for support.

Gulong Cells was an immensely powerful skill even just on its own.

However, what made Draconic Emperors truly a force to be reckoned with was their *other* special skill.

This skill was the reason why those who knew the nature of the job would call the Draconic Emperor an abnormality. Its name was "Draconic Heritage."

The gulong had created Draconic Emperor as a vessel — it was a job, yet not a job, for it didn't fully adhere to the world's rules.

Unlike other Superior Jobs, the Resources gathered for it were not emptied for the next inheritor — meaning that *Draconic Emperors were born with the levels and stats of their predecessors.*

The job's stat growth was uniform, and thanks to this skill, there was no limit to how high its stats could grow.

The magic that nearly matched Ignis Idea, the AGI that let him move at supersonic speeds, the STR that let him shatter Ignis's enhanced arm, and even the vast reserves of HP — all were the result of the levels Canglong had inherited.

The Draconic Emperor that had come before Canglong's predecessor was considered the strongest one ever, but that was because he exercised incredible control over his own powers.

In terms of pure stats, the current one — Canglong — was the strongest by far.

His level easily surpassed *3,000*.

This was the Draconic Emperor — a shapeless, abnormal vessel created by the gulong from their own existence in order to escape extinction at the hands of the Incarnations.

It was the humanoid Irregularity they had etched onto the world.

Born transcendental, the bearers of this abnormal job were human, and yet not.

They *could not* be human.

That was why the names given to them — Renwai, Renchao, or Renyue — had meanings like "inhuman" or "above man."

Royal Castle, Fourth Floor, Hallway

Damn it, what's going on? Morter thought, sensing the sudden appearance of a vast concentration of magic below.

It was different from the one he was chasing and the one that wasn't moving — a fourth source of magic.

Power-wise, it's up there with that fiery old geezer's. What's the deal with this castle?

The magic he'd sensed belonged to Draconic Emperor, Canglong, but since Morter couldn't know that, he was greatly perplexed.

Is this place actually haunted or something? He recognized this stray thought of his as the truth.

It accurately described his current situation.

Even now, he was being attacked by monsters. These obviously abnormal creatures chased after him, and he fought them all back, but he was immediately confronted with a new problem.

None of the monsters he'd defeated dissolved into light.

Upon death, they simply left the remains of what they had been: broken armor, shattered walls, collapsed flowers, torn paintings, and the like.

It was as though they had never been monsters at all — that they were nothing but objects that had gone out of control. No motes of light, no turning into loot... Something about them was different.

Morter didn't even feel like he'd received any XP or anything when he killed them — something that would never happen if they were normal monsters.

An illusionist's trick...? No way. Such illusions might've worked on someone else, but as Vespertilio Idea, who could move freely while remaining unperceived, he was nearly immune to illusions.

There *were* monsters here, even if they didn't obey the relevant laws.

...And then there's the biggest problem of all. Standing in front of a door, Morter glared at the magic he sensed on the other side.

There was the third abnormality — a fairly powerful magic signature.

The cause of all this weird shit could be on the other side, eh? The magic signature that had been moving through the fourth floor was now in front of him, behind this one single door.

It was as though it was waiting for something.

I got a bad feeling about this... I'd run if I could...but I can't.

Morter resented the fragment of Idea within him — the very thing that kept him from running away.

That piece was what maintained the bodies of the people modified by the Embryo — the Ideas.

It was also a leash that would take control of his body away from him if he acted against his orders. Once under control, Morter's body would be forced to do as he was bidden, but his movements would be far more awkward and less skilled than normal.

That would almost certainly lead to his death, so Morter had no choice but to obey.

Try to remove it and die, defy it and meet your end... This fucking setup, I swear...

He did like the powers he gained as an Idea, but the negatives had turned out to outweigh the positives.

I gotta do as Zeta told me and attack whoever this magic belongs to, he thought in resignation as he recalled the conversation.

"Important. The most important part of this request is to attack any strange person."

"Strange? You know that if you include Masters, there's strange people everywhere, right?"

"Aware. I know that. That's why the entire city needs to be attacked."

"...Huh?"

"Directive. I order Regina Apis Idea to destroy the city. The other three will assault the castle. You will sabotage the castle and attack anyone suspicious. It doesn't matter if they survive or not."

"...Are you insane?"

"Sane. I am of sound mind. This is part of the request we accepted, and chaos will help me achieve my own goal as well."

"Is everything all right with your and the client's wiring...?"

"Uncertain. I don't know if either of our mental states are stable. However, for the client, this might be an important enough matter to ignore the resulting sacrifices."

"...Man, if something's important enough to call for *that*, I don't even wanna know what it is."

"Agreed. With that in mind, I want you to do this job."

They had gone on to assault the castle, and Morter had followed an extremely suspicious magic signature.

Whatever's behind this door is obviously something pretty weird... Did I hit the jackpot?

The moment that door was opened, the victor would be decided. Morter knew that full well, so he considered how he would go about this.

I'll kick the door and activate the Darkness Boundary. They'll lose sight of me, giving me a chance to end it all with Sudden Death.

167

Darkness Boundary was a function La Crima had implanted in him. It briefly absorbed the visible light in a certain range, robbing anyone in the affected area of their sight.

Sudden Death was King of Raids' ultimate job skill.

It could only be used while undetected by the target, and it delivered a triple damage attack which ignored defense, endurance, and resistances. It also prevented the activation of the Brooches many people relied on to survive massive damage, and it was affected by the raider grouping's basic skill, Sneak Raid, which tripled the damage done while undetected.

Modified as he was now, he could deliver Sudden Deaths powerful enough to utterly obliterate his targets.

Even when dealing with high HP opponents, he could still instantly kill them by targeting vital areas.

"Hm…" Even though he had figured out all of this in his head, Morter's intuition and experience made him hesitate. He felt as though what waited for him behind the door was a bottomless pit.

But if he let fear hold him back, the Idea within him would forcefully take control, making him watch as his body headed to its death.

And even aside from that, there was the possibility of whoever was on the other side striking first.

Thus, Morter had only one choice here.

…Well, I guess I just gotta have faith. I'm a Superior Job — one of the few who rose above the rest. And even with all the dumb shit that came with it, I was given a crazy good body.

And so…

"Hh…!"

…he gathered his resolve and kicked open the door.

At the same moment, he activated the Darkness Boundary, drowning the surroundings in pitch black.

Even though he was also now plunged into darkness, being mixed with a bat-like Pure-Dragon-tier creature had granted him hearing good enough to perceive his enemy.

There's two of them...?! I see...so one's riding the other! Since they were so close together, he'd mistaken them for a single magic signature — assuming both of them had one, of course.

Below is a four-legged monster, above is...a really small human! The moment his hearing allowed him to grasp this, Morter instantly selected his target.

I'll go for the one on top! Following Zeta's order, he kicked off the floor and ceiling several times before approaching the strange, short person on the monster's back.

Sudden Death! He spoke the skill name in his mind before swinging his blade-like claws down towards the back of the tiny figure's neck.

Morter's attack, backed by the power of a lethal skill, struck the tiny target.

"...What?" he muttered, and he stared at his claws, thoroughly confused.

The attack that was supposed to end a life *didn't even break through the skin.*

It wasn't just that — it seemed like the target wasn't even affected by the attack at all.

Soon after, the effects of the Darkness Boundary expired, bringing light back to the world.

The moment his perception switched from sonar to visual...

"...HOW?!"

...he was overcome by immense shock.

His target — who had been unharmed by his deadly swing — turned out to be nothing but a little girl.

Mounted upon a four-legged beast, she looked at him with a disinterested expression and eyes that held no emotion.

I know she seemed small, but…an actual child?! A child was just hit by my ultimate skill and felt…nothing?!

Morter quickly used Reveal to find out more about her.

Theresia Celestite Altar

Job: None

Level: 0 (Total Level: 0)

The info he was given only made him realize that she had no jobs at all.

The only thing he'd learned was that according to her name, she was none other than the Third Princess of Altar.

"No… There's no way!" Faced with this impossible reality, Morter rejected the facts he had just been given.

There's no way this girl is powerless! She's not just a princess. "Strange" doesn't even begin to describe her… She has to be the most abnormal thing in the entire world!

Zeta's order flashed back into his mind. Theresia now disturbed him far more than any of the I.F. members or his fellow Ideas had ever done.

"There's nothing strange about this," Theresia said, as though she had read his mind. Morter instantly jumped back to put some distance between them. "I survived because of my Brooch. There aren't any fragments around because the Brooch just happened to not break. Your attack really scared me."

Theresia described the situation in a way that made her seem like a normal child. Morter didn't have Truth Discernment, but he didn't need it to know that she was lying.

After all, *Sudden Death was a skill that couldn't be negated by Brooches.*

In his mind, it would've been far better if the Brooch *had* activated for some reason.

He also felt that just like Reveal had failed him with her, Truth Discernment would also mean nothing against this girl even if he had possessed the skill.

"You followed the magic, didn't you? You must've felt Dor, then. I mean, he's my protector. He's very strong…strong enough to destroy the world," Theresia said as she pet the beast — Dormouse.

Perhaps she was right that Morter felt Dormouse's magic, but despite that — or perhaps because of it — he found the girl herself so abnormal that the magic signature meant nothing, no matter how vast it was.

"I'm just a normal girl, and Dor is my very strong protector. Your attack just happened to be blocked by my Brooch. There's nothing here that your leader would want. That's a reasonable explanation for all of this, but…" Theresia said as she looked at Morter with unreadable eyes, "…you won't just accept it and leave, will you?"

The little girl's aura was so overwhelmingly powerful that it might just be enough to make any ordinary person lose their minds or even die.

"Huh… Gh…" Morter couldn't even bring himself to respond.

"…Very well. If you want information, then you can bring this back."

Before he could say anything, the girl's tone became more mature as she continued to speak.

"I am… ▪▪▪ ▪▪▪▪."

Her words, however, failed to reach him.

Or, more precisely, they reached him as nothing but meaningless noise.

"You probably couldn't hear that. My job as ▪▪▪ ▪▪▪▪ is camouflaged, and I can't say the name to anyone myself. Though, I'll still tell you what I know. You might not hear certain bits, but I want to convey it to you as is. The general meaning should still get through to you. This assault was orchestrated by someone who wants me eliminated, so the capital was attacked so that they could find out *who I am*. I'll give you the answer, and that info by itself should satisfy them."

"Wa—" Morter wanted to say "Wait," but Theresia continued before he could finish.

"Also, it'd be troublesome if you died this close to me. Progression is slowed down thanks to Dor *handling it*, but if there are too many deaths nearby, some of it will get through. Also, the amount absorbed is the greatest when I or ▪▪ ▪▪▪▪▪▪▪▪▪▪ do the killing directly, and Dor doesn't have the authority to eliminate you because of the Embryo you've been mixed with. Not many people die in the castle, and the barrier prevents ▪▪▪▪▪▪▪▪ ▪▪▪▪▪▪▪▪▪▪ from the outside, so this would be inconvenient. ▪▪▪ ▪▪▪▪▪▪▪'s appearance would be pushed forward."

Morter couldn't understand — or even hear — a lot of what she said.

"Dor can destroy the world, but the ▪▪▪▪ ▪▪▪▪ would ▪▪▪▪ it."

Morter's very cells understood that he was just too insignificant to hear her words.

They were meant for those far more special than him.

He felt as though hearing this alien information would rob him of everything, even the prospect of a normal death.

Why must I hear this? Morter thought with the remaining fragments of his sanity.

"That's why I want you to stop attacking me. Otherwise, more safety functions will be activated. The more danger I am in, the more of them are freed. Like how ▪▪▪▪▪▪▪▪ ▪▪▪▪▪▪▪▪▪▪▪▪▪▪ was unlocked because of Sechs."

She spoke the name of the leader of I.F. — the one who outranked even those who had defeated him, modified him, and used him — but Morter was in no state to acknowledge that. But for some reason, he felt that some of the words he couldn't hear had something to do with the bizarre monsters he faced back in the hallway.

"Back when Gloria attacked, I thought that I could end it all by taking it down with me. You just aren't enough to deal with me… And now that I think about it, Gloria was modified too, so maybe not even that monster could've touched me."

Theresia's expression slightly changed.

"My safety functions are automatic. They're activated to eliminate any threats and to keep me alive. You can see it in the ■■■■■■■■■■ that attacked you. You can't hurt me because you've been mixed with a foreign object, but it still reacts to your attacks and skills. The reaction is weak because they caused no damage, but if you keep this up… it will surely be released. Eventually, ■■■ ■■■■■■ will show about half of its face…and that's *terrifying*."

She said that last word with a truly worried expression.

She was terrified not of Morter's attacks…but of something within herself — the automatic defensive reaction of the power lying dormant inside her, ready to create unnatural monsters and whatever else it took every time she was attacked or put in danger.

This scared her like nothing else.

"I don't want to release more of this power. I might kill my sister with it. So please…don't touch me," she said. With that, she had finished giving Morter his information and laid a hand on her chest. "…Don't touch the GAME OVER."

An ultimatum, delivered calmly.

What Is Untouchable,
What Shouldn't Be Touched

5XX years ago

Deep under the ruins of the industrial city, there was a cavern even larger than the shelter.

Its ceiling easily surpassed a hundred metels in height.

And yet, there was something large enough to take up the majority of this vast space.

Possessing both humanoid and beastial features…it seemed to be a corpse of some kind.

However, through its fossil-like exterior, a pulse could be sensed.

These pulses carried enough energy that it almost seemed as though the corpse might stand up at any moment and wreak havoc upon the world — but then it suddenly stopped. Everything became deathly still.

"…Con…firmed. On the surface…the current…The Evil…died. That made…The Demise…The GAME OVER…go dormant…"

"Good grief… I guess this trouble's finally dealt with, eeh…?"

The gloomy-looking woman received a response from a youth with a cat perched on his head.

The other people there with them looked up at the *thing*.

Perhaps "people" wasn't the right word. Many of them had a human appearance, but there were a few who did not.

"This is the first time we've found the true body, and I suppose this thing works similarly to Jabberwock...Evolution," said the entity made up of four floating orbs, which from some angles looked somewhat like a *caterpillar*.

"The Evil that the Sacred King and his brethren defeated must be this thing's brain-frame. This time, the brain-frame died before this combat-frame, preventing it from waking up. Or perhaps our activities have made it so it lacks the Resources required for activation."

"Based on the measured valuuues, we were preeetty close to the limit!" A pair of twins — a spectacled boy and a girl with headphones — gave their analysis.

"If the retrieved texts are correct, the last time it was activated was before we arrived. Back then, the forces were adequate. We had difficulty subduing just The Evil this time, but they didn't have much of a problem even with this."

"Hmm... That means it was weaker last tiiime! I mean, we eeaasily wiped out the 'adequate' forces they used! This time, it was probably stronger than each of uuus! Ohh, Bandersnatch is an exception, of coouurse!"

"Does that mean that it spent the last millennium — and more — reconstructing itself and growing stronger?" asked a slender, fussy-looking youth.

"Likely. Now, Red King...attack it with your Space Fracture."

"Understood." The slender youth quickly used his power on the fossil-like object.

A moment later, the world was split in two along a straight line, and a colorless void peered out from beyond it.

A few seconds later, it closed, splitting everything in its path... except for the fossil-like object.

It was right in the center of this immense destructive power… and it wasn't affected whatsoever.

"…Same as it was with The Evil, huh?" said the youth with a cat on his head and distress on his face. "If not even Space Fracture can hurt it… This is baaad."

"Indeed. Space Fracture destroys objects and phenomena regardless of toughness, yet it did nothing here."

"Ah ha haaa! It's *sooo* bad! Should we try calling Bandersnatch?"

"Let's not… In the worst-case scenario, everything we've done so far might go to waaaste," the youth rejected the headphone-wearing girl's suggestion.

"So those who defeated it last time had offensive powers greater than Red King's Space Fracture? Maybe it would be possible with the Sacred King's blade…" said the caterpillar.

"No, this is a matter of fundamental mechanics. As those who came from the *outside*, we cannot affect this thing in any way. It's the same as with The Evil. This is probably a safety function of this world's system itself," said the spectacled boy.

"…So this thing can only be harmed by tians, eeeh?" said the youth with a cat on his head. "What about UBMs?"

"They probably couldn't harm it either. In fact, I doubt any monster actually could. Queen gave them all the item transformation function."

"Ah ha haaa! We reeeally messed up there!" the headphone girl laughed, but no one else found it funny.

"Wait. The Evil was defeated by the Sacred King, right? Isn't The Primeval Blade an Irregularity? As in, a UBM?"

"When it comes to the phenomenon of 'severance,' that thing can do anything, no matter how ridiculous. It probably negates even The Evil's defensive functions. It also shows just how absurd something needs to be to get past them… From the looks of it, even the Masters we will eventually welcome will be powerless against it."

"That much is obvious. There is nothing we or any other Embryos can do against it."

"What do we do now? What will become of our plans if something like this remains here…?"

"We can only hope that by the time it activates again, our goals will already be achieved," said the caterpillar. It seemed as though all of them were truly troubled by the difficult problem before them.

"Why…does this…exist…anyway?" asked the gloomy woman.

"It's a trial," said the four-legged beast that had been silent until just now.

"Dormouse…"

"The environment we are creating is meant to nurture Superior Embryos, and to that end, Jabberwock is gathering SUBMs. If this land was meant to nurture strength through jobs, this might be intended to fill a similar role — a powerful force to test them."

"But…something like this…would destroy…the world…"

"'Surpass this trial or be destroyed.' That might've been the idea behind it."

"…Such short-tempered…creators…"

"Is that conjecture, Dormouse?" asked the spectacled boy.

"It is. This is a conclusion I reached by using all of my processing power… Though, it incorporates some of my intuition."

"Animalistic intuition is something we do not have. The idea is worth considering," the spectacled boy — one of the twins who had the greatest machine-like calculating power among everyone present — said in agreement.

"Based on the data we've gathered so far, it seems that the brain-frame's rebirth happens not far from the main body. The Evil who was just defeated was also born in the city right above us."

"So it's likely that the next one will be here too?"

"We should keep an eye on it, then, and when The Evil appears, we should just deleeete it! Like we did the previous tiiimes!" said the headphone girl.

The beings present knew of The Evil and The Demise — this fossil-like object — from the writings of the pre-ancient civilization. They had decided that these creatures would surely ruin their plans, and thus had made an effort to prevent The Demise from appearing by defeating The Evil every time.

Having discovered The Demise this time made them all the more certain that they had done the right thing.

"But this is the last time we can use our previous method... Employing tians, I mean," said Dormouse, looking sour.

"...Yeaaah. We overused the makeshift solution," said the youth with a cat on his head and a bitter expression on his face.

"So far, we've managed to lead tians into beating The Evil after discovering it early..." Since their own attacks wouldn't work on The Evil, they hired or otherwise enlisted powerful tians to defeat it on their behalf; however, this was the last time that would work for them.

"The Evil returns stronger every time. This one was so powerful that even as a child, he was able to automatically counter the Superior Job we sent after him. As an adult, we led the most powerful tians we could find against him...and it was still a Pyrrhic victory."

"...It won't work at all next time." The Evil that would come after this would be too strong for any tian to kill.

In fact, careless contact with it would only accelerate its functions.

After all, the deaths caused by The Evil or the monsters it created — monsters called "dependants" — gave it more Resources than any other deaths, accelerating its leveling and the arrival of The Demise.

"We will change our approach," said Dormouse.

"What do you mean?"

"From now on, when we find The Evil, I will stay by its side and absorb the Resources meant for it. At the same time, I will slow down their activation by protecting them and keeping them away from danger."

"We have no data supporting this idea, so I cannot say much about it… But if it works well, there is the possibility that The Evil will die a natural death before The Demise is activated."

"But what if it happens after we welcome the Earth's Masters? There will no doubt be a great deal of turmoil, and the amount of Resources flowing to The Evil will increase dramatically. Not even you can absorb that much, can you?" asked the caterpillar.

Dormouse thought about it for a few moments before saying, "…We can only pray that we achieve our goal before that happens."

The words made the rest of them grin wryly.

"'Pray,' huh? I find it hard to comment on that."

"…The ones who destroyed religion in this world are now clinging to a divine hope to protect the world from a doom mentioned by those veeeeery same religions. It's so ironic that it's not even funny."

Despite the comments, they all knew that this was the only hope they had.

"Very well. That will be our approach. No one objects, I assume…?" the spectacled boy asked, and the others all nodded. "So we now have the approval of myself, Dee, Red King, Caterpillar, Duchess, Dormouse, Cheshire…and Alice — she just gave it to me through the avatar. That is a majority, so it's decided."

"Well, it's not like those who *aren't* here would say nooo… If you ignore the big tin can, anyway," said the youth with the cat on his head — Cheshire.

"...Bandersnatch is very stubborn, after all. If there are enemies, crushing them is the only option for him. That's the only job he can do too, since he can't even have an avatar," said the fussy-looking youth — Red King.

Their massive, mighty, and mad colleague always had to be taken into account.

"Now, we need to conceal not just The Evil itself, but this thing too. Caterpillar, place a save point somewhere on this land and begin adjusting the environment," ordered the spectacled boy — Tweedledum.

"A save point? As in, an environment maintenance marker? But I've already removed them from this area once," said the gathering of orbs — Caterpillar.

"I am aware. I will have you make the arrangements, Cheshire. Needless to say, Dee and I will also help by using DIN to spread info."

"What are you planning?"

"We will create a narrative that the death of The Evil at the hands of the Sacred King has blessed this land. People will flock to build a city here. The more people we have close to this thing, the higher the chances that The Evil will be born here, making them easier to observe. Also, the save point here will be given a resource absorption function."

"I see. That would help," said Dormouse.

"Additionally, Red King, I will have you reconstruct the space here to keep people away from this thing," Tweedledum said as he pointed at The Demise.

"How?"

"Create multiple layers of extra dimensions, making it impossible to arrive at this place by simply digging down. In fact, let us make an entire created dungeon. It will seem unnatural if it's *just* a reconstructed space. We will use DIN to spread the idea that this phenomenon was caused by the death of The Evil. You help too, Duchess; I will be counting on you to convince Queen."

"Very…well…" said the gloomy woman — Duchess.

"A created dungeon… We only have the Overlord job change dungeons left behind by the previous manageerrs. This'll be our first time making ooone."

"This one will be more difficult than the others. I will talk to Jabberwock about that. We will use the UBMs he retrieved as guard dogs — Extinction Dragon King and the like will do just fine."

"I seeee! Oh yeah! What about the dungeon's naaame?" asked the headphone girl — Tweedledee.

Tweedledum looked up at The Demise — those fossil-like divine remains — and said, "The dungeon will be called…the 'Tomb Labyrinth.'"

Following this, the Royal Capital, Altea, was constructed, along with the created dungeon known as the Tomb Labyrinth.

Various myths and legends sprung up about it, but most of them were eventually lost or forgotten. The truth behind it remained hidden, even as the city and dungeon both stood for centuries, surviving even into the present day.

About her…

She has been lying since the day she was born.

Theresia C. Altar was the third princess of the kingdom.

She'd lost her mother soon after birth, and she herself was born sickly.

Likely because of those tragedies, her father and sisters had showered Theresia with love for her entire life.

Even if all of that hadn't been the case, then the doctor's statement that she wouldn't live into adulthood would've been more than enough reason for them to cherish her.

Within her cradle, surrounded by love and sadness, Theresia thought, *So this is the life I was born into this time.*

Even back as an infant, she already had a functional mind and an awareness of the world.

It was as though the brain inside her head wasn't the only thing that stored her thoughts and memories.

In fact, there actually was a *vessel* that fulfilled that function — the Special Superior Job, The Evil.

This job served to prime, rouse, and stimulate The Demise — the other half of the world-ending god.

It was part of The System left behind by the previous observers, who'd created it to test this world.

Because of this, The Evil was equipped with functions that made it truly unique among jobs — a whole five of these functions, in fact.

First, The Evil possessed the memories of the job's previous holders, and the job itself served the role of the user's brain in producing thoughts.

Second, The Evil automatically leveled up by absorbing Resources from dead people all over the world.

Third, the information regarding the job was completely hidden until The Evil reached a certain level.

Fourth, The Evil was completely immune to all "outsiders" that didn't exist within the realm of The System.

Fifth, the newest The Evil had greater stats and stronger skills than the one that had come before.

I was just born, but I already feel tired of life. For Theresia, the greatest problem was the first point — the memories she had. The Evils didn't inherit the natures of the previous ones, so her personality was her own, but memory and personality weren't completely separate.

Because she possessed the memories of every previous person who had held the job, Theresia already had a great deal of knowledge as a mere baby. This had forced her to mature mentally far past her actual age. If the memories and capabilities she had as The Evil didn't come with a mental safeguard, her mind would've shattered moments after she was born.

Still, having multiple memories of her own death made her mentally exhausted.

But at the same, she understood that The Evil was an entity that would eventually have to die.

If The Evil lived, The Demise would arrive, likely causing the end of the world.

The problem with that was that The Evils couldn't kill or hurt themselves, and if exposed to danger, their job skills would automatically react to it.

By merely existing and maturing, Theresia would bring harm to the world, so she would eventually be killed.

Among The Evils of the past, there were those who had just silently awaited their end, as well as those who had bared their fangs at the world. Her ancestor had killed one of the latter kind; she herself was the former.

In spite of their similar memories, their approach was different, which must've been due to the difference between their souls.

Theresia understood that she would eventually be exposed and killed. Having just been born, she decided to simply wait for the end.

But until she was exposed…she chose to lie.

When Theresia was about a year old, she had an understanding of her surroundings.

Altimia is the Sacred Princess. While my level is still low, she could easily lop off my head.

She looked back through the memories of The Evils' previous deaths and came to that conclusion.

The Primeval Blade was now a UBM, but despite having been mixed with some foreign substances, it had still been able to cut through The Evil's impenetrable defenses.

In fact, the sword was exactly like The Evil in one key way — it had been specially prepared by the creators of this world. If they had made it to cut through anything, then that quality would remain even if its very nature was tampered with.

This much was evident from the picture book read to her in the cradle — Altar's most famous legend.

The bearers must not abandon the god's remains… Azurite knew that The Evil would reincarnate here and said that so that the bearer of The Primeval Blade would quickly kill them. Though, I can't imagine that he expected The Evil to be his own descendant.

The god's remains… In other words, the main body of The Demise lay dormant underneath the capital.

It was unknown if the Sacred King of that era knew that The Evil would be born close to The Demise, but he had still happened upon the correct approach.

The most effective way to deal with The Evil was to use The Primeval Blade to lop off their head while they were still young.

The more they matured, the more defensive potential their skills provided. Eventually, there could come a point where even the current bearer of The Primeval Blade would have to struggle as much as, if not more than, the first Azurite to defeat their opponent.

The level growth is…slow. Leveling for Theresia was harder now than it used to be when she was born.

The reason for that was the sterilization barrier that had been placed on the castle for her sake.

Though it wasn't created with the purpose of blocking the Resources coming to her from all over the world, it did protect against curse-type status effects, which effectively shut out most of the Resources she should have been absorbing.

That isn't a problem, since the Resources just return to nature instead… Well, actually, my leveling speed was slower than for the previous The Evils even before the barrier came up — which I guess is obvious, given that this isn't an age of war.

Theresia had no way of knowing this, but Altea's save point was also equipped with the function of absorbing stray Resources. The control AI had built it that way to counter The Evil, and it was slowing down her leveling speed.

…Not that I mind it. It will all be over when my level rises too high, so the slowness is welcome…even if it doesn't change much in the end.

The Evils of the past were all put in mortal danger before turning five, activating their safety measures and forcing them to undergo their first awakening. If this ever happened to Theresia, it would become obvious that she was The Evil even if that fact had been hidden from skills like Reveal. When that happened, she would be killed.

Since that's the way things are, I think I'll just enjoy this lavish life, she thought with nothing but sincerity.

Though Theresia knew that Altimia would kill her one day, she still loved her, as well as their father and Elizabeth.

None of The Evils that had existed in the past had been as blessed as her.

This reminds me that the last one was from a poor family. Born in the ruined ex-capital of Adrasta, Theresia's predecessor was from a household that had been forced to sell their children in order to survive through the winter. He'd had siblings, but they were sold off and he never saw them again and...

...*Wait, is that really how it was?* Theresia had almost remembered something, but couldn't quite grasp it.

Though this wasn't true for all of The Evils, the memories they had of their past lives tended to become more hazy as they aged. Perhaps this was just how the job handled the memories of The Evils who became insane enough to break the limits of their mental safeguard.

Regardless, The Evils who had a happy life were few and far between. At best, they simply understood their nature and eventually accepted their death.

That was why, in her unnaturally mature mind, Theresia had decided to enjoy life as a princess until her time came — to maintain the lie that she was nothing but a sickly young girl.

I'll be exposed in a few years, anyway...

Nearly four years had passed since then. Almost five years old now, Theresia looked at the scenery outside and whispered, "...I'm *too* blessed."

As a princess — a sickly one, at that — she was given perhaps the warmest upbringing possible in this world. The concept of danger was almost alien to her.

"I didn't expect this..." She thought that she would have certainly been revealed as The Evil by now.

Normally, that happened when The Evil was exposed to things like monster attacks or war, activating their safety measures and unlocking parts of their power. For most of The Evils so far, that had occurred in their early years, leading to their death soon after.

However, Theresia was a princess who was kept inside all the time, shielding her from any danger that would activate those safety measures and expose her true nature.

No one in this world — not even those actively looking for The Evil — had any inkling that she was the one.

I can't hurt or kill myself, and no one would believe me if I told them... They wouldn't even listen to me, actually.

Theresia's status as The Evil was not only hidden from skills like Reveal, but censored when she tried to say it herself. "The Evil" would come out as some different word or gibberish — and given her age, it would just be written off as childish baby talk.

And for some reason, the stories regarding The Evil were extremely simplified, with large gaps in the information they conveyed, so as a result it was likely that anyone she explained it to wouldn't understand anyway.

It's not impossible that The Evil will actually reach its final state like this... But at my current leveling rate, that would probably take decades.

Theresia could actually *feel* her level.

Since the time of The Evil several generations before her, the world had begun displaying detail and stat windows. Before then, people had to rely on particular skills and intuition, but now, everyone was able to bring them up at will.

However, her status as The Evil as well as her true stats were hidden even from her, forcing her to figure out her true level using her own sense of it.

And based on that feeling, she believed that she wasn't even level 30 yet.

Her leveling speed might've actually been the slowest among all The Evils that had ever existed. It wasn't out of the question that she would actually die of old age or disease before she became complete.

Imagining that scenario filled her heart and cheeks with warmth, for that would no doubt be the best death she could hope for.

"Is anything the matter, Your Highness?" asked the maid by her side.

"No. I'm just a bit warm," she replied with a lie.

"It has been rather sunny recently." As the person tasked to accompany Theresia, the maid actually had Truth Discernment, but she didn't realize that the princess was lying.

This was also because of her status as The Evil.

Just like she was protected from Reveal, she was immune to the effects of Truth Discernment.

In a world where lies were limited by skills, Theresia could lie with complete freedom.

The lie she had told just now, though, did not even begin to compare to the one that had existed since her very birth.

"I want to go to my room and nap," she said.

"As you wish," the maid replied before helping Theresia into her sizable carriage and pushing it to her room.

Since she was believed to be frail — which wasn't true due to her stats as The Evil — she was advised against traveling any longer distance on foot.

That was one of her few complaints in life. Despite actually being less than five years old, with her immense knowledge and long memory, the girl couldn't help but wonder if there was a more dignified way for her to travel.

"If you need me, I will be in the neighboring room."

"Thank you."

Following that exchange, Theresia was left in her chambers alone.

The room was as fancy as one might expect for a princess, but was also noticeably clean and hygienic.

In the canopy bed, there were the adorable plush toys she'd received from her sisters.

Next to the bed, there was a bell she could use to call the maid in the other room.

Among all the things of note, Theresia was focused on…the space between her and the bed.

She opened her mouth…

"Who are you?"

…and spoke to the empty space.

However…

"I did not expect to be addressed before I addressed you."

…the empty space replied in an unfamiliar, masculine voice.

A moment later, a green cloak appeared in the empty space.

The person wearing it took it off without a sound before giving Theresia a bow.

"My name is Sechs Würfel," the black-haired, plain-looking man introduced himself. "I am here to take you away," he added, in the tone of an actor on stage.

"What a wonderful line. I would love to hear it when I'm ten years older," Theresia replied, unfazed by the potential kidnapper in front of her.

Sechs was at a loss for words and his eyes opened wide in surprise — a sight which would no doubt shock those who would come to know him.

After observing her for a good few moments, he said, "Pardon this question, but are you truly the third princess of Altar?"

"I am. Why are you asking?"

"Because you just made me feel like I'm looking at some sort of aberration."

"...What a dreadful thing to say to a lady."

"That is true. My apologies."

Though Theresa's replies were calm, her heart was beating faster than ever before in her life so far.

Does he know I'm The Evil? How? Who is this man, anyway...? She looked him over to figure out what she was dealing with and noticed a crest on the back of his left hand.

It was a symbol in the shape of a droplet — a simple thing, signifying water and its ability to change into anything.

"Are you a Master?"

"Yes. I started last month."

Theresa was aware that since about a month ago, more and more Masters had begun to appear.

She saw these beings somewhat differently than other tians.

So he's like The Lynx... One of her predecessors had fought a Master bearing that job. The Lynx fought using an Embryo that allowed him to multiply, but The Evil remained undamaged no matter how many of his doubles attacked.

Theresa knew that was due to one of The Evil's characteristics — immunity to anything *foreign*.

Masters are foreign to The System. They can't hurt me no matter what. Why would one of them establish contact with The Evil?

The situation was so strange that Theresa couldn't help talking to him to get more information.

"Was that your Embryo you were just wearing?"

"No. It was an MVP special reward. Originally, it was an Epic chameleon named...'The False Tone, Soundcolorless,' I believe. I don't know for sure, because our encounter was sudden and *began with a devouring.*"

The smile on the man's face as he casually mentioned being killed and eaten by a monster gave Theresia the feeling that he wasn't exactly normal.

"And that's why he's now my special reward."

"Hm...?"

"I have a question for you, as well... How did you know I was here?"

Theresia said nothing at first. Given that he had been hidden by a special reward, it was only natural that she would spot him.

What Sechs's reward did was make him blend into the surroundings to both the eye and ear. Its effectiveness was proven by the fact that he'd snuck into her room completely unnoticed. Of course, there were security elements that could sense him in other ways, but he must've dealt with them, as well.

Regardless, as potent as the special reward was, it was an item derived from a UBM — creatures with powers considered foreign — meaning that The Evil, Theresia, was immune to its effects.

She'd actually *seen* Sechs standing in her room as if he wasn't camouflaged at all.

"That's because..." she said before losing herself in thought for a moment, "...I am ▪▪▪ ▪▪▪▪▪."

"Hm?"

Theresia had revealed what she was, but the words didn't reach him.

So it works against Masters too. Then why did he call me an aberration? Not just that — if he doesn't even know that I'm The Evil, why is he here in the first place...?

One of her questions had been answered, leaving even more behind.

That was why she went ahead and just asked, "Why are you kidnapping me?"

In response...

"Because it's one of the greatest crimes you can commit in this country."

...Sechs readily revealed his motive, if it could even be called that.

"...Huh?"

"I am committing grievous crimes to become a villain, and one of the most grievous ones I could think of was kidnapping you. That is why I am here."

To become a sinner, he would commit a crime. If Sechs truly meant what he said, his goals and the means to achieve it were one and the same — he wanted to commit crimes, with no expectation of reward, to become a criminal.

Neither Theresia nor any of her predecessors had ever met someone as strange as him.

Perhaps this is just how Masters are... Odd as he was, however, he was still someone who'd made it past the castle's tight security and arrived in her room, meaning that he couldn't be taken lightly.

Masters are foreign. They can't hurt or kill me. But still, I...

She couldn't just ignore him, but if she were to raise her voice, the maid would rush in from the neighboring room, and Sechs would most likely kill her.

As she wondered how to go about this...

...she heard Sechs's voice *from right behind her,* and a wet cloth was pressed against her mouth.

"Huh...?" After a single breath, her consciousness began to fade.

Before she completely fell unconscious, Theresia saw the Sechs she had been talking to until this very moment...as well as the one who put the cloth on her mouth.

The man was in two places at once.

"Ah...!" Theresia woke up about two hours after she had lost consciousness.

Moments after she recovered, she realized that she'd been put to sleep by some drug.

She was now somewhere she didn't recognize.

It looked like a wooden cabin, and she could see the forest outside. As a princess who had lived her whole life in a castle, Theresia had never seen something like this before, but the memories of her predecessors made her assume that this must be a lumberjack's cabin.

She realized that after she'd been put to sleep, she had been taken to this cabin and locked inside it, and that she was likely in the Noz Forest near the capital.

Theresia wondered how she — The Evil — had been put to sleep by a Master, but she quickly realized what had happened.

...Ohh. There was that one exception, she thought.

As a rule, what was foreign couldn't harm The Evil, but there were three ways to get around this.

The first way was using things like The Primeval Blade, which bent the laws governing The Evil's existence.

The second way was to gain influence over the very system in which The Evil's foundations lay...to take control over the entire world, basically.

The third and the simplest one...was to use consumables made by tians.

The drug Sechs used to put Theresia to sleep, offensive magic Gems, anything like that...as long as it had been created by tians, even Masters could use such consumables to harm The Evil.

193

Due to the monster-loot transformation system, this didn't work if the consumables were made using items or materials gained from monsters, but the drug that Sechs used happened to be made entirely from natural ingredients.

It probably wouldn't have worked if my level as The Evil was higher, but since it's so low and I don't have any safety measures unlocked... It makes sense that it put me to sleep.

Another notable thing was that the safety measures had *remained* locked.

Her body was unharmed, making it clear that, at the very least, her kidnapper hadn't hurt her.

Sechs was nowhere in sight. Perhaps he, like a proper criminal, had gone to the castle to declare the kidnapping and make his demands.

Theresia also had a question regarding him.

She wanted to know why she'd seen *two* of Sechs before losing consciousness.

Multiples of the same person... If it wasn't an identical twin, it could only be the effect of some skill he has. The fact that I saw it means that the other person was real, not an illusion. I guess it was either the effect of his Embryo or a skill like Art of Shadow Clones. I mean, it's not like he just split himself in two like a slime...

At this point, she had no way of knowing that this was, in fact, exactly the case.

As she continued to wonder how Sechs had accomplished that feat, she realized something.

"...It went up."

Her senses told her that there had been a change in her true level. It had been stagnating for a good while now, but she realized that it had gone up while she was asleep.

This was only natural. She was not only outside the castle's protective barrier, but the capital itself — away from the save point designed to absorb Resources.

Though close to the city, she was still out in nature, allowing her to gather the Resources of the dead just as The Evil normally would.

Every second she spent out here shaved more and more time off her limited life span.

Though, so far, leveling had only raised her stats. She still had no skills.

If she was exposed to danger now, the safety measures would be activated, unlocking her true power — her skills — as The Evil.

The first skill that would be unlocked was Dependent Transformation, which changed the nature of the surrounding matter. It responded to any apparent danger by automatically turning surrounding objects, such as rocks and trees, into monsters... her "dependents" that would leap to her defense.

When that happened, she would be exposed, and her death would quickly follow.

She wasn't against that. In her mind, it was far better than the world being destroyed.

She had a faint hope of living out a full life, but if that turned out to be impossible, then there was no way around it.

The problem is that Altimia is studying in Dryfe right now. Can my automatic defenses be broken without The Primeval Blade...? Can they really kill me?

Worrying about whoever would have to kill her, Theresia let out a sigh of resignation.

It was likely that many people would die.

Right now, the best thing she could do to avoid that was merely staying in this cabin.

She was capable of destroying it even with her current stats, but she would not be able to return to the castle without encountering any danger.

Even ignoring Sechs himself, the area here was full of monsters ready to attack her on sight.

Though her stats and their status as outsiders made them harmless to her, they would still be recognized as a threat and activate the safety measures.

Sechs seemed to know nothing about Theresia's situation, but this shabby cabin in the woods turned out to act as The Evil's cage.

…If only there was someone who could escort me safely back to the castle, she thought before silently chuckling at herself. Someone that convenient wouldn't just appear out of nowhere.

Suddenly, she noticed a faint sound.

"…Rain?"

It was the sound of rain droplets hitting the wooden roof. It grew in frequency and intensity, but stopped before becoming too intense.

She focused on listening to the sound.

"…I never thought much about the weather." The sickly girl had always stayed inside the castle. That had been all she ever knew, and since she'd only inherited the memories of the outside world from her predecessors, she'd never truly cared about it.

That was why this was the first time she experienced rain so close at hand.

It's noisy, but somehow a bit soothing too… I wonder why? She closed her eyes and strained her ears.

Did she stay like that for a minute? A few? Or perhaps longer?

An uncertain amount of time passed by, and then…

"…He's here."

…she heard footsteps mixed with the rain.

Sechs is back… I wonder what will happen now.

Would he exchange her for a ransom? Would he hand her over to some people outside her family? Or did he intend to kill her to add another grievous crime to his name?

If he'd kidnapped her just for the sake of committing any crime at all, Theresia believed that this lunatic might also kill her to make his transgression even worse.

Whether or not that was indeed his intention, based on Theresia's impression of him, she wouldn't be surprised if it was.

Sechs can't kill me, but he can still activate the safety measures. I guess I only have minutes left until my life as a princess is over.

The lie that had lived with her since the moment she was born was now coming to an end.

After this, she would be The Evil — nothing but a threat to the world.

Even if they wouldn't be able to defeat her, it was impossible that she would be able to live as she had until now.

Still...I lived a better life than The Evils so far, she thought, as if to console herself.

However, despite her preparation and resignation...Sechs wasn't entering the cabin.

In fact, he seemed to be struggling with something in front of the door. She heard metallic sounds that made her assume that he was trying to unlock the lock.

Sechs was the one who locked it. He should have the key. Did he drop it...?

As the sounds continued, she realized something.

Is this actually...? Before she could finish that thought...

"GRRRRR! I CAN'T BEAR IT ANY LONGER!"

...she heard the lock break, accompanied by a somewhat-comical, angry voice.

A moment later, the door opened with a creak, and a large silhouette walked in.

"I just wanted some shelter from the rain. Why's it locked? The old lumberjack said that he doesn't lock it since there's nothin' here worth gettin' your paws on. What happened to tha— Hm?"

Silence. The person who had just entered was a man in a dog — or wolf — costume, who for some reason was using bear puns.

He was all black with the exception of his back, which was red.

Needless to say, it wasn't Sechs.

"What's a little cub doin' in a place like this?"

"…Who are you?" The fact that he spoke human language and had no name over his head made it clear that he wasn't a monster. However, she still had no idea who or what he was.

In response…

"I'm Shu. A Master, thank you beary much… I mean, woof!"

…the Master introduced himself as "Shu" and finally seemed to realize that his bear puns didn't make sense at the moment, switching instead to simple barking.

"Are you a dog? Or a bear?"

"A human. In a dog suit, as you can see. I used to rock a bear suit not long ago, and I still haven't managed to kick the bear pun habit. I can't *bear* to part with them… I mean, woof."

"…Heh." Theresia chuckled at the strange person before her and also at the realization that he was just a passerby who had nothing to do with Sechs.

"If it made you laugh, then mixing up my quirks was worth it. And what's your name, li'l lady?"

"I'm…" Theresia said before thinking for a moment. "I'm Tee. I don't know how I got here."

She chose to give him a fake name.

If she'd used "Theresia," he might've realized that she was a princess, and that might've negatively influenced his actions even if he had nothing to do with Sechs.

Giving a fake name seemed like the best option.

I'm The Evil. It's not like he'll realize I'm lying— "Hmm? And what's your *real* name? It's hard to contact your parents if I don't have it. Woof."

"Huh?" She was more shocked by those words than anything else she'd experienced since she was born. Not even facing Sechs had surprised her as much as this.

"Wh-Why…do you think…I'm lying? Truth Discernment should…"

"Don't have that. Woof."

"Then how…?" Not even the highest level Truth Discernment could see past The Evil's lies.

Theresia was so perplexed that she couldn't help but ask how he'd figured it out.

"It's easy to tell that you have no attachment to that name. You glanced around and paused before saying it. Woof."

"Ah…!"

It wasn't even the effect of some skill.

It was actually a *sense*. Shu's own power, born of his experience and intuition, had done what the most powerful Truth Discernment could not.

The lie of The Evil, which avoided all orthodox skills and was protected from everything the world had, was easily exposed by Shu's perception.

"Well, I get that it ain't easy to trust some guy in a costume you just met. You said you don't know how you got here, and I want to take you back home. Woof."

Silence. Theresia wondered how to process Shu's words.

She didn't have Truth Discernment herself, so she didn't know whether he was being honest or not.

But ultimately, she...

"My... My real name is...Theresia."

...chose to reveal the truth.

Shu had seen through her lie, so she decided to give him the truth this time.

"Theresia Celestite Altar."

"That name..." That was enough for Shu to realize who she truly was.

"Mr. Costume...I have a request," Theresia continued.

Her request was related to a path she'd given up on only moments ago — one that could let her continue to live life with her family as The Third Princess of Altar, Theresia.

The possibility of a hopeful conclusion.

"I'm listening."

"I'm a princess...and it's very dangerous to have me around..."

"Mhm..."

"Could you... Could you take me back home to the castle?"

"I'm not going back on what I said. I'll bring you back home. You can beary much count on that."

Shu's reply came quickly and without any hesitation.

He understood that she was a princess and suspected that there was something more to it than that, but he still declared that he would take the girl back home.

[Quest Received: Escort — Theresia C. Altar, Difficulty 7.]

[Confirm the quest details in the quest window.]

Thus, a message announced the start of a quest.

???

"…Odd."

"What is it, Dormouse?"

"There's something strange about the movement of Resources around Noz Forest."

"Noz Forest? Speaking of which, I just had to set the difficulty for a strange quest over there."

"A strange quest?"

"A quest to escort the kidnapped third princess to the castle. I set the difficulty to 7, since the kidnapper is still in the zone and a fierce UBM currently roams the area."

"Hm…"

"Are you curious?"

"Mhm. I will check on it. Perhaps…I will find the one we are looking for."

That incident would come to be known as the Third Princess's Kidnapping.

It was the first meeting between Theresia and those who would eventually learn her secret.

The kidnapper, who would later be dubbed King of Crime, Sechs Würfel.

The savior, who would come to be called King of Destruction, Shu Starling.

And the control AI who would be tasked to stay by her side and protect her, Dormouse.

This was the beginning of an important series of events that created a number of strange connections between people, some of them completely unrelated to The Evil at the center of it all.

About him...

Morter Cortana was born to a distinguished family in Caldina.

One day, though, his parents both died and he was separated from his sister, quickly bringing his smooth and easy life to a screeching halt.

He was forced to join a gang of thieving street urchins in order to survive, and his life quickly became one of crime. He continued stealing even after he grew up and found legitimate employment, and after he got his Superior Job, he took to making a living by hunting treasure hunters in ruins.

Not even he himself fully understood why he went down this path.

Perhaps, as someone who once had everything but had lost it all, he had some negative emotions towards those who were in the opposite situation — those who started with nothing and gained a great deal.

Regardless, this way of life had led to his defeat at the hands of Rascal and eventually, his transformation into an Idea.

And now, he was facing a creature no one should ever have to face.

In this situation, he couldn't help but wonder why his life was going *so* wrong.

Royal Castle, Fourth Floor

After hearing the final warning, Morter reached the greatest depths of despair. His own cells told him that Theresia wasn't joking; everything would be over for him if he didn't turn back.

If it had been possible, he would've fled already. The reason he was panicking now was that he found he *couldn't.*

Ahh...damn it... Why is this happening...? His life began to flash before his eyes in disjointed moments... The moment he chose to become an Idea, the moment he attacked the sub-leader of I.F., the time period where he made his living assaulting treasure hunters, the time he lived among the criminal street urchins, the time he lost all his worldly possessions and was left alone....

Damn it...! Why is my life so...! He lamented the many bad choices he'd made at all of the most critical moments in his life.

However, this moment was different. Right now, it was like the time it all began to go wrong for him — the very instant when he had lost everything he had.

Here, in this moment, Morter didn't even have the right to choose.

"I can't back down...even if I want to..."

"Hm?"

"My body won't respect my desire." He spoke the truth — he was being forced to do something against his will. "There's an Embryo... in my body. If I go against my orders...my body will...damn it!"

While he spoke, his body began to act on its own.

"Damn it! La Crima, you...!" This was accomplished by the piece of La Crima's Embryo implanted inside of him. What he just revealed was meant to be a secret, and Idea decided that Morter had violated his orders enough to justify taking control of his body.

And, with movements far less precise than his natural ones, the Embryo made Morter's body charge towards this overwhelming force.

Even a moth flying directly into a flame would have higher chances of survival than him.

"I don't wanna die…! Not like…not like this…!" Vespertilio screamed as Idea forced him to attack something he could never hope to defeat.

Theresia looked at him with emotionless eyes before suddenly putting her hands together.

A moment later, giant arms sprouted from the floor at an incredible speed and moved in sync with her movements to crush Morter.

"Ghuh…" His body was shattered and immobilized, but he was still alive.

"…Dear me. I'm even stronger than before. My level really *is* growing."

The damage done was greater than Theresia expected, and this seemed to trouble her.

The stone arms that grew from the ground were her dependents — the monsters just like the ones Morter had fought earlier.

However, while those had appeared automatically as a response to danger, these were deliberately created by Theresia, making them far faster and more precise.

In fact, they would even be a match for Legendary-tier creatures.

The attack itself turned out to be overkill, but what mattered was that it stopped Morter's body from moving.

"Dor." She said only a single word, but Dormouse instantly understood what she wanted and brought her closer to Morter.

Theresia then slowly reached towards him…

"…This must be it."

…and tore out the piece of Idea from his body.

"Ah…?!" Shock appeared on Morter's dying face. Theresia had just taken the Idea that had been completely merged with his body right out of him, as easily as plucking a caterpillar from a leaf.

Ignoring him, Theresia then took the starfish-like creature in hand…and crushed it like a piece of fruit.

"Huh…? Ah…"

At that moment, Morter was set free.

However, before he could rejoice, an overwhelming pain assaulted his body.

"Gh… AAAAAAHHHHHHHHH…?!"

"…I took it away. Can you leave now?" Theresia asked casually.

"Theresia. He and that Embryo were linked. Obviously, if you take it out of him, he's going to fall apart. It's like opening a huge hole inside his body."

"Oh. That makes sense. Sorry. I didn't realize."

Theresia apologized, but Morter was in no state to even acknowledge it.

"With the Embryo gone, I can finish him off," said Dormouse. "That will minimize the Resource absorption… Hm…? Is there something on your mind?"

"…So he needs something to bind him together?"

"Indeed."

"Dor. I have an idea."

"Hm?"

"Remember the insurance we talked about? It would be difficult with just us, would it not?"

"Well, mostly because my avatar is not humanoid."

"That is why I believe we need an adult. Shu knows about us, but we cannot rely on him more than necessary."

"I do think that he would help if asked."

"…That is the problem. I need to *prepare*."

"Prepare…? Do you actually intend to do it?"

"Is it possible?"

"…If you believe it is."

"Thank you." On the brink of death, Morter couldn't hear most of what they were saying.

"Hey, you," Theresia said as she looked him in the eyes. "If given a choice between dying here and now or giving up your humanity… which would you pick?"

That was a choice much like the one he'd been given back then. Morter's response was quick.

Once the choice was made, only Theresia and Dormouse were left in the room.

"He has been taken care of. I suppose I should go meet up with Liliana now. She's looking for me." Though there was still no emotion on her face, she did give the impression that she'd done away with something troublesome.

She knew that Liliana was looking for her, but if Theresia was with someone during such an emergency, Dependent Transformation could lead to them finding out what she was — or even worse, it might hurt someone. That was why Theresia had run off on her own — if you didn't count Dormouse, anyway. Liliana was her elder sister's friend and her friend's elder sister, so Theresia really didn't want her to die.

Though she'd been found out by Morter, she was able to *silence* him.

"Theresia, there is something I must ask," said Dormouse.

"What is it?"

"Why did you reveal your secret to him?" Even though she'd gone on to silence him, Theresia had told him what she was of her own accord. The important words were filtered, but the information Morter had heard was enough to fully expose her if he brought it back to a person who was actively looking for The Evil.

The many twists and turns of her life so far had led to her beginning to awaken as The Evil, but thanks to Shu and Dormouse, she was still able to live on as the third princess.

However, what she had done just now...was almost destroy the last thing that allowed her to be herself.

She'd told Dormouse not to do or say anything, but when Theresia had begun to explain the situation, he was actually fairly perplexed.

In response to his reasonable question, Theresia said, all without changing her emotionless expression, "Some people can see through lies even without Truth Discernment. That is why it is best to just be honest. And there was a chance that the man would retreat upon gaining the necessary information, which would have been acceptable in its own right."

"What do you mean?"

"That would have given me the time I needed to run far, far away. I am immune to your colleagues' abilities, so I can only move by walking. If I am to run, I need the time."

"Time to run?"

"Tell me, Dor — what is the worst-case scenario for me and for your group?"

"...The activation of the GAME OVER."

"Exactly. Preventing that is more important than my current lifestyle or even my life itself. Nothing would be worse than me becoming complete and that *thing* awakening. However, that is not directly linked to whether or not my secret is known."

"Hm...?"

"Even if someone finds out that I am ▪▪▪ ▪▪▪▪ (The Evil), I can simply leave Altar and hide somewhere else. As long as you are with me, we do not need the barrier to slow down ▪▪▪▪▪▪▪▪ ▪▪▪▪▪▪▪▪▪▪ (Resource absorption).

And as long as we are not facing Masters or Embryos, you would also deal with any dangers that came along, would you not? Your most important task is to prevent that thing from awakening until your goal is fulfilled."

Dormouse saw Theresia's point. With The Evil's masking function, she would be fully protected from search-oriented job skills, and with information organizations like DIN belonging to the control AIs, they could easily find a good destination to escape to.

"I feel like the idea relies too much on me personally, but…are you certain about this?" Dormouse asked. Could Theresia truly abandon the country and family she'd grown up with?

"I am. I believe it would be better for both sides," she replied, her expression determined.

Dormouse didn't really understand whom she meant by "both sides," but chose not to ask.

"…Well, now I'm glad it did not have to happen," he said. Theresia was able to silence Morter, so the truth regarding her was safe.

"As am I… Though, it does seem like the time is close."

"Indeed. Someone is looking for The Evil, so the limit is no doubt drawing near."

"Here in Altar, the menace of ▪▪▪ ▪▪▪▪ (The Evil) is seen as a thing of the distant past, but it seems that it is not so everywhere. Or perhaps we're simply seeing our first High-End tian in centuries. The extremely talented High-Ends are provided information regarding us and even ▪▪▪ ▪▪▪▪▪▪ (The Demise) by the Archetype System…the job-managing system itself. It would not be unexpected if they were to try to find and kill me."

"The world is full of those who do things they should not."

"You were the ones doing just that until the time of my last predecessor, were you not?"

"...I cannot deny that. I am ashamed," Dormouse said, glancing down. With their makeshift solution of getting The Evils killed whenever they were discovered, the control AIs had only made The Evils grow in strength at a faster rate than normal.

"I am not angry. I feel bad for my predecessors, but it is you and your colleagues I have to thank for being able to live as I am."

"...It is good to hear that the measures we took are effective. Though, it is regrettable that we did not find you before release."

"We met after I encountered Shu and Sechs, after all."

"...Having welcomed the Masters from Earth, we are now one... no, perhaps two steps away from fulfilling our ultimate goal. It would be especially troubling to get a game over now."

Though it didn't show on his hamster-like face, Dormouse's tone made it clear that he was deeply troubled.

A moment later, he seemed to remember something and said, "I can imagine a certain someone saying 'Online games can be shut down, but they don't have game overs.'"

"'A certain someone?'"

"...Oh, never mind." Dormouse simply ended the brief exchange, and Theresia didn't push him to keep talking.

"We were lucky this time," he said instead. "We faced a unique kind of opponent and ended the exchange without much issue."

If they faced tians, monsters, or mechanical weapons, they could've silenced them by simply destroying them, just as Tom had done in the ruins when he'd destroyed Prism Soldiers.

They also had special means of dealing with Masters, as well.

However, a tian-Embryo hybrid was a unique case that had caught them off guard. In light of that, the final outcome was actually fairly positive.

"...Duchess, are there any Masters who saw the fight or heard what was said?" Dormouse addressed those words to someone who wasn't there.

[No...there weren't. As far as...I can observe...there are no Masters...who acquired any knowledge...of the happenings... conversations...or phenomena...that happened there... The Embryo fragment also...wasn't constantly linked...to the main unit.]

The response came to him in the form of a window that suddenly popped up in front of his eyes.

"That is good to hear." The message had been from control AI no. 7, Duchess, who was responsible for the vision of all Masters as well as information windows. She was the entity tasked with implementing whichever of the three visual styles the Masters chose while also processing the information they saw or heard, as well as assisting the control AIs in managing the situation.

By Dormouse's request, she was now focused on the Masters in Altea so she could tell him if any of them were close to discovering Theresia's secret.

If she said that none of them were aware of what happened here, it could only be the truth.

"...If you have such a surveillance network, could you not have used it to prevent this attack from happening in the first place?" Theresia asked.

"We are prevented from limiting the freedom of Masters, and Duchess's observation network is not *that* thorough. Most of her processing power is dedicated to producing the visuals, so she cannot gather information from too many people on top of that."

This begged the question of how much counted as "not too many people" by his standards, but Theresia once again realized that even the godlike observers of *Infinite Dendrogram* had their limitations.

"Well, you also could not eliminate the person we just dealt with… You seem to have some truly inconvenient restrictions."

"The control AIs that have the right to attack Embryos and Masters are few. In fact, we have a colleague who must be restricted in this way even if it means restricting us, as well," Dormouse said, recalling the most short-tempered and aggressive control AI.

Theresia said nothing in response. They had a lot of information, but not all of it, and though they had authority, they had limitations, making their measures less than perfect. In her eyes, this made the control AIs seem less like machines and more like living beings.

[Dormouse…a moment…please.]

Suddenly, Duchess sent a new message.

"What is it?"

[One is coming…towards you… Oh…she's preparing…to attack.]

"What?"

A moment later, the room they were in was blown away.

"…Confirmed. The fusion reaction from 'Absolute Dominion Over the Sky — Uranus' has hit something."

The speaker was the bandaged King of Thieves, Zeta, who stood on the roof above the fourth floor of the castle.

She had confirmed the signatures of three of the four Ideas she'd let loose upon the capital — Regina Apis, Aranea, and Vespertilio — had already been extinguished.

Claudiah's request for Zeta went as such: "Indiscriminately attack any unusual persons in Altea and discover who has an odd reaction to these attacks. Eliminate them if possible; if not, stop attacking them and observe."

The target of the request was so vague that she'd entrusted the role to the Ideas.

She'd sent Vespertilio after the most unusual signature; the way that his own signature had vanished had struck Zeta as suspicious, so she stopped her search for Treasurebeast Orbs and chose to investigate instead.

She discovered the room where the fight had occurred, used information provided by Uranus to confirm that Vespertilio's opponent was still inside...and used her ultimate skill against them.

...Based on the fact that she said "if possible," she must be almost certain that the target cannot be killed, Zeta thought, reviewing the request. She hadn't been told what she would be dealing with, but she knew enough to understand that the target was either really strong or had some unique qualities.

There would be a problem if the one I attacked just now was the target and, in spite of her assumption, they actually died just now. If they completely vanished without showing any odd reactions to the attack, I would be unable to confirm if they were truly the target.

She worried that completing the task would be impossible then, but...

"...They're...alive?"

...unfortunately, the target withstood the immense heat Zeta had created.

The hellish fusion reaction that would kill any animal and evaporate any material hadn't been enough to kill the target.

However, Zeta couldn't figure out what kind of creature had survived her blast, for she saw nothing but a jet-black vortex.

"A nuclear attack. How nostalgic. I have not felt one of those since the war all those years ago," Dormouse whispered from within the vortex, which completely drowned out his voice.

His form had completely changed. He was no longer the round, adorable creature with short limbs, but a dreadful beast straight out of a Japanese yokai picture scroll. His entire body was enveloped in a dark force field and he stood in the center of a surging vortex, a storm in which he was the eye.

The vortex had consumed all the heat and electromagnetic waves created by the nuclear fusion reaction.

That wasn't all — it also quickly drained the surroundings of all warmth, freezing them at an incredible rate. Since it consumed even light coming from the outside, seeing what lay within the vortex was impossible.

It was as though it consumed all and any energy coming towards it.

Perched on Dormouse's back, Theresia remained silent and expressionless.

Though she was just within a nuclear explosion, her safety mechanism hadn't activated.

As The Evil, she wouldn't have suffered any damage from it to begin with, but that wasn't the reason why her defenses remained inactive — it was because she knew that there was no safer place than Dormouse's back when he donned his black vortex.

[A message… The kingdom is winning…the battle at the border… It might…end soon… It's possible…that the castle attackers…will also retreat…]

"That means that we only have to bear this a little while longer. The seventh form's output should be enough for that. Though I have to suppress my body size, so this feels a bit cramped."

Dormouse responded to Duchess and cracked a warped grin. He couldn't have used this against a special case like Morter, but Masters were a different story.

"I cannot attack Masters, but there are no rules against protecting or hiding something from them."

Thus, Dormouse went on the defensive.

Zeta tried to use her all-powerful Uranus to disperse the unidentified black vortex.

However, her efforts were futile.

He was control AI no. 8, tasked with dealing with hazards and someone who had eliminated countless Irregularities.

Consuming all heat energy, he was the being who stood above all in the art of extermination, as well as an impenetrable defense.

He was Type Infinite Fortress — Infinite Conversion, Schwarzer Tod.

The Incarnations that had attacked the pre-ancient civilization two thousand years ago were beings far above what anyone had ever seen — even The Demise they'd brought down before was weak in comparison.

There was the Incarnation of Blasphemy, which created countless puppets that carried the power of their deceased champions.

There was the Incarnation of Scales, which turned creatures into dust and vice versa.

There was the Incarnation of Nature, which could bring forth calamities like plagues, heat waves, droughts, and cold snaps.

There was the Incarnation of Cages, which couldn't be reached or escaped.

There was the Incarnation of Dreams, which rid various creatures of their reality.

There was the Incarnation of Armaments, which used thousands upon thousands of Legendary weapons as though they were nothing.

There was the Incarnation of Influence, which rendered any and all tactics completely meaningless as though it could see the future.

There was the Incarnation of Seconds, which could instantly slice through anything regardless of speed or toughness.

There was the Incarnation of Beasts, which could multiply to the point that it was capable of covering the entire landscape in itself.

However, there were three Incarnations which were more feared than the others:

The Incarnation of Mortar, which could effortlessly grind entire mountain ranges.

The Incarnation of Evolution, which grew more powerful without limit the more it fought.

The Incarnation of Death, which simply had countless inconceivably powerful abilities at its disposal.

Those were twelve of the thirteen Incarnations besides the Extra-Continental Vessel.

The last one was the Incarnation of Maelstroms — Infinite Conversion, Schwarzer Tod.

It wasn't the strongest, toughest, or the most destructive among them.

It didn't have the greatest ability to destroy, nor did it have the greatest potential for use in war.

In terms of sheer battle capacity, it likely did not have a single area where it was not surpassed by another Incarnation.

But despite that, both the pre-ancient civilization and his fellow Incarnations alike believed that despite its relative lack of strength, the Incarnation of Maelstroms was no doubt the most troublesome of them all.

Zeta was thoroughly troubled by the unexpectedly difficult opponent she had stumbled upon.

…*Nothing I do is working,* she thought. The room had been melted by Uranus's ultimate skill, yet the black vortex remained.

She tried firing air-bullets and using any weapons she had, but they all seemed to be negated by the vortex. Upon touching it, everything lost its kinetic energy and latent heat; they would stop, freeze, and fall to the floor as inert objects devoid of energy.

She tried to create a vacuum or poison gas within the vortex, but it was actually cutting off her very ability to control the air.

…*This isn't even a case of bad compatibility.* Compatibility meant nothing against an opponent that absorbed all energy and rendered it useless.

I suppose the only exception would be people with skills that can attack whoever's inside without interacting with the vortex at all. Curiously enough, Xunyu — whom Zeta had just defeated — was one of those people. It would have been difficult even for her, though. The slightest targeting mistake and her prosthetic limbs would touch the vortex, which would instantly consume them.

The vortex is a wall that completely separates the outside and the inside. Not even light or sound can reach through it… That means that they shouldn't be able to see me either.

Zeta guessed that the vortex remained stationary in the ruined room because whoever was creating it also could not see what was happening outside.

It seems to be a defensive barrier, but it's abnormally powerful. It seems like the energy-damping ability of the ocean element taken to an extreme, but I have never seen anything that drains energy to this extent.

The fact that it was able to negate the heat from Uranus's ultimate skill — a nuclear explosion — made it clear that it had enough power to match Superior Embryos.

Also, if it isn't damping the energy, but absorbing it...it's possible that they may also be able to repurpose the energy for some kind of attack. Zeta knew that she had to be wary of counter-attacks like the ones Ray Starling had used to defeat her pupil, Logan.

Also, it was clear that whatever this was had defeated Vespertilio Idea, meaning that it was immune to surprise attacks. That meant one couldn't be too careful.

Thus, for the time being, she chose to stop attacking and see what they would do next.

Besides the one about Morter, Zeta's assumptions were actually correct. This black vortex was actually Infinite Conversion's energy absorption ability, Infection Citadel.

Everything that touched it *had all of its energy drained from it.*

Fire would lose its heat, sound, and light, while anything living would lose its warmth, kinetic energy, and even the electrical impulses running through the nervous system. All energy-based attacks would be nullified, while all living beings who touched it would die. The energy absorbed would be used to maintain the skill and make it grow.

Resistance against it was not only futile — it made it grow stronger. There was nothing one could do against the approaching *maelstrom*. Like the Black Death, the wielder's namesake, this vortex was feared by countless beings all over.

However, that wasn't the full story of this creature. The energy absorption of Infection Citadel was actually related to its ultimate skill, Schwarzer Tod, which was as terrifying as the name suggested.

Dormouse, though, had no intention of using it this time.

To him, this was solely a defensive battle. He didn't have the right to attack Masters.

"The absorption has weakened. The attacker must have stopped to observe what we will do next."

While spreading Infection Citadel in every direction, Dormouse was unable to see what was happening outside, but he could still tell if he was being attacked based on the amount of energy he had left.

"Duchess. How is the situation…?"

[…King of Beasts…has stopped fighting… She's negotiating… with the High Priestess… King of Thieves…the one who's attacking you…has also stopped…]

Following the message, the window began showing him Zeta's perspective. He couldn't see outside the vortex himself, but he had Duchess conveying the situation to him.

Her ability didn't adhere to any ordinary laws of physics, so it wasn't blocked by the vortex. On their own, the control AIs had flaws, but their experience had taught them that most of them could be made up for through cooperation.

In fact, under normal circumstances, merely keeping up Infection Citadel would require copious amounts of energy.

It wouldn't be a problem if there was energy to absorb — but if there wasn't, he would have to use his own until there was nothing external left. While this wouldn't matter if he was using his original body, as an Infinite Embryo in his seventh form as he was now, he couldn't keep it up for long without an outside supply.

However, this flaw was irrelevant now. With most of the castle's barriers having been deactivated, more Resources were free to flow towards The Evil, but Dormouse was absorbing them and using them as energy for Infection Citadel.

As long as he kept the vortex up, Dormouse was akin to an impenetrable fortress for Theresia.

[However…the kingdom's…what was it, again…? The Royal Guard knightess…is coming closer… She's with…K&R Masters…that entered the castle…]

"Liliana is coming?" *That's not good,* Dormouse thought.

It was impossible to guess how she would react to this situation. There was the chance that her arrival would accelerate The Evil's awakening, so he wanted to deal with this situation before that happened.

The attacker is still observing us because their goal is to gather information, so it's possible that they will not leave until they find out exactly what we are... That would prolong this until Zeta chose to leave, and that was risky for him.

That was why he chose to, as an exception, rely on a fellow control AI.

"Duchess, are you able to use your Invitation to the Second World — Daydream? Even limited use of it would suffice."

[Yes. I can use it anytime...*and on anyone.*]

Zeta had no means of breaking through the vortex-fortress before her.

...I'm just not good against these kinds of outliers, she thought. Uranus's control didn't extend to the inside of the vortex, and phenomena from the outside couldn't break through it. She considered covering the outside in a vacuum to suffocate whoever was within, but since she couldn't influence the inside, this could easily be countered by a simple inventory filled with air. Having such inventories was common practice in Granvaloa, and there was no way that someone with an omnidirectional, long-lasting defense ability wouldn't have prepared something similar.

Perhaps Zeta's skills as King of Thieves would've worked better than her Embryo abilities, but she couldn't use them without coming close to whoever was inside within the vortex. Merely extending her hand to touch them and take their heart would mean going through the vortex, and that was certain death.

She also had a third ace up her sleeve — the Superior MVP special reward, Moby Dick Left — but there was no viable way to employ it in this situation.

Zeta was well-rounded, but if nothing that she had worked, then that was it.

But if I retreat now, I would not have enough information for the task... I need to at least see their face...!

The moment she thought that, a part of the vortex vanished.

Perhaps from lack of energy, the dark maelstrom was undone, exposing the person within.

"Ah...!" Zeta didn't miss the opportunity to etch the person's appearance into her mind.

She also assumed an offensive stance and prepared to take out a camera, but before she could, the seam in the vortex was fixed, once again hiding the person from view.

...Was that a failure on their part or an intentional trap? That much isn't clear, but I now have enough to report.

There was no doubt that, as requested, she had discovered and confirmed the existence of a "strange person" inside that vortex. *Perhaps I can retreat and focus on stealing the orbs again,* she thought, when suddenly...

"Zeta. It's me."

...she heard her client — Claudiah — call to her through the comms device inside her bandages.

The fact that Claudiah had called her at all definitely indicated something, but since she couldn't ignore her, Zeta replied with, "Acknowledged. Since you are using this device, I assume that your efforts ended in failure?"

"Yes. We lost. What about you?"

"...Incomplete. As per your request, I have discovered the target and confirmed their identity, but elimination is proving difficult.

I thought I'd finished them off, but it doesn't seem like any of my Embryo attacks are reaching them."

"Oh, so that really *is* how it works. I wanted to confirm that as well."

Hearing that, Zeta realized that Claudiah had made her request while fully aware that Zeta's attacks would be futile.

"What about your own goal? Were you able to steal them?"

Zeta had to stop herself from saying "I would've been well on my way to stealing them right now if you didn't call me." Instead, she said, "Rejection. I refuse to answer."

"I see." Despite having asked, Claudiah didn't seem to be terribly interested in the topic.

It was clear to Zeta that Claudiah cared mostly about the black vortex before her.

Though, the information Zeta had on the vortex wasn't quite what Claudiah had in mind when she'd made the request.

"Directive. Since elimination is impossible and your situation isn't favorable, I request that you give me a new order."

"We are moving on to plan C. Make the preparations we discussed and retreat from Altea."

Zeta had actually forgotten about that particular plan until Claudiah mentioned it. It was only meant to be executed if Dryfe lost at both the negotiations and the battle, so she had pushed it deep into a corner of her mind.

Zeta did remember what it entailed, however, so she readily agreed.

"Commencing. Present the reward using the designated method. That is when I will provide you with information on the target."

Zeta then cut the comm and faced the vortex again.

Anyhow, I am done with this. I'll execute plan C while moving underground. Perhaps the ones who have the orbs are taking shelter there.

She had her next job and her own goal. Thinking that she could still accomplish them both, she began to create distance between her and the vortex. Then, she quickly accelerated down the outer wall, following a path leading downwards.

Speaking of underground, that's where Ignis went. He seems to have done that by melting the bulkheads from the first floor, so maybe I should follow him...?

With that in mind, she proceeded along when suddenly, a chill ran down her spine.

Then, with a strange uneasiness in her heart, she took out a device given to her by La Crima — the one that displayed the status of the four Ideas.

Three of them were inactive, while the fourth one — Ignis Idea — was not only active, but *becoming more active.*

The body temperature data displayed was far too high even for a wielder of flame magic.

"Question. What is happening?"

Cold sweat soaked through her bandages as she realized that something unexpected was happening again.

"...She seems to have retreated."

[Yes. She left...and went...underground... It doesn't seem like... she'll come back...]

Upon hearing Duchess's words, Dormouse canceled the vortex.

"I have not used Infection Citadel to its fullest for quite a while. That was tiring."

[...Tiring?]

"Apologies. I am fairly sure I am not nearly as tired as you are."

The apology was earnest. Duchess was tasked with the arduous duty of managing every Master's visuals. She had been operating at full capacity every waking hour for over four years now. Dormouse with his single battle couldn't even begin to compare.

"Dor," said Theresia. "I am aware that if Liliana finds us in a room that seems to have been a battlefield, explaining that to her would be difficult."

"We need to move to somewhere less destroyed. Duchess, lead the way so they do not find us before we arrive," said Dormouse.

However, Duchess didn't respond.

"Duchess, I truly am sorry for my careless words. Please forgive me." Dormouse apologized again…

[Dormouse…take The Evil…and leave Altea…immediately.]

…but in response, he got a warning, spoken with all possible urgency.

"…What happened?"

[…You don't know? Ohh…you aren't in the…control room… In that case…I will say it…]

And so, Duchess…

[In a few more minutes…

the castle will be…

blown apart.]

…announced an approaching calamity.

Chapter Twenty-Six Supernova

Fire

While fighting Canglong, Ignis Idea…or rather, Feuer Lazburn, became certain that he could not win.

His long years of training and fighting as a Lazburn Pyromancer and his staggering defeat at the hands of the Arch Sage had given him enough experience to know that he would almost certainly die here.

It was only obvious. His fire couldn't hurt Canglong — the Draconic Emperor would instantly regenerate even if the majority of his body was blown away.

In fact, it didn't seem out of the question that he could come back even if he was reduced to a single scrap of dragon-flesh.

Canglong, on the other hand, had more than enough strength to bring about Feuer's demise.

…*How long will I last, I wonder?* Half-giving up, he was buying time by firing spells at the people all around.

This couldn't continue forever, though. The Altarians who could still walk were slowly helping the immobilized leave the area.

Once everyone Canglong had to protect was gone, he would be able to kill Feuer with little effort.

How did it come to this…? he wondered.

Why was he in a place like this, fighting such a foe?

He had yet to find the Arch Sage, whom he was sure was here in this castle, yet he was now facing an enemy who was likely even worse than him.

And now, he would die without having even encountered his target.

This was a battle he couldn't win, nor could he retreat from it. The Idea-piece implanted in his body wouldn't allow him to run. It was part of the contract that had given him his warped body and vast reserves of magic.

He wouldn't have run even if he was able — retreating with such obscene amounts of magic at his disposal would have been a defeat in and of itself, the ultimate proof that he could not win even after exceeding his limitations.

For one who wanted to prove that Lazburn magic was strongest, retreating was not an option.

For what purpose did I...? Feuer Lazburn looked back at his life — or perhaps it was flashing before his eyes just like many others who were near death had experienced.

The many days of training, his father's death, the fight against the Arch Sage, the heavy defeat by his hand, the days that followed, the contract with La Crima — it all passed him by in a brief moment that felt like an eternity...

"Hm...?"

...but it stopped when it reached the matter of his life's goal.

At its core, this goal was simple — to prove that he was the strongest. Specifically, he wanted to show the world that no magic was greater than fire, and prove that the Lazburns, who dedicated their minds and bodies to fire magic alone, were the most powerful casters of all.

To that end, he and his father had made it their goal to defeat the Magical Apex — the Arch Sage.

However, his father expired before he could even challenge him, while Feuer himself had been effortlessly defeated.

Since then, he had been reborn and had once again attempted to seek out the Arch Sage in order to prove that he was the strongest.

Indeed — the Arch Sage's defeat was *nothing but a means to an end, not the end itself.*

Feuer didn't *have* to defeat him.

"Heh heh…ha ha ha ha ha ha ha!"

"Hm?" Feuer's sudden laughter made Canglong and the Altarians who were still in the shelter stare at him with confusion in their eyes.

The laughter wasn't a sign of the man losing his mind.

He was merely laughing at *himself* for taking this long to realize his error.

"I lived my whole life for the sole purpose of becoming the strongest and proving that fact." Indeed — he had been misguided, mistaken… just plain *wrong*.

Perhaps Feuer was this way because his father was mistaken before him. His final words might've carried more weight with Feuer than they had deserved.

The Lazburns' ultimate goal wasn't to defeat the Arch Sage.

Bringing down the Magical Apex was but a means to prove his own strength.

The Lazburns merely wanted to claim the Arch Sage's title as evidence of their absolute power.

That meant that he could achieve his goal of proving his power using other means.

This realization cleared his mind, in spite of his rapidly approaching demise.

"…What are you planning?" Canglong asked, confused by Feuer's change in demeanor.

To some, the Idea was now more fear-inspiring than he had been when he was firing flame spells in all directions, so Canglong couldn't help but ask this simple question.

In response, Feuer said, "The Parting Sea between Tenchi and Huang He, the great desert of Caldina... The wounds etched onto this very continent are evidence of the existence of those who inflicted them."

These words barely made sense at first, but it didn't take long for Canglong to realize their meaning.

The separation of Tenchi from the continent at the hands of the Incarnations, the exclusion zones created as a result of the fights between one of Canglong's predecessors and the King of Kings, the contaminated areas left behind by Huang He's civil war... Such scars on the land were there because those capable of creating them had actually *done that.*

They were evidence that those who held immense power had changed the very lay of the land.

So, what Feuer Lazburn intended was...

"I will use this land itself as proof... Proof that the strongest spellcaster of all was once here!"

...to prove his magic was strongest by using it to change the shape of this landscape beyond recognition.

Canglong approached, intent on stopping him — but before he could, Feuer's warped body began releasing waves of intense heat in all directions.

Hot enough to make people evaporate in an instant, these waves rushed towards the Altarians who had yet to escape.

"Kh...! Please, run...!" Canglong said before spreading out his Dragon King Aura.

This rendered him immobile, but it was the only way for him to prevent the Altarians from dying in an instant. The aura acted as a wall, protecting them as they rushed out of the shelter.

"All restrictions...abolished. Supercritical transformation... all magic into heat. Heat escalation...activate."

While Canglong was holding him off, Feuer began crafting his spell.

The magic unleashed thus far was only the beginning. The true spell would follow soon.

Or, more precisely, would be *created* soon.

What he was about to use was a spell he was crafting from scratch at this very moment.

"Exchange loss...cause is bodily structure...incinerating cells to enhance magic flow." He disregarded control in favor of pure power. Conjuring this spell even started to harm his own body.

This was a self-destructive effort, and it would surely wipe him out with it...but Feuer didn't care.

He had already realized that to achieve his true goal, his life was a small price to pay.

Did I want the glory and fame that came with proving that I am the Magical Apex? Did I want society to sing my praises after I defeated the Arch Sage? No. That certainly wasn't the case. His only goal in life was to prove he was the strongest; he didn't seek to live a life where he was *revered* for that.

The battle and his own feelings were all distant — all that mattered to him now was the culmination of his obsession.

"Question. Ignis, what are you d—?" Zeta, realizing that something was happening, tried to question him, only to be cut off.

"Be silent," Ignis said as he tore out the comms device in his ear, ripping out some of his own flesh in the process.

At this moment, he sought nothing but the spell he was crafting. His fixation on the Arch Sage and even the deal with La Crima had lost all meaning to him.

Once complete, this spell he was creating would destroy the castle, scorch the capital, and render the entire area a wasteland of molten ruins.

"Ha ha ha ha! HA HA HA HA HA HA HA HA!" The Lazburns sought nothing more in life than firepower, so his very blood was set ablaze by the mere thought of the magical might he would soon exhibit. He couldn't help but laugh.

One of his four arms fell to the floor. The brains implanted in his body, which provided his magical power reserves, were boiling. Even the Idea-fragment couldn't withstand the heat and died.

The very cells of his face began to melt, his vision washed red, his eardrums burst; the collapse of his already barely stable body was fast approaching.

None of that is of any consequence now. All that matters is that I cast this final spell.

He didn't care what he would lose. His life was already fleeting. Dying a bit sooner meant nothing.

He would construct this spell even if he gave all that he had to give.

"This will be the last spell of my life, and it will incinerate the entire capital."

This would be King of Blaze's new final attack, never before seen or heard of.

About the dragons of the east…

Draconic Emperor, Canglong Renyue, had no recollection of his birth.

Just like anyone else, he had no memories of the time when he was still a baby. Even being the Draconic Emperor didn't change that.

His earliest memory was a moment where his vision was completely drowned in *red*.

He didn't even know what it was he had seen — he didn't understand the meaning of the color.

When he grew old enough to understand the world around him, he realized that he was being shunned by his siblings and father.

Even in the Imperial Court, the fact that he was the Draconic Emperor was kept secret. The only ones who knew were the emperor, his children, and a few of the closest aides.

The clueless retainers gave Canglong the respect a third prince deserved, while the nursing mother who'd raised him treated him well despite knowing what he truly was.

However, his family was different. They almost seemed to look at him like he was their enemy.

Canglong didn't understand why. He had been taught that Draconic Emperor was a Special Superior Job that, to Huang He, matched or perhaps even surpassed the emperor himself in importance.

That was why, one day after he had matured enough to wonder this, Canglong had approached his father and asked him directly, "Why do you shun me?"

What he'd seen next was the emperor's face twisting into an expression Canglong had never seen him make before throwing his fist at the boy.

Because of the insurmountable gap in stats between the two of them, only the emperor himself had been injured.

Despite that, he — Canglong's own father — had attacked him.

Then, as though to release everything he had been keeping inside until now, he'd screamed, "*Because you took the life of my beloved!*"

At first, Canglong had almost seen his point but had then become confused.

He knew that his mother had died while giving birth to him. However, it wasn't unheard of for mothers to die during childbirth.

Canglong did understand that the treatment of children born in such circumstances could vary, but it didn't seem like enough of a reason for the emperor to loathe him as he did. The man had never shown even a hint of love for Canglong.

The emperor's attitude towards Canglong was far, far different from how anyone might expect a parent to treat their child. Rather than his own son, the emperor treated Canglong like a callous murderer who had brutally slaughtered the person he'd cherished most in the world.

"...Ah."

And just like that, Canglong had found the answer.

His mother had died at the moment of his — or rather, the Draconic Emperor's — birth.

Draconic Emperors inherited the levels of their predecessors, granting them stats that far exceeded even those of specialized Superior Jobs *from the moment of their birth.*

That was both the cause of the emperor's rage and the answer to Canglong's question.

Canglong's mother hadn't died from a fever or any other common risk of childbirth — he had actually torn her apart.

While still inside his mother's womb, the baby Draconic Emperor had struggled and writhed...and in the process, his excessive power had destroyed her.

That was the reason his father and his siblings shunned him so.

They might have even seen the infant Canglong tear the emperor's wife — his children's mother — to shreds. That would have been reason enough to make them loathe the sight of him.

Not even human, Canglong was an Irregularity — a monstrous creature since birth.

But at the same time, he was also a symbol of Huang He and the strongest being in the country, making it impossible to get rid of him even if they wanted to.

They must've been bottling up their rage for quite some time, and Canglong's careless question had set his father off.

For all he knew, the emperor might've attacked him fully prepared to die, thinking that this monstrous being who'd taken his wife would now take him too.

However, the emperor was Canglong's father, whom he didn't have the slightest intention of killing.

He also hadn't intended to kill his mother merely by being born, but he had done it regardless.

On that day, however, neither Canglong nor the emperor died.

However, Canglong's relationship with his family became unsalvageable.

After that moment, Canglong continued life as both a prince and the Draconic Emperor. He participated in festivals and ceremonies in his warped, dragon-like form with his face hidden behind a mask. He also received education befitting a prince and fulfilled his duties as such.

However, he never once spent any time with his family.

Canglong had "siblings" who were raised alongside him and nursed by the same mother, but his blood relatives completely stopped interacting with him the day after his father struck him.

There was no violence between them, but nor were there any words. Their relationship never went beyond the bare minimum conversations required for official purposes.

Canglong also made no effort to interact with them in return. Since his power was so vast, he believed that he could unwittingly kill them just as he'd killed his mother.

If it weren't for the nursing mother who'd raised him well in spite of knowing what he was, or Meihai who looked out for him while unaware of his secret, he might never have grown to know love and friendship.

However, he was terrified of even touching them.

The only times he allowed himself to touch anyone without reserve were during the duels that were protected by the barriers.

He'd dueled to prove the power of the imperial family and the Draconic Emperor. The arenas, where anyone who was broken would emerge unscathed, were the only places a born monster like him wouldn't kill anyone.

He had a robust stature and a dragon-like appearance, so when his face was hidden by the mask, no one could tell that he was the young third prince of Huang He.

By fighting in the duels again and again, he effortlessly became the duel champion of Huang He, showing everyone the glory of the imperial family and the power of the empire's great symbol.

However, his family never once praised him for any of that.

Through his duels, he even learned to control his power, but he still made no attempt to touch anyone.

One day, he read the letter left for him by Honglong Renchao — the Draconic Emperor that had come before him.

The text gave Canglong the impression that his predecessor had known what would become of him. He even guessed that Honglong had perhaps gone through something similar himself.

The letter said, "Do not be bound by your sins," but Canglong felt that that would be difficult.

The sin of matricide bound his life like a chain.

However, his life changed somewhat when many more Masters began appearing in the world.

Masters were immortal beings bearing unique powers — the kin of The Lynx that one of his predecessors had faced.

For the first time, he began to meet abnormal entities besides himself, and in great numbers.

Eventually, he dueled one such abnormality — Xunyu.

Canglong won, of course, but it was the first time he'd ever met anyone who could compete with him — someone he could treat as an equal.

Because of that, he quickly became attached to this particular Master, for he had always wanted an adult who would coddle him like the little boy he was.

That only made it all the more shocking, though, when he learned that Xunyu was actually a girl about his age.

In this year, Canglong's father, the emperor, gave him an official order to travel to Altar and meet the girl he would most likely have to marry.

Canglong didn't understand why he picked the shunned son instead of one of his brothers for the marriage, but he had no intention of refusing either.

To hide his true form and power while in foreign territory, he picked an appropriate Treasurebeast Orb left behind by one of his predecessors, defeated the UBM inside, and assumed the form of a powerless child.

Then, with Xunyu as a bodyguard, he went to the kingdom.

He then caught the local epidemic, but things had gone smoothly otherwise.

And not too long ago, he had met his fiancée, Elizabeth, for the first time.

She was a naive, simple girl who smiled and laughed a lot. He was a prince, and she a princess, yet he couldn't help but feel that despite their similar positions, they were vastly different.

Her smile, however, had vanished — and he was the cause.

Elizabeth's sister had told her that she would have to marry Canglong and move to Huang He.

Part of the reason the sister had resolved to do this was to protect Elizabeth from the flames of war that could soon engulf the kingdom.

But Elizabeth stood against it. She didn't want to flee Altar and leave her sisters behind.

The sisters argued, but any onlookers would know that they did so because they all wanted what was best for each other.

Canglong quickly understood that this was the difference between them — the existence of a loving family.

He had no family he loved or family that loved him. The relationship the princesses had was dazzling to him, and it hurt his heart that he'd caused them to argue...and because he would ultimately take Elizabeth away to the loveless court of Huang He.

That was why, on the morning that followed, he visited Elizabeth and apologized.

The very same day, thanks to Xunyu's planning, the two went on a Love-Duel Festival date. This came as a surprise to him, but it was true that he wanted to learn more about Elizabeth, so he didn't refuse it.

The two walked through the lively city of Gideon until they found a festival stall selling various masks.

One of those masks was made to look like the Zifu Longmian he usually wore.

His masks were created by forcing magic into metal to change its shape, so the crafted mask in the stall actually looked more presentable than the ones he crafted for himself.

"Did you find something, Canglong? Hm... That one is a bit scary." Upon hearing that, Canglong didn't know what to say. If even the mask meant to hide his warped face was scary to her, what would she think of his actual face? Would she be able to accept him?

He also wondered if it was right for him to take her as a wife and bring her back to Huang He without revealing how monstrous he truly was.

But at the same time, he couldn't deny that he was more and more drawn to this incredible girl.

During the date, he became exhausted and had to rest.

Normally, the very idea of him running out of stamina would be absurd, but the Self-Sealing Wraps he was wearing had given him the attributes of an ordinary child.

During this break, however, Elizabeth had noticed the Self-Sealing Wraps underneath his clothes.

"Are you hurt or sick?"

"...I suppose you may call it an illness. These bandages are a measure to hold back a certain handicap I was born with."

It wasn't exactly a lie.

The bandages were there to seal away the power of the Draconic Emperor — the handicap preventing him from living as a human.

Canglong had never once been glad to be born as he was — the revered and blessed job was a burden to him.

"...I'm sorry," Canglong apologized. "I didn't mean to let you see something so unsightly."

"Don't apologize! What's so unsightly about that?! So what if you were born with an illness?! If you think *that* bothers me, you're sorely mistaken!" Hearing that made Canglong's heart ache, for he realized that Elizabeth wouldn't find him unsightly even if he had suffered from some kind of sickness.

It made him hope that he could reveal himself and she would accept him as he was.

However, he still hesitated enough to stop himself from telling the truth.

Elizabeth then told him how she felt about her sisters and that if it meant protecting them, she would readily leave for Huang He.

But before she could promise that, Canglong asked for a postponement. He felt that he also needed to gather the resolve to tell her the truth.

The truth that he was the monstrous being known as the Draconic Emperor.

And now, tongues of flame had engulfed the both of them, forcing Canglong to reveal his true nature before he could properly tell her.

He was still frightened of Elizabeth finding out what kind of abomination he was. However, he hadn't hesitated to reveal himself, nor did he regret doing it — for it was the only way to protect her.

"Protect what you wish to protect."

"Accomplish what you believe you must."

"Do not be afraid to do as you will."

The words left behind by his predecessor came back to him as he resolved to protect and fight for the girl who had captured his heart.

Royal Castle, Underground Shelter

As Feuer crafted his spell, the flames grew ever stronger.

Their heat began to overcome even Canglong's Dragon King Aura and reach his scales.

Such magic and heat… There will be an explosion even if he dies now…! Canglong thought. The spell's activation and the explosion caused by the caster's death were the exact same thing.

If that volume of heat was released, the entire shelter would melt in a split second. Not even those who fled would survive. The heat waves were so intense that they would instantly kill even someone equipped with a Brooch.

The castle, as well as Altea as a whole, would be absolutely devastated by this heat.

To prevent that, Canglong had only two options — either he could take Feuer somewhere else or somehow dampen the heat that was being released.

The former wasn't possible because they were deep underground, but the latter also held its own problems.

Will my Dragon King Aura be enough...? Canglong wondered. The legendary Draconic Emperor that had come before his predecessor had possessed countless techniques he could use to counter this situation, but the techniques had died with him. Neither Honglong that came after him, nor Canglong, the title's current holder, could use them.

The most he could do with his latent Dragon King Aura was to stop the preliminary heat waves.

Because of his Gulong Cells skill, the Draconic Emperor himself could focus on defense and survive even if he was at the heart of the explosion, but everyone else would die.

If I do not prevent this, then the city...and Elizabeth would...!

There were limits, but he had to surpass them.

...I will transform my life force into magic to enhance my Dragon King Aura.

He resolved to do this, even if it cost him his life.

Ready and prepared, he faced the burning Idea — when suddenly...

"Ah...!"

...he felt a presence behind him. Most of the people had already left the shelter, but there was still one person behind him.

"Cang…"

It was the very girl he wanted to protect more than anyone else.

"Elizabeth! Why are you still here?!" Despite his Dragon King Aura, the heat in the surroundings was growing ever higher. It wouldn't take long for it to become powerful enough to incinerate someone — even before the explosion actually occurred.

Despite that, Elizabeth was standing behind him.

"Cang…run away with us!" Those words were enough for him to understand that she'd returned because she was *worried* about him, left alone in the flames.

She was concerned about Canglong, even after seeing him exposed as the monstrous entity that he was.

That fact almost made his heart waver, but he kept it steady by clenching his teeth.

He then took off his mask and looked at her.

Neither human nor dragon — his was a face as distorted as that of the Idea he was fighting.

And he was now baring it to her.

"I am the Draconic Emperor…an abomination," he said. "*This* is what I am — nothing like you. So please, run…"

His words were those of rejection…

"*You are not an abomination!*"

…but they were rejected in turn.

She raised her voice as though to blow away his self-loathing and low opinion of himself.

"You are my friend…" she said. Draconic Emperor or not, they *were* still friends. "You are also my fiancé… *And you will be my family!*"

Shock overcame Canglong. She just said that, in spite of it all, she still saw him as one she would spend her life with.

"So, please…! There are still so many things…I want to talk to you about…and ask! So…please…! Let us…" Whether it was due to the feelings in her heart or the fear of the oncoming flames, she was crying too much to finish her sentence properly.

However, he clearly heard her say, "Let us live together."

It didn't need to be voiced to reach him.

In silence, Canglong looked away from her and put on the mask again.

As he did, a tear running down his cheek disappeared in the coming heat. However, in his heart, there was now something that could never vanish.

"Your Highness! Your Highness Elizabeth!" Marquis Findle cried as he rushed into the shelter. Upon seeing the princess, he rushed to her and took her in his remaining arm.

"Marquis Findle, take care of Elizabeth."

"…Of course!" Canglong entrusted Elizabeth to the man and faced the flame once more.

"Cang…!" Elizabeth called.

"…I *will* come back to you. So please, leave this to me."

"…Very well!" With that promise made, he listened to them leave behind him.

As the sound of them going up the steps faded, he began to speak.

"…King of Blaze." He was talking to Feuer Lazburn — the Idea slowly turning into a roiling mass of flame. "Up until moments ago, I intended to stop you even if it cost me my life."

Canglong had planned to subdue the explosion using all his magic as well as his own life force.

"I would never do that now. I cannot give you my life. It belongs to her. I will stop your flames *and* keep myself alive. I apologize if that seems greedy, but I cannot give up on anything!"

He was now resolved to protect his life…for the sake of the promise he'd made to the one he loved and their future together.

"That…*is what I have decided!*"

With that, he faced the all-consuming flame of destruction.

The fire said nothing in response. With his eyes and ears gone, he probably hadn't even heard what Canglong had said.

However, he felt *something*, and it was enough for him to warp his nearly destroyed mouth into a grin and…

"Supernova."

…speak the name of the completed final attack.

Supernova was the pinnacle of fire magic — a school focused on turning magic into pure heat.

It was in many ways the direct opposite of the ultimate job skill of King of Blaze, Fixed Star.

While Fixed Star was focused on concentrating and controlling immense amounts of magic to create an all-melting orb of fire, Supernova had no such concentration or control.

None of the magic used was directed towards managing the power involved, and since the MP needed to manage spells was proportional to the MP used by the spell itself, this allowed him to release all of his magic at once.

Since there was no control, the vast amount of magic that would normally be used for that purpose would all become heat instead.

Indeed — Supernova was nothing but a skill that merely put layer upon layer of heat escalation and then released it all. It was omnidirectional and indiscriminate, harming even the user.

It was a self-destruct skill, and that was exactly what made it impossible to deal with.

Feuer now had absurd amounts of magic even compared to Superior Jobs, and since he was converting it all into heat…stopping him was impossible.

Canglong himself knew that well.

Despite that, he hadn't given up. To do so would be to give up on his own life and that of his beloved. Even if it took him past his limits, he would protect everything he could.

After Canglong gathered his resolve, Feuer activated his final attack, turning him into what looked like a human-sized sun.

A moment later, heat that turned everything into ash before evaporating even that began to push in all directions.

If it was released, it would not only scorch the passage Elizabeth was in, but also turn the entire city into a burning hell.

"*OOAAAGHH!*"

Thus, Canglong gave his all to spread out his Dragon King Aura and enhance its mitigating effect. The effort was such that it affected even his gulong body.

He released vast amounts of Dragon King Aura in order to envelop Feuer and his exploding flames.

The heat and the aura clashed, sending the temperature around them roaring up to three thousand degrees Celsius. The shelter now looked like the inside of a furnace, but thanks to the Dragon King Aura, the effect was mostly confined to the immediate area.

"Gh…!" Smoke began to rise from Canglong's scales and flesh, but he didn't weaken his aura one bit.

His fight against the heat was like sealing away a small star. Even the Draconic Emperor's absurd power was pushed to the limits with this task.

He threw his hands, along with the Dragon King Aura, right towards the heat, suppressing it.

The knowledge that weakening his aura could mean his beloved's death stopped him from even *thinking* of doing so.

He was immovable, but the coming heat was unstoppable. It was still anyone's battle.

"Ah...!" At the core of the heat he was suppressing, the sun-like orb was growing more luminous...and larger.

Despite the immense heat, the sight sent a chill down his spine.

Even this immense heat was only the beginning...? Like an earthquake, there were fast, weaker advance waves, followed by intense, slower waves.

The weak waves so far already carried more heat than the Fixed Star Rain that had melted Golem Bellcross. The heat of the true Supernova was far above what Canglong had expected.

"Even so...!"

Even so, he wouldn't run or move, for he *had* to push this heat back.

He was the Draconic Emperor — perhaps the strongest tian of these times — as well as a boy who had found a girl he loved.

Thus, he resolved to stay here and continue subduing the heat.

Would Canglong burn first, or would the overflowing heat consume the castle and the city while he still stood?

Or perhaps there would be some miracle that would let him claim victory?

It was as though his fate depended on a dice roll by some heavenly *observers* far greater than even him...

"Need a hand?"

...but then someone else came, taking the dice in their own hand.

A person was standing in this furnace-like space, talking to Canglong.

He had no idea how long they had been there, but someone was right behind him.

The presence of a person in this room that he'd thought contained only him and the flame filled Canglong with shock.

The person asking that question seemed to have appeared from thin air.

"Oh wait. 'Need a hand?' isn't the right thing to say in this case. I don't want this castle blown away, so I won't accept your refusal. 'Please let me help' is more apt. Neither you alone nor I alone are capable of dealing with this magic anyway."

The unfamiliar voice belonged to a *young woman*, but Canglong didn't even have the capacity to ask her who she was.

This space would instantly burn any normal person to death. Yet she appeared here as though she'd planned it — which she had — and talked to Canglong with an unfittingly casual tone.

"Oh, if you don't mind me saying, the Dragon King Aura you're using now isn't suited to phenomena like this. The standard Dragon King Aura is a defensive function that mitigates both physical and magic attacks. If you're using it against a single phenomenon, the magic-mitigation effectiveness isn't that great. With something like this, it would be more effective to use an aura focused *solely* on heat mitigation. I would like you to shift to that, please."

"Huh?" Not only was she speaking casually — she sounded like a laid-back professor.

"Ohh. Well, one of your predecessors was...*apparently* very good at such fine-tuning of the aura, but you aren't at that level, I assume? Sorry for demanding something you can't deliver. Oh, and sorry for giving you a lecture before even introducing myself. You are the current Draconic Emperor... 'Prince Canglong,' was it? Sorry if I seem rude. Unfortunately, back when I was a girl, I swore that I wouldn't use polite language with anyone but my late teacher. I do keep my letters formal sometimes, but I'm actually quite stubborn about this."

Canglong was on the verge of just directly asking what she was, and the woman could sense that.

In response, smiling in spite of the situation, she said, "Ha ha hah! You must wonder who I am. Well, I'm basically the one King of Blaze was looking for."

"Ah…!" Shock overcame Canglong. He could scarcely believe it.

"Though, with his eyes and ears melted, I don't think he even has the ability to acknowledge me. Still, here's an introduction."

The person faced the Draconic Emperor — as well as Feuer behind him.

"I am the one who inherited everything from my teacher." She then folded her arms, put a finger over the rim of her monocle, and said…

"Arch Sage, Integra."

Royal Castle, Fourth Floor

"...Now *this* is truly troublesome."

It was the moment after Feuer Lazburn had activated Supernova. Upon hearing that it was possible that the explosion underground could blow away the entire capital, Dormouse prepared to take Theresia away from the site of the blast.

Infection Citadel could absorb the great amounts of Supernova's heat and protect Theresia, but if she was found unscathed within a crater left by an explosion that obliterated the city, it would become far too difficult for them to operate in the future.

If Dormouse went there to stop the explosion from even happening, the same questions would arise.

That meant that Duchess's suggestion — running away from the explosion — was the most reasonable one, and he intended to follow it.

"Wait, Dormouse. No need to evacuate. Stay where you are."

However, he was stopped by another colleague addressing him.

It was Humpty Dumpty — the one in charge of Embryos. While Duchess used message windows, Humpty talked directly to Dormouse's mind.

"What is your business, Dumpty? What do you mean there is no need to evacuate?"

"The signature of the Embryo within the tian who is trying to blow himself up has vanished. Now — at least in theory — he is nothing but a tian."

"What does that matter?"

"Don't you understand? A tian's attack would work on The Evil, wouldn't it?"

"Ah…! Humpty, you…!"

Dormouse instantly understood what Humpty intended. The Evil would no longer recognize Feuer Lazburn as a foreign entity, so she was suggesting that they should just let his explosion take Theresia.

Saying nothing, Dormouse thought of the girl sitting silently on his back.

If The Evil died, it would take quite a while for a new The Evil to achieve completion.

The time span depended greatly on the previous The Evil's level of completion upon death, but it was certain that if Theresia died now…the next The Evil would not arrive before their plans were complete.

The Evil and The Demise — the greatest problems the control AIs had. Letting Feuer's explosion blow them away was nothing but a good thing for them.

"Humpty, that is…"

However, Dormouse hesitated to follow her advice.

"Oh? What's the delay?"

"…If I continue observing her as I am, the likelihood of her becoming complete as The Evil is low. In fact, by letting her get caught in the explosion, we might activate her safety measures and suffer unforeseen consequences…"

Dormouse argued against Humpty's idea, but his words came off as mere excuses.

249

"I see. Unforeseen consequences or total erasure…which do you think is more likely?"

"I…"

"Dormouse… You're just being sentimental, aren't you?"

Dormouse was unable to say that he wasn't.

In fact, she was completely right. It was his job to protect The Evil, Theresia, but he hadn't exactly remained emotionally detached from his job.

In fact, his relationship with Theresia was no longer just about the role to him.

"The Evil of this era is like your Master, so you're just making up emotion-based reasons for protecting her. It's not rational."

Dormouse was shocked by the truth of those words. When he was but an Embryo, his Master had been a sickly little girl — a frail child who would surely die without help.

Perhaps his power to protect, as well as his plague-like true power, came about because he had been born from her.

He and his power had grown for the purpose of protection, eventually making him a Superior Embryo; then, they had allowed him to pass the final test and become an Infinite Embryo.

And the girl that was his Master, having grown into a woman by then, was there to watch him reach that point. Relieved that he could now live without a Master, she had then gone on to pass away.

It would be a lie to claim that Dormouse didn't see his late Master in Theresia — a sickly girl who needed his protection.

"But all of that is meaningless, Dormouse. Regardless of whether The Evil lives or dies, when the project is over, *Infinite Dendrogram* will—"

"I understand! I just…!"

"You seem to be quite troubled. I suppose that is an expression of your feelings for your Master?"

As she spoke, Humpty's words seemed cold.

"Sorry, but *I just can't relate*."

Perhaps Cheshire, Rabbit, or some other control AIs would've been moved by Dormouse's words. However, he knew well that that could never happen with Humpty.

He knew that she could never have any strong emotion towards her Master...and that very quality was why she was in charge of Embryos.

"*A philosophical zombie* like you would never understand..."

"Oh? But Dormouse, insulting me like that seems like you're expressing a wish to die." Humpty wasn't even present, but her words carried true murderous intent.

Dormouse knew well that Humpty was one of the few who could break through his absolute physical and chemical defense. Once called the Incarnation of Death, she was a being that no Infinite Embryo could defeat by themselves.

In spite of the threat, Dormouse refused to back down. He was preparing to say something back when...

[Stop...right there.]

...Duchess stopped them.

[You can no longer...run away in time...regardless. So, Dormouse... stay there...and decide...whether to protect or not...when the timec omes...]

"...Very well." Dormouse nodded.

Humpty had already cut the comms line.

"Your Highness! Your Highness Theresia!" Shortly after that, a voice calling for Theresia rang out through the fourth floor. It belonged to Liliana, who'd been looking for the princess all this time. She was accompanied by the K&R Masters, who'd rushed here after seeing the explosion at the castle.

They quickly found Theresia and Dormouse and rushed over to them.

"Your Highness... I am so glad you are well...!"

"I'm glad you're okay too..." Finding Theresia filled the search party with relief.

However, Dormouse realized that this made it nearly impossible for them to leave the capital.

"Let us head to the underground shelter, then. Your sister and the others are already there…"

Going there would be really bad, Dormouse thought. Liliana had yet to be informed that the underground shelter was perhaps the least safe place in the entire castle.

As Dormouse wondered how to convey that information…

"Huh?"

…a message window suddenly appeared before them.

No, this wasn't a semitransparent, board-like message window, and it certainly hadn't been summoned by Duchess.

It was actually a hologram created using illusion magic, and it said, "Refrain from approaching the area. I am currently below, dealing with explosive material. Stay away from the underground shelter and *the walls.*"

Behind the hologram, there was a wall that seemed to be made using ocean magic. Circular in shape, it covered a part of the fourth floor, and if the inside was empty, it could be described as a cylinder.

It was likely that it continued all the way down to the first floor, if not lower.

The barrier felt like the border of a construction site, or perhaps *something* that was aimed towards the sky.

"Who could have created this… Oh?" Confused, Liliana continued reading the message, and she quickly saw the text saying "Arch Sage, Integra."

"Integra?! When did she come back?!" Seeing the name of an old friend surprised Liliana, but Dormouse didn't know much about her. All he knew was that she was the Arch Sage's disciple as well as apparently the creator of the barrier around the castle.

What mattered here was that she was doing something about King of Blaze's explosion.

He didn't know if she would be successful or if the city would be blown away in spite of her efforts. But if she wasn't able to…if the explosion actually happened…not even Dormouse himself knew if he would decide to protect Theresia or not.

Even the processing power of an Infinite Embryo wasn't enough for him to fully understand his own heart and mind.

Royal Castle, Underground Shelter
Upon hearing the girl introduce herself as the Arch Sage, the star that was the core of the heat seemed to tremble slightly.

It was strange, considering that his eyes, ears, body, and even his brain must've been completely obliterated by now.

"I am the Arch Sage you've been waiting for, Feuer Lazburn. If you wanted a duel against my teacher, I'm here to inherit that too. Oh, and even if you no longer need it, let me tell you that I'm not one to let go of what I've rightfully inherited."

As though his soul was still present somehow, the Supernova that was the remains of King of Blaze was reacting to her words — the words of the Arch Sage.

"Let's continue where we left off, shall we? This time, instead of doing what my teacher did, I will win against you in the most effective and relentless way I can think of. This was my teacher's response, and it will be our final offering to you."

Integra — the new Arch Sage — cracked a confident grin.

There was little time left until the Supernova detonated.

The only thing they could do was rely on Canglong's Dragon King Aura and Integra's magic.

As the Arch Sage, Integra could cast a wide array of spells belonging to the greater elements of atmos, earth, and ocean, as well as spells outside of that framework. She'd used teleportation to suddenly appear in this shelter, and she could even use the grand dark magic composite spell of Imaginary Meteo that her teacher had perfected.

However, that was the limit of her power. Armed with only a normal tian's magic, she would have to face heat even greater than that of Gloria's Overdrive. It was reckless to even attempt something like this.

It was likely that she couldn't withstand King of Blaze's onslaught even if she cast her strongest defensive spells or barriers specialized against heat.

That was just how intensely hot the Supernova was.

And it was why they needed a bit of trickery.

"Now, young Canglong. Sorry, but can you keep your Dragon King Aura running at full capacity for about two more minutes? Definitely no more than that."

In response, the Draconic Emperor nodded.

The Arch Sage of Altar. Canglong had heard of such a person, and he had heard them called the strongest caster of the west. The Arch Sage had been described as an old man, but since she spoke of inheritance, it was easy to guess that this woman was simply the new holder of the title.

Canglong found it strange that she'd suddenly appeared at such a time, but more than that, he appreciated the reinforcement.

And if she had a means of overcoming this predicament, his only real choice was to do as she asked.

"Well, it will all end in two minutes, anyway. That's about when the capital will be blown away."

"Huh?!" The shock from her words was such that Canglong almost weakened his Dragon King Aura.

"Well, I'm not saying that that's how long we'll last or that the spell's peak is coming in two minutes... Two minutes is just about how long it'll take for the walls to melt and the underground water to pour in."

Canglong already knew that this underground shelter was designed for long-term stays and thus included a water supply. That meant that this place was linked to an underground water main.

And if the water so much as touched Feuer as he was now, there would be a violent steam explosion that would flip the city upside down.

"Honestly, it's already pretty bad with the heat that's being conducted alone. We need to hurry and do something...by which I mean removing his heat from here."

Those words reminded Canglong of the moment Integra had appeared.

She'd probably achieved this by short-distance teleportation, which in this world was some of the rarest magic, usable only by a select few.

He guessed that she intended to take Feuer out of here using the same means, but...

"Oh, and by 'removing,' I don't mean teleportation. I can't do that. The spell only works on me, and it can't cover a great distance. And even if I could use it on other people, I'd burn up the moment I touched that thing. That's why the method I'm thinking of is simpler... and more basic," she said as he raised a hand up. "Though, it required some difficult preparation. Oh, and forgive me if it seems like I'm talking too much," she added as she winked with the eye that didn't have a monocle over it. "After all, all I've said so far was a *Chant* for this spell... High-End Heat Resist wall, ultra-multilayered expansion."

The moment she said that, nothing happened in their immediate vicinity — but up above at the castle, reaching up to the fourth floor, holograms appeared with a message on them, as well as something circular...or cylindrical.

It was a tube-like barrier spell that reached from the first floor all the way to its top and beyond.

The caster could freely choose the words used in a Chant, but Integra had used such a long spiel as a Chant that no one could guess that it was, and the enhancement from it was now used on this barrier spell.

A magic barrier of the ocean element, meant specifically to shut out heat, covering a long distance and composed of hundreds of layers, immediately activated.

The barrier felt like the edge of a construction site, or perhaps *a chimney* that was aimed towards the sky.

This was Integra's simple and basic counter against Supernova.

"Now, young Canglong, are you familiar with the principles behind the composition of fire spells like Crimson Sphere?"

"Huh...?"

"Thanks to the Archetype System, they can be used as job skills, so if you have the level, you can cast them without even knowing how they work. However, they can be broken down into three components," she Chanted as if giving him a lecture. "The transformation of magic into heat energy, the control to prevent unnecessary spread, and direction, which grants the attack a vector. You can use job skills without considering these things, but like King of Blaze before us did, if you understand the structure, you can construct your *own* spells. What he did was disregard everything but the transformation of magic into heat energy."

Canglong listened, saying nothing.

"Whether you can create original spells depends on whether you have the intelligence and talent to look past the simplification used by jobs and delve into the actual workings of the magic itself.

Oh, and even though Draconic Emperor isn't a caster job, I remem… read that the one from two generations before yours excelled at this technique."

Casually mentioning the Draconic Emperor who had surpassed all others, she pushed up her monocle…

"And if I wasn't able to do all of that…I wouldn't even have inherited this job."

…and activated her own modified Crimson Sphere.

"Well, that was another long-winded speech, but this is about all I can do." She had crafted this spell while removing one of the three factors making the sphere the fireball it was supposed to be.

It was control. Controlling the extent of a spell required more magic than the actual magic-heat transformation, so if she focused on the transformation alone while facing someone who had greater magic than her, not even someone of her caliber would be able to insert the control factor.

However, the situation was different with direction. Supernova was a magic-heat transformation spell without regard for control of any kind.

In other words, it was nothing but a release of heat without direction.

That was why Integra wove a spell that was effectively the *opposite* of Supernova — a spell that gave the heat direction.

She was warding off Feuer's final attack by influencing it from the outside and giving its heat a specific vector.

And the only direction…is up, she thought. They were underground. Focusing it in any other direction would cause the ground around it to melt, increasing casualties on the surface.

And in the worst case scenario, the heat would make contact with the underground water main and completely destroy the whole city.

That was why she could only release the heat upwards — towards the distant sky.

It was something like adding a chimney to an active furnace.

And I've already prepared the chimney. She'd set up the insulation barrier to make sure that the castle wasn't incinerated as Supernova's heat traveled up.

If it was directed upwards without this barrier, it would no doubt burn the castle down. However, now that the insulation barrier was complete, the heat would travel up without causing much harm… at least, according to her calculations.

"Young Canglong, focus your Dragon King Aura upwards. And when I give the sign, increase your output. Can I count on you for that?"

"…Yes!"

Following Integra's order, Canglong modified his Dragon King Aura. At the same time, Integra activated the heat-vector spell.

Now…let's see how this goes. With the Dragon King Aura that had once contained it now gone and its direction set, the heat of Supernova began to flow upwards. The searing heat melted the reinforced walls of the shelter, reached the surface, and passed through the insulation barrier to flow towards the sky while piercing through every floor of the castle.

The heat made the clouds in Altea's sky begin to evaporate.

It was a cataclysmic sight, but it was done with the precision of a laboratory experiment. Its scale was actually a bit subdued, given the context.

Success…so far. The heat was following the path set out for it, and the chimney-like insulation barrier seemed to be holding.

The temperature increase inside the shelter also began to slow down, and so far they seemed to have spared the walls leading to the underground water main.

According to my calculations, this should be good enough, Integra thought. However, it was still uncertain if this would be enough to contain the true explosion…if all that heat would actually escape to the sky.

Could the insulation barrier bear the heat that would accompany that blast? And would they be able to protect themselves from the inferno raging at the heart of the explosion?

Even if most of the heat escaped to the sky, it would still be the most powerful where the two of them stood, next to Feuer.

If the insulation barrier Integra had created and Canglong's Dragon King Aura weren't enough, the capital would be leveled by the steam explosion that would result when the heat touched the water main. The chimney wouldn't help with that.

Approximately twenty percent of the total heat will not escape through the chimney. Twenty percent of a temperature that can destroy the capital… Considering the water main, this might not be good. Will we be able to block the real explosion? If not, then all I inherited from my teacher and those before him would be lost. All because of me.

Integra had remained calm while talking with Canglong, but on the inside, she was worried. A cold sweat, caused by tension and terror, joined with the sweat running down her face from the intense heat.

"Ngh…!" However, Integra slapped her own cheek, banishing her worry.

Though she was afraid, she wouldn't admit it. She knew that fear was something she could not afford to have.

She was certain that the magic she'd been taught wasn't weak enough to lose to some last-ditch spell woven and cast at the cost of a mere single life.

Thus, she focused and waited for the right moment.

When the explosion came, she would add her own insulation barrier.

Beyond the Dragon King Aura, she saw the Supernova — the remains of King of Blaze, Feuer Lazburn. It was still growing and would reach its full extent in less than a minute.

That moment would be like a fork in the road for both her and her predecessors — and before it split, she looked back at the past. Specifically, she remembered the time the previous Arch Sage had dueled King of Blaze, taking his specialized spell and showing just how much difference there was between them.

Perhaps if the Arch Sage hadn't used fire magic back then, it wouldn't have come to this.

However, Integra knew the two reasons why her teacher did what he'd done.

First, he wanted to show the power and presence of the Arch Sage. Masters had begun to increase in number since that fateful duel. An all-rounded caster crushing a specialized caster at his own forte — this had shown his unmatched power to the world, which resulted in certain developments later.

Second, he wanted to make King of Blaze, Feuer Lazburn, better himself. By showing what lay beyond the magic Feuer wielded, the Arch Sage had urged him to seek it.

If that had broken him, the Arch Sage would have deemed Feuer useless.

However, everything had turned out exactly as the Arch Sage had intended, but in some ways completely different than he imagined.

Feuer Lazburn hadn't been broken, and he had indeed renewed his vigor for training to become stronger.

However, in the course of this, he'd also become an Idea — a being that could completely destroy the Arch Sage's plans.

The Arch Sage could not have anticipated something like this.

And that's why I need to fix my teacher's mistake. King of Blaze had been inspired by the last Arch Sage, and as a result had become an obstacle. As the inheritor of all of this, Integra was resolved to settle things once and for all.

Finally, the time came.

The star-like orb of fire pulsated, signifying that it was reaching its limit.

"Dragon King Aura! Full power! Now!"

"OOAAGHH!" In response to Integra's order, Canglong created an intense aura that used even his own life force as fuel. At the same time, Integra activated the greatest insulation magic she'd ever prepared.

"Hundred-fold insulation barrier...activate!" Flat barriers, twenty in number for each direction, surrounded Feuer like a box.

The barriers hid away the star inside, and the Dragon King Aura enveloped it.

Then came the fateful moment...and the space was filled with a light so intense it seemed like it might swallow up the whole world.

Fire

How many people have learned the meaning of their life only at the very final moments of it?

It was perhaps impossible to know the exact number. No one could truly know what someone else was thinking right as their spark was snuffed out.

Why were they born? For what purpose had they lived? And did they leave this life with a feeling of satisfaction?

Only the person in question could come to know the meaning behind their birth...or they vanished without ever learning it at all.

Feuer Lazburn's life was a flame — a life dedicated solely to fire.

He'd sacrificed his time, way of life, morals, and even his body to that flame.

His life was lit by fire and had been consumed by it.

And ultimately, he'd transformed his very body into flame itself.

He understood that he'd given everything he had to create the strongest fire of all — to prove that his kind of magic was the strongest.

However...the meaning was still lost to him.

His life had been dedicated to fire, but for what purpose?

He recalled that his reason for trying to defeat the Arch Sage was to prove that fire magic reigned supreme. He'd taken on his family's goal and trained from a young age to prove the power of fire.

But no matter how hard he tried, he couldn't find a *reason* for delivering that proof.

He lived to prove he was strongest, but what would that proof accomplish? While he dedicated himself to pursuing that proof, he couldn't think of any reason for it.

Feuer Lazburn was like a fire himself.

A spark caught and burned, shone for a moment, and then was reduced to ash.

His life had been one of light and heat, and it left behind nothing of consequence.

And if he wasn't even able to prove that he was the strongest, it would all be even more meaningless.

He wouldn't even leave a corpse, and his entire life would be...

"I'm...alive. Well...that was some intense magic..."

As the mind Feuer Lazburn had used to comprehend meaning gradually slipped away, he suddenly perceived a voice praising him.

With his eyes, ears, and flesh lost, Feuer still somehow felt the voice of a woman.

It was his first time hearing it, for when she'd first spoken, his ears were already gone.

The voice belonged to Integra...who had survived his flame.

She was still standing in the shelter.

Their surroundings had completely changed. The walls between them and the water main that supplied the castle had melted away, creating a small river on the floor.

It was evaporating as it touched the heated walls and floor of the shelter, but the reaction wasn't intense enough to cause a steam explosion. The walls had only superficially melted away, and the source of the heat — Supernova — was already dissipating.

Now, the water main was slowly cooling all it passed by.

Beside Integra, who was standing near the center of the shelter, there was Canglong, lying down on the wet floor, but still breathing.

The destruction of the capital had been prevented, and the ones responsible for this feat were still alive.

There was now a hole piercing everything from the shelter to the top of the castle, but the castle itself was still intact.

That meant that Feuer Lazburn's final spell had been prevented from demonstrating its immense destructive power to the entire world.

"The hundred-fold insulation barrier, the Dragon King Aura of the strongest Draconic Emperor so far, and this fire damage-cutting accessory made by my teacher himself...and I'm still coming out of it like this." Integra was in an awful state. Her entire body was covered in burns; some parts of her had serious injury-based status effects. Her heat resistant clothes were now nothing but burnt rags.

"My eyes and ears aren't working either. The barrier only stopped heat, so light and sound still passed through. My eyes were burned away even though they were closed, and my ear drums were ruptured too. Honestly, I'm talking here, but I don't even know if anyone can hear me. Or maybe I died and I'm just a spirit now. No — my entire body hurts really bad, so I've got to be alive."

Perhaps Integra was speaking in spite of her heavy wounds because she wanted to convince herself that she wasn't actually dead. That was just how much of a close call this was.

"You might've already burned up completely, but let me tell you just one thing, Feuer Lazburn." Integra continued to address the man before her, who now had no proper shape or shadow.

Would she berate him for harming her so severely, or would she mock him for being a fool?

What she actually said...

"I am the Arch Sage and the inheritor of two thousand years' worth of knowledge."

...was neither of those things.

"As such, I assure you that your fire magic is by far the strongest in this entire era. No one alive has mastered the flame like you."

She actually praised his power.

And these words of hers actually reached his lingering soul.

"Your magic won't be forgotten. We remember *all* spells, and we will never forget yours."

Hearing that about the magic he'd woven, Feuer Lazburn found that his life had, indeed, held some kind of purpose...and was satisfied with it.

I see... In that case...there was meaning to it all...

A moment after that, the soul vanished as though it had no grudges or regrets.

The man who'd lived a life of fire...burned away.

Riser woke up due to a slight warmth on his cheek.

He blinked to fix his hazy sight. Slowly, his focus returned.

When his vision became clear, he found himself looking down at the capital from high above it, watching an immense amount of heat rise to the air.

He could feel the heat, but it wasn't great enough to harm him all the way up here.

"That's…"

"Ah! Riser! You're awake!" The voice belonged to a fellow member of the Babylonian Battlegroup, Lang. That was when Riser realized that he was being carried on the back of Lang's hippogriff.

"…What happened since I was out?"

"You beat the leader of the bee-men. That made the other bee-men stop moving, so I flew up into the sky, saw you fall, and went to catch you."

"And that pillar of fire?"

"I don't know. It just appeared a bit ago… But the people at the castle seem to be fine."

"…I see." Realizing that everything would work out, Riser was relieved.

Shortly after, the hippogriff landed in the fountain plaza where they had first encountered Regina Apis Idea.

After dismounting, Riser looked around and confirmed that little had changed since he took to the sky.

Having seen them land, everyone he'd left behind started to approach him.

"Mr. Riser, I'm glad you're...o...kay...?" Kasumi said, only to tilt her head in confusion mid-sentence.

Io and Fujinon also seemed puzzled.

"What's the matter?" Riser asked.

"You *are* Riser...aren't you?"

"Yes. Why ask— Hm?"

That was when he realized that something wasn't right about his head.

Touching his head in several places, he realized what it was.

"Oh, right. I lost my mask."

The full-face mask that defined him had been broken during the midair fight, so his (or rather, his avatar's) face was now completely exposed.

It was the sort of face one might see on twentieth century tokusatsu heroes before they transformed. It wasn't all that special, but the very fact that you could see his face at all shocked everyone present, including Babylonian Battlegroup members.

"So that's Riser's face... First time seeing it."

"That guy had a face...?"

What did you think *I was?* Riser thought in response.

"Mr. Lang doesn't seem surprised, though..." noted Kasumi. Lang was the one who picked up the maskless Riser, but he didn't seem the least bit shaken by the sight.

"Yeah. I actually saw his face when we took a bath together."

"A bath," the three girls said in perfect unison.

Oh yeah, that happened, Riser thought. It was back when he and Lang had visited Quartierlatin and went to the large bath at the inn. He wasn't unreasonable enough to wear a mask in a situation like that.

Actually, Riser only wore a mask as a matter of personal pride. The fact that his face was almost completely unknown was merely a side effect.

"Bathing…together," said Kasumi.

"Two men, completely nude," said Fujinon.

"Very nice! Thank you very much!" said Io.

"'…Nice?'" Riser and Lang tilted their heads in unison. The next moment, Fujinon threw a body blow into Io's side.

"Ghh…?! Th-That's not fair…! Yours was pretty bad too…!"

"Yours was too blatant."

"Nnh…! But your collection is *way* worse than…"

"That's a declaration of war."

"Awhawha… Y-You two…stop it…" The girls' exchange made Riser smile wryly, and some of the others around them began to laugh.

He looked around and saw both Masters and tians here.

This moment of calm after the storm made Riser once again realize something.

"…I protected them this time." He repeated the words he'd spoken before he'd lost consciousness, as though to confirm that they were indeed true.

Royal Castle, Underground Shelter

After Feuer Lazburn's Supernova was prevented from destroying the castle or the capital, only the sound of running water remained in the underground.

Elizabeth and the Altarians had evacuated, Feuer had vanished, Canglong had fainted, and Integra, though heavily injured, had carried him away, leaving the place empty.

The water from the main was pouring into the shelter through a hole in the wall; through the hole melted into the ceiling by Supernova, sunlight streamed in from several dozen metels above.

Suddenly, a bandaged woman appeared in this previously vacant space.

"Close. This place almost collapsed before the next plan could succeed," she whispered as she waded through waist-deep water.

Feuer... The Idea La Crima had given him had gone out of control. Because of that, Claudiah's plan C had almost fallen apart before it could even begin.

Saying nothing, Zeta privately questioned La Crima's ability.

Besides the mass-produced Apis Ideas, the hybrids she'd deployed here had all been modified while maintaining their personalities. That was good if you wanted to make the best use of the tians' combat experience, and it was especially important if they were meant to operate independently.

La Crima could also make Ideas without any remnants of past personality, but they couldn't function without operating towers such as La Crima herself or Regina Apis Idea.

To I.F., which was far harder to fill than most clans, the Ideas were precious firepower. Logan could provide incidental firepower by summoning devils, but overall they lacked the pieces needed to play on this ever-growing board.

However, if these Ideas could go out of control, Zeta felt that they might be more trouble than they were worth. If they often did as Ignis Idea had and decided to destroy themselves using the very magic they'd been granted, ultimately they'd be nothing but a problem.

I will have to file a report to La Crima about this. Even if he'd caused trouble, though, Ignis Idea had only been capable of crafting a spell this powerful exactly because he still had his mind. It seemed like managing the positives and negatives of Idea creation would be a difficult and dangerous task.

To them, however, the fact that the "material" involved was *tians* was neither a positive nor negative.

"Commencing. Moving over to prepare for plan C."

Zeta walked through the shelter towards the hole in the wall. As she took out a white whale-like accessory, she looked down at the flowing water.

"…Abundance. This place has a wealth of water and air," she whispered, touching the water in which her lower body was submerged.

That was what she'd said back when she'd first appeared in Granvaloa.

Her real self couldn't even imagine having enough water to get this wet.

That was also the reason why she'd picked Granvaloa as her starting country.

"…I'm jealous." She let her honest feelings show for once. The world of *Infinite Dendrogram* was full of water and air, and she couldn't help but be jealous of that — as well as loathe it.

It was the sentiment of the have-not. To some, *Infinite Dendrogram* was a means of escapism…a shelter from reality…and she knew that better than anyone else.

And exactly because she *could escape* into this world, she understood that it couldn't be just a game.

Zeta slowly looked upwards.

The ceiling blocked the view of the sky, but she could still picture it clearly in her mind — both the sky and *even what lay beyond it.*

"...I imagine that no one here has ever reached for a world beyond what their hands could touch..." She spoke words that reached no other ears.

And suddenly, her vision was lost.

She'd been thrown into a pitch-black darkness, akin to a starless night. She couldn't even guess which direction was which.

What is this? A darkness where she was blind even with her eyes wide open... Zeta hurriedly tried to use Uranus to create a defensive barrier of compressed air, but before she could, a slight shock ran through her body.

The darkness then vanished, and her vision returned.

She then looked down to see a warped hand sticking out of her chest...and holding her heart.

For a moment, she thought of Xunyu, whom she'd defeated, but it couldn't be her. This wasn't a metal prosthetic, but the arm of a living creature.

Before even looking back, she tried to attack behind herself using Uranus's compressed air bullets, but the owner of the dark hand pulled out his arm and quickly backed away.

Having lost her heart, Zeta almost collapsed, but she used air control to keep herself upright.

The wound was fatal. The attack had taken her by surprise, and her Brooch had already been destroyed by Xunyu.

Before she fell, she gazed at the one who gave her this wound.

"Vesper...tilio..." It was Vespertilio Idea, otherwise known as Morter Cortana, whom she'd thought was dead because the signature of his Idea-fragment had vanished.

The darkness that took her sight had been caused by his Darkness Boundary.

But this just didn't make sense. The Idea-fragment that was keeping his modified body together was gone.

And yet, Morter's body was still intact.

No... As a living creature, he was actually more refined *now* than he was back when the Idea had been connected to him.

He looked like a human that hosted a devil, like something out of a certain famous manga series.

His agility just now, as well as the ability that allowed him to tear out Zeta's heart without even being noticed...

This was a different Morter than the one she knew.

Saying nothing more, Zeta lost all of her HP and collapsed into the water before beginning to sink.

As her avatar vanished, she thought, *I'll really have to complain to La Crima.*

He watched as Zeta disappeared in the water.

He even checked that the disappearance wasn't some optical trick using echolocation.

Then, he spoke without even opening his mouth.

"It's me. I took care of the previous owner."

"...I see. I will call you if I have need of you again, so stay in the capital for the time being."

"...All right." With that, he cut the telepathic exchange between him and the girl that now owned him.

Morter's life was now supported by Theresia.

Given the choice to live or die, Morter had once again chosen to live.

It was entirely possible that living on, in this case, would be worse than death.

However, he also couldn't help but think that he didn't want his life to end here... After all, he had yet to do anything with it.

He was completely unlike his ex-colleague, King of Blaze. While Ignis had died to find purpose in his life, Morter was still unsatisfied and unfulfilled, so he chose to extend his.

Thus, he took on The Evil's Dependent Transformation and was once again reborn.

He was now neither man nor monster.

Losing his humanity had made him lose all his jobs — King of Raids included — but he still had enough power to make up for that loss.

He was even stronger as a Dependent than he'd been as an Idea.

However, he didn't intend to get comfortable with this power or wallow in it.

In his mind, there was only one question.

"I didn't make the wrong choice again...did I?"

The man who'd abandoned humanity to become an Idea, then abandoned that state to become a Dependent of The Evil herself, vocalized exactly what was on his mind.

Royal Castle, Medical Office

On the castle's first floor, there was an infirmary equipped with various medicines.

Since it was built right after an era of war and the struggle against The Evil, this place was well-equipped for long stays during sieges and similar situations.

The attack had destroyed most of the castle's equipment, but since the only magic used in the medical office was for preserving medicines, it could still function as normal.

In this room was Liliana.

Around her lay several coffins, each one containing a person.

The abundance of coffins made the place seem like a morgue, but they were actually filled with Lesser Elixirs and other liquid medicines, and the people inside were none other than Theodore and the other ten or so Paladins who had fought with him.

They were still alive, but they couldn't leave the coffins.

This was the result of their fight against Aranea Idea.

They were able to destroy the creature, but the price they paid for that victory was great. They had all touched the poison Aranea released while alive, as well as those he'd spread upon death.

The poisons weren't temporary, and because they'd absorbed as much of them as they did, their cells had actually begun to mutate. As a result, they were now in a critical state that mere medicine couldn't fully cure.

Thus, they were now kept in coffins full of Lesser Elixir to slow down the progression of the disease; additionally, they were subjected to sleeping magic so they did not have to suffer through pain. Magic had been used to put them under instead of conventional drugs, in order to avoid any potential reactions with the Lesser Elixir.

Liliana stood in the room, looking at her subordinates… her fellow knights.

Suddenly, someone tapped her on the shoulder.

"Hey, don't look so gloomy. I mean, you're gorgeous, so a poignant expression really suits you, but here it just makes it look like you're about to hold a mass funeral."

This unfunny joke was spoken by…

"Integra…!"

"It's been a while. We haven't seen each other since I left on the journey to broaden my horizons, which was…two years ago?"

"So it was that long already...?"

The speaker was Liliana's childhood friend — Arch Sage, Integra.

"...Thanks for what you did down there. That *was* your doing, right? And thanks for taking care of the poison on the first floor too."

"Yeah. I came back to the capital a short while ago, and I sensed some serious magic downstairs. And when I went there, I found King of Blaze ready to blow. I knew I had to hurry up and do *something*. The poison was just a bonus."

After the Royal Guard was overcome by the poison, Integra had gone to them, cleansed the poison, and done what she could to keep them alive. The timing of her arrival made it seem as though she'd been observing the whole thing and had only gone to clean up once it was over, but no one had questioned it.

Integra had also suffered heavy injuries during the Supernova explosion, but she now had no noticeable wounds. She had treated herself using healing magic and a few precious items she possessed.

"Back to your sad face, though. Is it because of these knights sleeping here?" Integra asked.

"...Yes. Once again...I was powerless..."

"Hmm? But I heard that you were looking for the lost princess."

"I was. But while they fought a deadly battle, I...the current leader of the knights...went through this entire ordeal without facing any danger. That's why, I—"

"You just prioritized what you had to. It is what it is." While consoling her friend so casually, Integra thought, *Not like* she *needed to be found, or any protection for that matter.*

Integra knew that Theresia was The Evil and that Dormouse was related to the Incarnations.

During the kidnapping where Theresia had encountered Shu and Sechs, the previous Arch Sage had confirmed that all of this was true.

The records clearly show that the Incarnations erased all The Evils so far. And since they can no longer kill them with tians, they're now trying to delay The Evil's completion by protecting her. Even a battle-focused Superior Job was nothing to her.

Integra considered this, as though she had actually seen Morter try to attack Theresia.

The only real danger was from King of Blaze's final attack. If they'd decided that the explosion would be enough to kill her, there's no telling how they'd act.

The Incarnation accompanying Theresia had neither retreated from the castle nor tried to stop King of Blaze. Integra had actually gone down herself because she'd considered it just that dangerous.

There's been no activity from their side since then. They didn't even get in the way when I was preventing the explosion. Does that mean that their goal wasn't to eliminate The Evil no matter what, but to eliminate it if possible? I can't tell. I have two thousand years' worth of records describing their actions, but I still don't truly understand them... Not that I want to understand this invasive species.

She cut her somewhat dark thoughts short, focusing once again on the conversation with Liliana.

Integra had thought about a lot of things, but her entire thought process hadn't lasted even a second of actual time. High-speed thinking was a basic technique of all skilled casters.

Not noticing even a fraction of what was going on inside Integra's head, Liliana vocalized her worries. "I...I can't ever save anyone by myself... Over and over again, I'm the one being saved."

"Hey, don't worry about it. These guys are thankfully still alive. Once Altimia...I mean, Her Majesty is back with that High Priestess who's supposedly with her, I'm sure she'll heal them with her magic."

"That is true... The idea does put me at ease."

Even as she consoled her friend, Integra's thoughts were turning dark.

Altimia's accompanied by Masters, eh...? Unlike the previous king, my teacher didn't mess with her outlook on this. I guess her conclusion is different despite the king's influence.

Regardless, Altar was already open to cooperation with Masters, so she had no intention of objecting. Instead, she'd decided to observe the situation between Altar and Dryfe as they both joined forces with Masters.

Perhaps I should get some information from these Masters too? In that case, I should focus on the strongest among them — the ones they call Superiors. Or perhaps the specific one responsible for Altimia's change of heart...

While considering her next move, Integra searched Liliana's face.

Integra had been sincere when she tried to cheer Liliana up, but it seemed like the knight's regret and sadness weren't so easy to disperse.

She was distressed about the current situation, certainly, but the core of her sadness was a hatred of her own weakness.

This sentiment had been building up inside her for quite some time. She was weaker than the princess she was charged to protect, and she had only barely contributed to solving the many problems facing Altar.

All of that combined was more than enough to justify her gloomy expression.

Integra was good enough friends with Liliana and Altimia to notice all of this. At the same time, though, she felt a bit bad about their intrinsic difference in position.

"If it bothers you that much that you weren't able to fight, there's nothing I can do about that — but if it's your weakness that's the problem, I may be able to help."

"Huh?"

That was why, Integra felt she needed to bring this up, as a friend.

"Out of all the things I've learned, I think there's a way to make you stronger. If you can achieve this, you will no doubt become a great deal more powerful than you are now."

That just happened to be exactly what Liliana wanted in her moment of weakness.

"And that would be…?"

Looking up at her taller friend's eyes, Integra…

"Wanna try becoming the Celestial Knight?"

…spoke the name of the Superior Job that had belonged to her late father.

Royal Castle, Guest Room

Canglong woke up to find himself on a canopy bed.

He tried to get up, but there was a slight weight on his left hand.

Glancing at his right one, he realized that he had a human body again.

He then looked at his heavy left hand…

"Zzz… Zzz…"

…and saw Elizabeth, clutching at his hand in her sleep.

A glance at the window made it clear that it was already dark outside. A few hours had passed since the battle underground, and he could only guess that Elizabeth had been holding his hand the entire time.

He scanned the surroundings for any presences and sensed one that belonged to a knight beyond the door.

Canglong and Elizabeth were alone in this room, and it was all because she had asked for this.

He'd lost consciousness during the explosion underground, and the next thing he knew, he was here.

All that was certain to him was that both he and Elizabeth had survived.

Canglong slowly raised himself, reached for her head...and after some hesitation, caressed it.

"Mnh..." She moved a bit, but continued to sleep as peacefully as before.

"A lot has happened. You must be tired..." What had happened underground, the attack itself...many things were still unclear to Canglong.

However, for now, he just wanted to enjoy the fact that they were both still alive.

"Let us talk when you wake up... There are many things I must tell you, as well as things I *want* to tell you..." he said before caressing her head again.

Some time after Canglong woke up, there was a knock on the door — so silent and subdued that it did not even wake Elizabeth.

"Come in," said Canglong. The door opened, and he saw the face of a giant rodent.

"Pardon the intrusion." The giant rodent — Dormouse — entered the room, and Theresia, who was perched on his back, apologized while being careful not to wake her sister.

"Your Highness?" Canglong wondered why she'd come here. Since it was a bit late to pay him a visit, he guessed that she was here for her sister, but then...

"Sorry for leaving the tea party early."

"Huh? Ohh..."

Theresia's words instantly reminded Canglong of the tea party they'd held earlier today.

Elizabeth had arranged the party. She'd resolved to leave for Huang He, and she wanted Theresia to meet Canglong before she left. Elizabeth wanted to show her sister the person she would spend her life with and to introduce Canglong to the family that she so treasured.

The two had ended up barely talking during the tea party and had been entirely separated once the assault began.

Now that everything had subsided, they were finally together.

"Dor." With just that one word, Dormouse placed Theresia on the floor and walked out of the room.

Now it was just Canglong, Theresia, and Elizabeth, who was still sleeping. Between them, there was nothing but a silence that felt both unbearably long and far too short.

Canglong said nothing and merely waited for Theresia to speak.

Theresia briefly exchanged glances with him before looking down at her sister, still clutching Canglong's left hand.

Then, she caressed Elizabeth's head like Canglong had done and…

"Protect her for me…"

…said only four words.

Theresia's real emotions were hard to read, but Canglong was certain that those words came straight from her heart.

She had come all the way here just to say that.

For all that anyone knew, perhaps she'd actually been gathering her resolve and waiting for the chance to say this even back during the tea party.

After all, these words were a goodbye. Her sister would soon leave for a distant land, and with these words Theresia had entrusted her sister to him.

Canglong understood that.

"I will… No matter what."

And that was why he swore this with his very soul.

No matter from what or from whom…he would protect Elizabeth.

Thus, Canglong and Theresia — Draconic Emperor and The Evil — exchanged a promise.

The Gaol, Café "Dice"

On that day, Dice ended up not receiving a single customer.

You couldn't even hear any voices outside.

The gaol was a rowdy place full of commotion, so this was an abnormally peaceful day.

With her head on the table, Gerbera turned the pages of some documents, lost in thought.

She wouldn't say it out loud, but she felt that her clan leader, Sechs, wasn't quite himself today.

After talking about the final boss, his peaceful, hard-to-define aura became more like…uh…the pressure of a beast sharpening its claws? Well, I don't really know how to describe it…

All that she knew was that Sechs was different than usual.

I guess I'm weird for noticing this in the first place. Wait, I guess it's the other way around. If he seems dangerous enough that even I'm picking it up… That explains why we didn't get any guests today.

She nodded to herself in understanding before resuming her scan of the documents.

These documents contained data that the other I.F. members sent Sechs in reality. He memorized it all and wrote it down here by hand for Gerbera.

This wouldn't have been necessary if they could just send an email to Gerbera's real-world self, as well, but she hadn't shared her address with the other members. In spite of how she acted in *Dendro*, Gerbera — or Kikuko — was actually fairly internet-literate.

I mean, I can't just give my email to people who do Dendro *crimes all day…though I guess I'm not in any position to say something like that.* Boredom was making her feel even more down than usual, but she continued skimming through the documents nonetheless.

"Hmm… Ignis, Aranea, Vespertilio, and Regina Apis… They sound like real villains."

She was currently going through the info regarding the assault on Altea and the Ideas that had been used for it.

What they're doing is pretty awful too… Being here almost makes me forget this fact, but we're a real group of bad guys, aren't we?

As Gerbera thought that, the bell on the café's door rang.

"Welcome! Oh? It's been quite a while."

"Helloooo! Everyone's favorite GOD is heeere!"

A voice that sounded like candy mixed with honey, fruit syrup, and artificial sweetener resounded through the café. It was so sweet it felt like it might melt your teeth away.

The person was wearing a dress styled like a heavily decorated cake with as many frills as possible, as well as small plush toys. It swayed as the figure came to sit at the counter.

"Sechsy and Gerby! It's been soooo long! Ah, one caramel macchiato, pleeease!" The painfully sweet voice that suited its apparel all too well spoke to Sechs and Gerbera with notable familiarity. Their drink order was just as painfully sweet — Sechs had created this drink based on recipes from real-world coffee shops.

"Egh… Candy." Gerbera spoke the visitor's name, her mood dropping even further down. "Like always…you gross me out."

"Ahhh! Gerby! That's sooo mean! I'm gonna shake my head at you!"

"I'm not in the mood for this…" Legitimately starting to become nauseous, Gerbera stared at the newcomer.

She'd first met this person in the gaol, and the times they'd interacted were few…but they were more than enough to leave a mark on her memory.

…The makeup's even better than before. If you ignore the absurd appearance and voice, you can almost feel like you're looking at a pretty girl… After reluctantly praising the person's appearance, she quietly added, "…Yet he's a guy."

"Tch tch tch! So naive! Lil' Candy is a *god* who's totally above gender!" the person replied, apparently not the least bit offended.

His name was Candy Carnage. By all appearances he was a girl, but as far as Gerbera knew, his avatar and real body were both male.

She also knew things besides his unusual appearance and personality that made him stand out… Knew them *too* well, actually.

"This is *Dendro*, where a *god* can be a *god*, so I will forgive your little act of disrespect, but if you push it, I might have to destroy yoouu!"

"…I know." Even Gerbera could tell that despite the joking tone, that was an actual warning.

After all, he was already *doing his thing*.

He was one of the Superiors locked up in this gaol — the worst and most far-reaching wide-scale extermination-suppression types of all.

He'd destroyed a city-state, massacred over a hundred thousands tians, and killed even The Hero.

The tian genocider. The "Legionkiller."

King of Plagues, Candy Carnage.

Gerbera knew that she couldn't win against someone like him.

Perhaps she might have a chance in such close quarters, but if Candy wanted to fight with all his might, he would be a complete calamity.

Our leader and Hannya beat this guy up, though... The Superior Killer too... Dendro really is all about compatibility...and about how broken and insane you are in real life.

Realizing the crushing gap in compatibility and power between them, Gerbera once again laid her head on the table.

"...By the way, the city is pretty quiet, considering you're outside."

Gerbera had met Candy once in a created dungeon and twice in town. *I died in that dungeon before even seeing him, though.* However, the two times she'd met Candy out in town, the locals had been panicking and running around as if he was some kind of natural disaster.

That was why Gerbera found it strange how quiet it'd been the whole day.

"That's because I killed everyone outside! Some ignoramus laughed at my *god*-ly clothes! I kinda snapped and did a little cleaning in town!"

"...Well, that explains the silence." *Man, he's powered up, hasn't he? He spread his infection so fast that they didn't even have time to escape,* Gerbera thought listlessly.

"Oh, but I made sure to leave the café untouched! Praise me!"

"Ah, sure, sure. Good job. Very nice."

"*Two* praises! That's enough to forgive the disrespect from before!"

...He hadn't forgiven me before that? I was in some serious danger. Gerbera knew well that Candy was hard to deal with even for a resident of the gaol.

Though feared by many, Sechs was tolerant and gentle in demeanor, so she had no problem with him. Hannya was also fine as long as you didn't set her off by being lovey-dovey with someone or bad mouthing Figaro.

Fu'uta would destroy you without question if you came close, but he never left his one spot, so he was no trouble either.

However, it was never clear how to deal with Candy. He came into town on a whim, approached her as he wished, and it was never clear what would set him off. Once he *was* set off, he would always go to extremes.

He's such a pain. I really don't wanna deal with him right now... Ignoring him was one of the things that usually displeased him, so Gerbera had no choice but to interact with him.

Maybe I should log out for the day, she wondered right as Sechs presented Candy the caramel macchiato and began to speak to him.

"So, Candy, what brought you here today?"

"Oh yeah! I have some grreeat news!"

"Great news...? Ohh, so you're done?"

"*Slurp slurp...* I knew you'd ask!" Candy sipped his drink through a straw and puffed out his chest. "I finally...*finally* did it! Lil' Candy has defeated the Disaster Bioweapon!"

"That is good to hear."

What Candy had just said was simply staggering.

The gaol had a created dungeon, but it also had a special area where a certain UBM was kept.

Called the Disaster Bioweapon, this creature was beyond even Mythical in power, with level well over 100 and the status of an Irregularity. Many Masters here had attempted to defeat it and take its MVP special reward, but all of them had been completely powerless against it.

Candy was one of the Masters that had challenged it, only to be defeated like all the others. However, he had been certain that he would eventually bring it down.

And today, after many attempts, he had finally succeeded.

Here, in the gaol, Candy Carnage had actually destroyed an Irregularity, all by himself.

"My determination was unswerving… I forgot how many times I tried, though!"

"…Oh, I'll praise you for real this time. That's actually amazing."

"Now I can…probably be super proud. But besides that, I can leave the gaol, so…" Candy smiled like a flower over-blooming. "…I can finally get back at that tasteless, black-clad hitwoman…" His face as he said that was, for the first time since he came, one of pure anger.

…*He's seriously mad about getting PK'd.* Gerbera herself nursed a grudge — or perhaps an antagonism or even a *vengeance* — towards Rook, so she felt a tiny bit of sympathy for Candy. "'Tasteless,' though? I really don't think the Superior Killer wants to hear that from you…"

"She wears masculine clothing despite being a woman. That alone makes it clear that our tastes don't match." *You sure that's not just a hatred for your own kind?* Gerbera thought, but didn't say out loud.

"This seems like a good time," said Sechs. "Your business here is done, and Gerbera is improving fast. With that in mind, Candy — about what we discussed…"

"Okaaay! This will delay my revenge, but I'll join I.F.'s care for a year!"

Upon hearing that, Gerbera made a face that said both "I wasn't informed of this" and "Are you serious?" but neither Sechs nor Candy noticed.

"Excellent… I would've preferred to have Fu'uta join us, as well, but he will likely walk his own path."

"But…do you really think it's possible?"

"Yes. Based on Hannya's attempts, it used to be about seventy-percent doable, but thanks to Gerbera here, we will no doubt be successful."

"Huh? Huh?"

The incomprehensible conversation continued, leaving Gerbera far behind. Her head was surrounded by question marks — more so than on any other moment today, even.

Paying her no heed, Sechs went on to say the most important part of the conversation.

"It is time for us to break out of this gaol."

The king of criminals was finally ready to abandon his temporary home.

Paladin, Ray Starling

The place I appeared once I logged in after my death penalty expired was the same one I'd logged into after the first time I'd died — the fountain at the capital.

There were two differences, though. First was that the sun was still high up, and…

"Nemesis…"

…Nemesis wasn't out of the crest.

I was well aware of the reason.

At the final moment of the battle against Behemot, I'd made her pierce through my body.

I knew Nemesis well enough by now.

She always accompanied me on my endeavors, but she also worried about me more than I did.

And yet, I'd asked her to stab me.

I wasn't so inconsiderate that I hadn't considered how hard that must have been for her.

"Sorry, Nemesis…"

"Mhm…" Nemesis replied, agreeing.

This was unlike the first time, when my apology was met with "No need." That made me realize that I'd actually done something that warranted an apology.

"…My bad."

"You say that…but it is not like you would ever limit what you do in pursuit of your possibilities, right?"

"…I wouldn't," I replied, with nothing but honesty.

"There is no helping it, then. That is how you are, and it is my duty to help you."

Following those words, she left her crest.

Her eyes were slightly red.

"You always do absurd things without considering yourself. You are always tattered… Look, even the armor B3 gifted to you is gone."

"True… I'll have to apologize to her." The armor had been completely destroyed by King of Beasts' attacks. I still had the casual clothes I wore in town, but I would clearly need a replacement sooner than later.

"But bear this in mind, Ray," Nemesis said as she turned away. "You ended up in this tattered state because you protected those things you needed to protect… That surely means that the anguish I felt while obeying your order…was also not without meaning."

"Nemesis…" I couldn't see her expression as she said that. She'd probably looked away to prevent just that.

I thought of what to say to her…and came upon two sentences.

"Nemesis."

The first was just her name.

In response, she said, "What is it?" without even turning back to me.

The second sentence contained what I wanted to convey to her.

It wasn't a "Sorry" or a "Thank you."

Her tiny back made it feel that she could disappear at any moment, so…

"Stay by my side."

...that was what I was compelled to say.

Nemesis still didn't turn around. With her back still towards me, she wasn't moving an inch.

No... She was actually shaking a little.

"...I-I'm your Embryo... Of course I'll stay by your side..."

"I don't want you by my side because you're an Embryo born from me. I want you to stay with me because you're Nemesis."

I wanted her to be with me not because the Master-Embryo system made it inevitable, but because she wanted to as her own person. She knew me better than anyone else and had always been there for me.

"Heh heh heh... Of course! I *am* the greatest Embryo, after all!"

"Yeah. You're the best, Nemesis."

"Nhm...?!" My honest reply froze her in place.

"Nemesis?"

"D-Do not mind this! It is nothing... I-I am going back to my crest! Farewell!" And so, with her face still covered, Nemesis returned to the back of my hand.

I didn't fully understand her attitude, but it seemed that she would stay by my side.

I walked through the capital, but I was still unable to meet up with my fellow Death Period members who got the death penalty before me. From what I'd seen, they weren't even online yet. In real time, the time between our deaths wasn't that great, so I supposed that I'd just happened to log in first because I had been waiting for the penalty to expire.

And according to Shu, who'd contacted me in real life, Azurite and the others had yet to return to the capital.

The reason for that was Azurite herself — she was in bad shape.

Apparently, the battle against The Ram had been extremely draining. Well, I was told she'd also talked to Claudiah right after the battle, and once Dryfe retreated, the relief of all that tension made her collapse like a loose marionette.

The reason for her fatigue was the ultimate job skill she'd used…and Shu'd told me that she'd been immobilized for two whole days.

According to him, she'd recently said, "I never expected to be nursed by the parasite…such humiliation." Regardless of whether or not she was serious, I saw that as a sign that she was recovering.

They'd departed yesterday in *Dendro* time, and they were on course to come back here by evening today.

Before meeting up with my clan members and Azurite, I decided to check on the situation at the castle. I passed the main street near the fountain and headed towards my destination.

"Hey, that's…" I was in my casual clothing, so there were fewer people that recognized me.

However, there were some who knew my face, and I could hear them speak.

"That's The Unbreakable…"

"The guy who matched KoB…"

…We were hardly *matched*, and it certainly wasn't just my doing.

Fuso had lowered KoB's stats, Rook gave me a chance to fill up my damage counter, B3 and I cornered her together, Marie and Tsukikage broke her Superior item — and in spite of all that, we weren't able to finish her off.

If Fuso hadn't been there to strike a deal and get Dryfe to retreat, all of those efforts would've been for naught.

However, there were rumors that I had fought KoB head-on and even ended it with a draw.

Their source was a certain video on the internet.

I didn't know how or from where it was taken, but it seemed to be hidden camera footage of our battle.

Additionally, it was cleverly edited in a way that was only apparent if you'd been at the scene yourself, and the purpose of that editing seemed to be elevating me...and Death Period.

That actually kinda creeped me out, for some reason.

I passed the gate to the noble district and arrived at the castle. Azurite had already given me permission to enter, and the guards who knew me let me into the castle without any trouble.

"...It's burnt," I muttered as I passed the gate. It seemed to have been broken...melted by some intense fire.

That was far from all of it — there were also holes in the walls as well as broken and scorched spires. Just how intense of a battle did this castle go through?

Were Liliana and the others okay? The state of the castle filled me with unease, but then...

"I was just informed that they will return in about two hours."

"I'm happy that I'll get to meet Her Highness again... Wait, she's Her Majesty now, isn't she?"

...I heard a familiar voice and turned towards it.

There, I saw Liliana, slightly injured but in one piece.

"Liliana!"

"Huh...? Ray!" Upon hearing me call out, she turned to me and ran over.

"I am glad you are well!" she said.

"That's my line. What about Milianne and the princesses?"

"...They are well... Though, there are some issues."

"Like...?"

"Hello, hello! A pleasure to meet you! So *you* are Ray Starling!" Before I got Liliana's response, an unfamiliar voice intruded on the conversation and called my name.

"Who are you...?" I asked. She was the person Liliana had just been talking to.

291

She was about as small as Nemesis, if not smaller, but she didn't *seem* all that young. Her tiny frame was swallowed by a wizard's robe straight out of a picture book, and on her head there was a pointy hat of the type you'd expect to see on a generic witch.

"I've been wanting to meet you! The one who brought down enemy Superiors in Gideon and Quartierlatin and thus saved the kingdom twice! No, now it's *thrice*!" Saying all this with a cheerful voice, she took my hand and shook it up and down.

Her voice and attitude both were brimming with friendliness. But for some reason — no idea why — I felt like there was nothing friendly about those eyes that were looking at me.

Was there a shine in them akin to that of a carnivorous beast that had found its prey...?

No... Her gaze was more like that of an insect that had found a cadaver it had to deal with.

"Whoops! Where are my manners? I haven't introduced myself! I am..." She let go of my hand, spun around, and gave me a slight bow before beginning the introduction. "I am the favored disciple of the previous Arch Sage, and now I am the current Arch Sage..."

Hearing the job alone filled me with surprise...

"My name is...Integra Sedna Clarisse Flagman."

...but before it could subside, she gave a name that was even more surprising.

"Pleased to make your acquaintance...Unbreakable Hero."

As I looked at her, still bowing, I felt uneasy...as if something had just been set in motion.

To Be Continued...

Cat: "It's time for the afterwooord! I'm the 'Cat,' Cheshiiire!"

Xun: "And I'm XunYu. 'Xun' for shOrt. We'rE in this aftErword 'causE we weren't in the lAst one."

Cat: "You worked hard even in the volume itself, didn't yaaa?"

Xun: "Yeah. It was mY first battle in a goOd while… Since volUme 3, actually."

Cat: "Nice fighting back theeere. Though, I gotta ask… Are all of your battles gonna end with you getting burnt to a crisp?"

Xun: "It's gottA be 'cause I'm undeAd. EveryOne and their mOm just wants to cremAte the corpse."

Cat: "I can't blame theeem. Just keep in mind that you certainly weren't the only one struggling in this voluuume. Even the author was attacked by his greatest enemyyy."

Xun: "What enEmy is thAt?"

Cat: "Page count. This volume is so large that putting it all together for printing was a real challenge."

Xun: "Well, I guess evEryone was fIghting theIr own battles hEre."

Cat: "Ray barely appears in it, but the battle count is probably the highest yet."

Xun: "The author mUst have it hArd. Though, I'm glAd I got my first illUstration in a while."

Cat: (…Doesn't it only show your arm?)

Xun: "By the wAy, with so many pagEs, there's barelY any parts that weren't in thE web novel, right?"

Cat: "Yes. But to make up for it, the author is working hard on an original short story that should be released during a twitter campaign on the official twitter account around volume 15's release. I believe it will be rather large."

Xun: "'Rather largE?'"

Cat: "…It's not finished at the point of writing this afterwooord… It's currently January, by the way."

Xun: "JanuarY…"

Cat: "The author usually gets work requests before January breaks, so he tends to be busy during the end and beginning of the year. Anyway, it's time for the author's serious comments."

Dearest readers — thank you for your purchase. I am the author, Sakon Kaido.

The number of people infected by COVID-19 has been growing, heavy snowfall has hit parts of the country… This has been quite an eventful time.

The snow has affected even yours truly, at times making it difficult for me to get around.

However, my dog found nothing but joy in the snow, charging into it at full speed and burying his head in it. He's a Pomeranian mix who's supposed to be an indoor pet, but he has as much energy as any big dog. Silly as he is at times, there's no denying that he's cute.

Oh, another volume of the manga adaptation should've come out shortly before this volume of the novel. It once again includes the shenanigans of the Pomera — I mean, Lobohta — in the form of a short story, so please take a look at it.

Now, about this volume of the novel… It marks the end of the events surrounding the peace conference that began in volume 13. We see what was happening behind the scenes while Ray was fighting, and we are introduced to something very close to the core of the *Infinite Dendrogram* setting… The Evil and The Demise.

Their relationship with the control AIs is a relationship between "a self-destruct device installed into an incomplete product" and "those who modified the incomplete product to complete it in a different way." They cannot possibly co-exist.

There are many such conspirators with incompatible goals and ideas, and their plots intertwine and compound each other seemingly without end.

The control AIs, The Evil, Flagman, the imperator, Caldina, and others… The world of *Infinite Dendrogram* has no shortage of schemers or their grand designs.

Please do pay attention to how the story of Ray and his group will go while they are caught up in this web.

The focus on Ray will have to wait until a later volume, though. The next book will shift the attention away from Altar and onto Caldina in the east, bringing the story back to the other Master-Maiden pair of Hugo and Cyco.

You'll have their encounters with new Superiors to look forward to.

Thank you for continuing to support *Infinite Dendrogram*.

Sakon Kaido

Xun: "…The guy wEnt on about his dog fOr a moment there."

Cat: "Why not a caaat?! The author isn't a cat persooon?!"

Xun: "You reallY gonna be jealous aboUt that? Oh and VOLUME 16'S SET TO COME OUT IN JUNE, 2021! By the wAy, why's it jUst the two of us this time?"

Cat: "Well, the Fox Lady wasn't in this voluume, while Brother Bear only appeared in a flaaashback."

Xun: "Yeah, I dunnO about these vagUe exclusions based on thE volume content…"

Six: "Then I suppose I can come out for a moment."

Cat and Xun: "HUH?!"

Six: "Hello. I am 'Six,' Sechs Würfel. I make a brief appearance in the tenth chapter of the Crow Record manga, and just like this volume, members of I.F. will have the spotlight in the following one. Do take a look at it if you're so inclined, and goodbye for now." *Sounds of leaving*

Xun: "The guy just sAid what he wanted and gOt the hell out…"

Cat: "…D-Did he do that just to assert that he was in the volume too?"

Xun: "…You'd think thAt a leader of a criminAl clan wouldn't hAve so much tIme on his hands."

Sakon Kaidou

Illustrator: Taiki

MANGA OMNIBI 1-4
ON SALE NOW!

NOVEL VOLUME 16
ON SALE
AUGUST 2022!

Infinite
Dendrogram

16. The Tartarean Possibilities

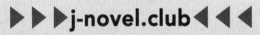

J-Novel Club Lineup

Latest Ebook Releases Series List

Altina the Sword Princess
Amagi Brilliant Park
Animeta!**
The Apothecary Diaries
An Archdemon's Dilemma: How to Love Your Elf Bride*
Are You Okay With a Slightly Older Girlfriend?
Arifureta: From Commonplace to World's Strongest
Arifureta Zero
Ascendance of a Bookworm*
Banner of the Stars
Bibliophile Princess*
Black Summoner*
The Bloodline
By the Grace of the Gods
Campfire Cooking in Another World with My Absurd Skill*
Can Someone Please Explain What's Going On?!
Chillin' in Another World with Level 2 Super Cheat Powers
The Combat Baker and Automaton Waitress
Cooking with Wild Game*
Culinary Chronicles of the Court Flower
Dahlia in Bloom: Crafting a Fresh Start with Magical Tools
Deathbound Duke's Daughter
Demon Lord, Retry!*
Der Werwolf: The Annals of Veight*
Dragon Daddy Diaries: A Girl Grows to Greatness
Dungeon Busters
The Emperor's Lady-in-Waiting Is Wanted as a Bride*
Endo and Kobayashi Live! The Latest on Tsundere Villainess Lieselotte
The Faraway Paladin*
Full Metal Panic!
Full Clearing Another World under a Goddess with Zero Believers*
Fushi no Kami: Rebuilding Civilization Starts With a Village
Goodbye Otherworld, See You Tomorrow
The Great Cleric
The Greatest Magicmaster's Retirement Plan

Girls Kingdom
Grimgar of Fantasy and Ash
Hell Mode
Her Majesty's Swarm
Holmes of Kyoto
How a Realist Hero Rebuilt the Kingdom*
How NOT to Summon a Demon Lord
I Shall Survive Using Potions!*
I'll Never Set Foot in That House Again!
The Ideal Sponger Life
If It's for My Daughter, I'd Even Defeat a Demon Lord
In Another World With My Smartphone
Infinite Dendrogram*
Invaders of the Rokujouma!?
Jessica Bannister
JK Haru is a Sex Worker in Another World
John Sinclair: Demon Hunter
A Late-Start Tamer's Laid-Back Life
Lazy Dungeon Master
A Lily Blooms in Another World
Maddrax
The Magic in this Other World is Too Far Behind!*
The Magician Who Rose From Failure
Mapping: The Trash-Tier Skill That Got Me Into a Top-Tier Party*
Marginal Operation**
The Master of Ragnarok & Blesser of Einherjar*
Min-Maxing My TRPG Build in Another World
Monster Tamer
My Daughter Left the Nest and Returned an S-Rank Adventurer
My Friend's Little Sister Has It In for Me!
My Instant Death Ability is So Overpowered, No One in This Other World Stands a Chance Against Me!*
My Next Life as a Villainess: All Routes Lead to Doom!
Otherside Picnic
Outbreak Company
Perry Rhodan NEO

Private Tutor to the Duke's Daughter
Reborn to Master the Blade: From Hero-King to Extraordinary Squire ♀*
Record of Wortenia War*
Reincarnated as the Piggy Duke: This Time I'm Gonna Tell Her How I Feel!
The Reincarnated Princess Spends Another Day Skipping Story Routes
Seirei Gensouki: Spirit Chronicles*
Sexiled: My Sexist Party Leader Kicked Me Out, So I Teamed Up With a Mythical Sorceress!
She's the Cutest... But We're Just Friends!
The Sidekick Never Gets the Girl, Let Alone the Protag's Sister!
Slayers
The Sorcerer's Receptionist
Sorcerous Stabber Orphen*
Sweet Reincarnation**
The Tales of Marielle Clarac*
Tearmoon Empire
Teogonia
The Underdog of the Eight Greater Tribes
The Unwanted Undead Adventurer*
Villainess: Reloaded! Blowing Away Bad Ends with Modern Weapons*
Welcome to Japan, Ms. Elf!*
The White Cat's Revenge as Plotted from the Dragon King's Lap
A Wild Last Boss Appeared!
The World's Least Interesting Master Swordsman

...and more!
* Novel and Manga Editions
** Manga Only
Keep an eye out at j-novel.club for further new title announcements!